COLLINS & BROWN

ULTIMATE

CROCHET

BIBLE

A Complete Reference With Step-By-Step Techniques

Jane Crowfoot

This book is dedicated to the memory of my Great-Grandmother Alice Martin who gave me the crochet gene.

contents

introduction

My great grandmother was a demon with a crochet hook and continued to produce "granny square" blankets right into her 90s. She would buy old jumpers from thrift stores, charity shops or yard sales and produce the most fantastic blankets from the unraveled yarn. I remember being enthralled by the speed of her hands and amazed by her artistic productivity. Over the years she must have produced literally hundreds of blankets of various sizes. All new babies received a cot cover; every bed had a blanket. Nana's creations were not only given to every family member, but were also donated to charities as raffle prizes or to keep people in need warm through the winter. Family members now live all over the world and I would love to know what Nana would make of her blankets adorning beds in countries that she never got to visit.

Even though I spent my childhood years surrounded by Nana's crochet blankets it was only relatively recently that I got to grips with the craft myself. Crochet is currently enjoying a huge revival with many people now wanting to pick up a hook in order to create lovely garments and projects for the home. Once mastered, crochet is incredibly speedy and portable. Equipment is minimal and inexpensive. It is easily stowed away in a small bag and can be carried with you on your travels. I am a complete crochet addict and hope that with the help of this book you will perhaps become one too!

If you are a complete novice I suggest you read the book from the very beginning, and then, once you have practiced a little and perfected your basic stitches, progress through the chapters. I have included many clear step-by-step illustrations to help you achieve accurate stitches. You will find that in the first few chapters these pictorial references are abundant, with each tiny step of the stitch process having its own illustration. As you progress through the book the techniques become more complex and thus the illustrations are more intricate. It is assumed that you have a good knowledge of the basic stitches by this point. For each technique you will also find a partnering image. There are over 200 images for you to refer to, each one designed to clearly show you how completed stitches should appear.

The *Ultimate Crochet Bible* follows a logical path, techniques become more complex from mid way and towards the end I have included a large "professional finishing" chapter designed to help you achieve the best results when putting together your project. So whether you want to learn how to add texture to your work, make crochet lace, add beads and color, or if you want to learn a specific style of crochet such as Tunisian, Irish, Freeform or Amigurumi then look no further than this book. Adopt the crochet religion, say your prayers, make this your bible and become a yarn disciple like me!

Good luck!

Jane Crowfoot

Jane Crowfoot

getting started

One of the advantages of the craft of crochet over many other crafts, is the relatively small amount of equipment you need in order to get going. Crochet is very portable because, a lot of the time, you are reliant on just a hook and a ball of yarn. However, it is worth spending time choosing the correct equipment and making sure that you have all the pieces you are likely to need.

choosing a hook

Crochet hooks come in many shapes and sizes; some have thick handles, and others are very fine. Some are made from metal, others from plastic or bamboo. The hook should be comfortable to hold and should not slip in your hand whilst you are working your stitches.

Hooks come in specific diameters, so that the crochet stitch can be made to the correct gauge (tension) for the article being made, and should be marked with the size. This relates to the size of the hook end and the shank diameter just below the hook. There are three main categories; US, imperial and metric. The US size will be given as an alphabetical and number reference (such as "C" for example), the size in imperial (UK) may be given as a numerical reference (such as 11 for example), while the size in metric will be given in millimeters (3.00mm). It is important that your chosen hook is compatible to the weight of your chosen yarn.

Unfortunately a universal comparison guide for crochet hook sizes does not exist. Hooks made by different manufacturers or produced in different continents or at different periods of time use different methods for sizing! The chart below can be used as a guide, but some hook sizes have no metric equivalent so be warned that comparisons in the chart are approximate and should be used for guidance only. If in doubt as to what size hook you have, try to match it to a standard millimeter size by using a reliable knitting needle and hook gauge. You may have to try a few different gauges until you find one that works for you.

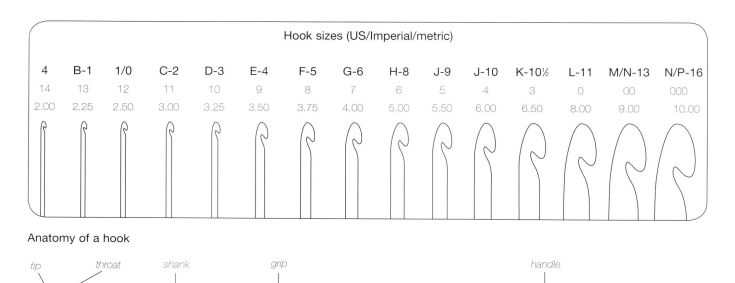

Hook sizes (US/Imperial/metric)														
4	B-1	1/0	C-2	D-3	E-4	F-5	G-6	H-8	J-9	J-10	K-10½	L-11	M/N-13	N/P-16
14	13	12	11	10	9	8	7	6	5	4	3	0	00	000
2.00	2.25	2.50	3.00	3.25	3.50	3.75	4.00	5.00	5.50	6.00	6.50	8.00	9.00	10.00

Anatomy of a hook

tip   throat   shank   grip   handle

▼ Plastic and aluminum hooks

Aluminum and plastic crochet hooks are perhaps most common. Both types allow the yarn to slip well through stitches, but can be a little uncomfortable when working on large or heavy projects, or when used for long periods. Try wrapping a piece of sponge or soft fabric around the handle to make it more comfortable.

▼ Steel hooks

Tiny hooks, which are used to make very fine lace weight fabrics, these are often made from steel because it is a harder metal than aluminum and thus is less liable to break at the hook end. Many of the really small steel hooks have a plastic handle to make the grip more comfortable.

▶ Wooden and bamboo hooks

Wooden (such as birch, for example) and bamboo hooks are a contemporary alternative to traditionally made hooks (see vintage hooks) and often have detailed handles. Wooden hooks are usually slightly longer than their plastic or metal equivalents, and can have quite a sharp cut in the throat of the hook. Wooden hooks are more flexible and lighter in weight than most aluminum hooks.

▶ Japanese hooks

These are probably the most comfortable hooks to use if you crochet holding the hook from the top, so that your thumb rests on the wide plastic handle. Japanese hooks usually come in sets, or can sometimes be purchased separately. They are relatively expensive so it is a good idea to keep them in a pouch of some kind to protect them.

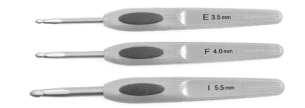

▶ Vintage hooks

You may come across old hooks that once belonged in somebody's collection, and which were made in the traditional way from turned wood or even from bone or ivory. If you do find some make sure that they are in good condition and that they are smooth and clean, and thus unlikely to spoil or snag your yarn. Use a reliable knitting needle and hook gauge to determine the size if they do not have any markings.

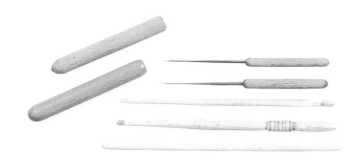

▶ Double-ended hooks

If you can get hold of one or even more of these, they will be a very handy addition to your hook collection. Most double-ended hooks will have a different size hook at each end, with a flat grip at the center.

▶ Novelty hooks

As the craft of crochet has become more popular, the range of different hooks available has increased considerably. There are many novelty hooks on the market—such as those that contain a battery and small light bulb to make crocheting in poor light easier. There are also brightly colored and glitter filled plastic hooks, which are easy to spot at the bottom of a bag.

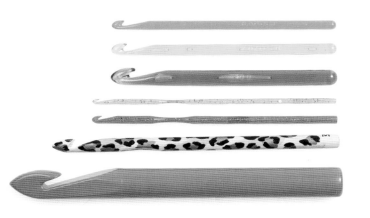

other equipment

Apart from crochet hooks, there are one or two other pieces of equipment that you will also find useful. You don't necessarily have to buy all of it at once—and if you also knit you may find you have some items already.

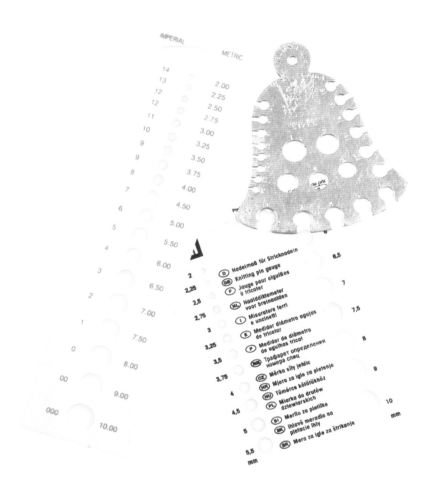

◀ **Hook and knitting needle gauge**
These gauges have a series of holes and you find the size of a crochet hook by pushing it through each hole in turn until you find the one closest to it in diameter. Do not force the hook through the hole, as this will damage both the hook and the gauge. It may take a little trial and error to find a reliable hook gauge that works for you, because there is no universal comparison guide. The hook gauge may also have a ruler down one side to help you to determine crochet gauge (tension).

Stitch markers
Usually stitch markers are made of plastic and brightly colored so you can spot them easily. They are used to mark the beginning/end of rounds or to mark the position of stitch detailing, such as increases and decreases for example.

Pins
The best pins for use on a crochet fabric are long, with brightly colored tips so you can see them against the yarn.

Tape measure
For crocheters, the best tape measure is the retractable dressmaker type. It should be strong and flexible but must not stretch. It is useful to have one marked with both inches and centimeters.

Small sharp scissors
You will only need a small pair of sharp needlework scissors. You can get the retractable type that fold down, but these tend to not be quite so sharp.

▶ **Yarn cutter**
These gadgets are a recent phenomenon and are very useful when traveling, or if you are in a position where you are unable to use scissors. They contain a sharp metal blade that can be used to slice through a yarn, encased within an ornamental casing. They are often decorative and can be worn as a pendant.

Row counter

These are handy when working complicated designs and if you struggle to recognize rows on your crochet fabric.

Bobbins

Bobbins are used to wind short lengths of yarn for color work, especially when doing intarsia (see page 152).

Yarn needle

When dealing with yarn ends or sewing crochet pieces together, it is best to use a large blunt sewing needle. These are often referred to as "knitters'" sewing needles or yarn needles. It is possible to get cranked sewing needles that have a slight dip towards the point end; these are very useful for sewing up because they make it easier to find the gaps between stitches.

Pencils, eraser, notebook or scrapbook, calculator

It is a good idea to jot down any changes made to an existing pattern for future reference. Small scrapbooks are handy for holding design ideas jotted down in a hurry, or cuttings from magazines to provide future inspiration. A calculator is useful for working out dimensions, particularly if you are making changes to the size.

▼ Rolls and cases

It is a good idea to keep your hooks and equipment clean and safe by storing them either in specially made tool wraps or in small cosmetic-type bags. Try to source a bag big enough to hold your hook, scissors, and a ball of yarn, so that your crochet is always handy and portable.

Hook storage

You can make a crochet hook roll in fabric or woolen felt, like the one that is shown here. Make sure the pockets are wide and deep enough to accommodate the hook, with a flap to cover the hook end to protect it. For added embellishment, you could make a crochet flower and tie together with a ribbon.

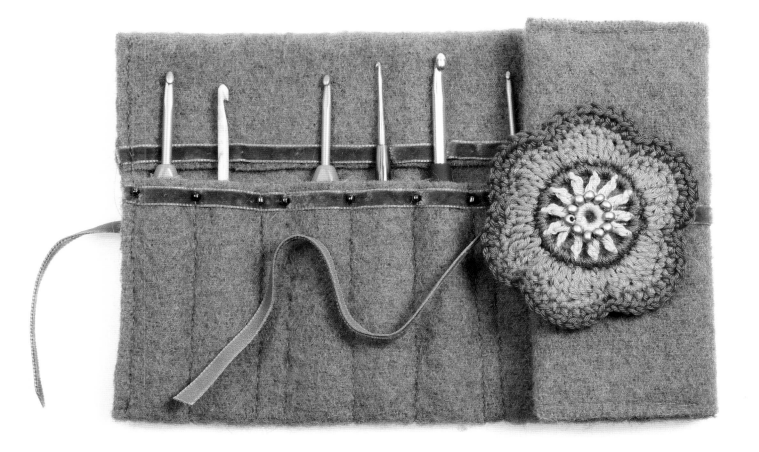

yarn

It is important that you take plenty of time to choose the correct yarn (and subsequent hook) for your project. Yarns come in many different types and are available in an amazing array of weights, colors, textures and fiber contents.

Yarns and ply

In order to be used to produce a fabric, fibers need to be processed in some way to form a yarn. Each strand of fiber is known as a ply and a yarn is made up of a number of these spun together. Choosing a yarn to complete a crochet project is the most important decision you will make. The finished appearance of the piece can depend completely on the quality of the yarn, whatever the standard of crochet and finishing, so it is imperative to consider a yarn's suitability for a project. Yarn content falls into three main categories: animal origin, plant origin, and synthetic (or man-made).

Animal origin

Wool, mohair, alpaca, angora, cashmere and camel hair
Traditionally, the most common yarn available has been wool from sheep—although many animals produce a fleece suitable for spinning yarn. Breeds of goat, such as the angora (which produces mohair) and the cashmere, are particularly suited to craft yarn. The hair from alpaca, camels and angora rabbits can also be spun. The advantage of wool is that it is warm and strong and is capable of absorbing up to 30% of its own weight in moisture without feeling damp. Wool is easy to dye but can stretch if loosely spun. Crocheting with wool will give a slightly fuzzy stitch definition.

Silk
A silkworm surrounds itself with two fine threads produced from the top of its head to form a cocoon. This filament is thread like and therefore does not need to be spun. The thread produced can be as long as 1500 meters from a single cocoon. Silk is available wild, producing a coarse thread, or cultivated, creating a finer thread. Both qualities are expensive, due to the intensive farming they require. As a craft yarn silk can be brittle and has a tendency to be a little slippery when crocheting, but the sheen and tactile quality of silk yarn easily outweighs its drawbacks.

Plant origin

Cotton

Cotton washes well and is cool to wear. It is also a good alternative to yarns of animal origin for people who suffer with allergies. Cotton is available in various grades of quality; the highest grade is Egyptian cotton, which is also considered to be the softest. Cotton yarns take dye very readily and are thus available in many vibrant and clear color palettes. However, it has little elasticity and can be quite heavy so it is important that you achieve the correct gauge (tension) to avoid stretching. Crocheting with cotton will give a crisp and clear stitch definition, especially if you use mercerized cotton, which has been processed to create a sheen on the yarn.

Bamboo and soya

These yarn varieties are relative newcomers to the craft market and have been produced as a reaction to concerns over the welfare of our environment. The bamboo plant is incredibly effective at absorbing air pollution, such as petrol fumes and is thus an eco friendly crop to grow. Luckily, when processed, it also produces a beautiful yarn with a soft sheen and smooth feel.

When grown responsibly, soya is also considered to be an eco friendly crop. Soya (like silk) produces a brittle yarn that breaks relatively easily. Soya fibers are often mixed with other more hardy fibers to produce a more reliable yarn.

Linen

Linen is made from the stem of the flax plant; it is very strong and washes well. Like wool, linen absorbs moisture and so is thought to be especially suited to hot climates. Linen can be quite stiff and is prone to creasing, and because of this, yarn manufacturers often mix it with cotton or a light man-made fiber.

Synthetic/man-made origin

Most synthetic fibers are derived from coal or petroleum. Nylon was first produced by Dupont in 1938 and revolutionized textile and fiber production. Acrylic and polyester are now the most widely used synthetic fibers, because they are easy to care for and inexpensive. Rayon is often used for both metallic and elastic thread.

Ply

Yarns are made up of a number of ply spun together to create a yarn and obviously the yarn produced can vary greatly in thickness or weight. Traditionally yarns have been referred to by the number of ply they contain, i.e. 4ply. This is now not so much the case because yarns are produced simply to work to a certain gauge (tension). The general rule is that the lower the number of ply the finer the yarn. Use the table below as a guide to identify the weight of a yarn if it is unclear.

Yarn weight category	Super fine 1	Fine 2	Light 3	Medium 4	Bulky 5	Super Bulky 6
Type of yarns in category	Sock Fingering	Sport Baby	DK Light worsted	Worsted Afghan, Aran	Chunky Craft, Rug	Bulky Roving
Crochet gauge (tension) ranges	21–28 sts	16–20 sts	16–18 sts	12–16 sts	8–12 sts	5–9 sts
Knit gauge (tension) in stockinette stitch 4in. (10cm)	26–32 sts	22–28 sts	20–22 sts	16–20 sts	12–16 sts	5–9 sts
Recommended crochet hook in metric	2.25–3.50 mm	3.50–4.50 mm	4.50–5.50 mm	5.50–6.50 mm	6.50–9.00 mm	9.00 mm and larger
Recommended crochet hook in U.S. size	Steel hooks, B-1 to E-4	E-4 to G-6	G-6 to J-9	J-9 to K-10 ½	K-10½ to M/N-13	K-10½ to M/N-13 and larger

Traditional crochet thread

So long as you match the hook size to the weight of yarn you have chosen, you can crochet with pretty much any weight of yarn regardless of the market for which the yarn was intended. Many knitting yarns work extremely well when crocheted, as do rug yarns and even unconventional materials such as string and metal wire.

Traditionally, however, crochet yarn has had a tendency to be on the fine side, often made from premium cotton or linen, to produce small, intricate stitches comparable to a lace weight fabric. Traditional crochet cotton is still available today; it is wound onto a cardboard tube and comes in small balls weighing either 1¾oz (50g) or ¾oz (20g), depending upon the thickness of the thread. The yarns are categorized using a number system rather than an indication of ply, with numbers ranging from 5 through to 100. The higher the number on the yarn, the finer it will be—and thus the smaller the required hook will be.

Thread Count	Hook Size
No 5	1.75/2mm
No 10	1.25/1.5mm
No 15	1.25/1.5mm
No 20	1.00/1.25mm
No 30	1.00/1.25mm
No 40	1.00mm
No 50	1.00mm
No 60	0.75mm
No 80	0.60mm
No 100	0.60mm

Scale

It is important that you understand how the weight of a yarn can affect the scale of the crochet piece produced. Here are 4 samples, each made with a different weight of yarn and the correct hook size. Each sample has the same number of stitches, and the same number of rows has been worked for each.

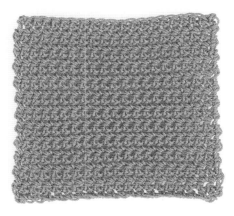

Sample in 10 count yarn

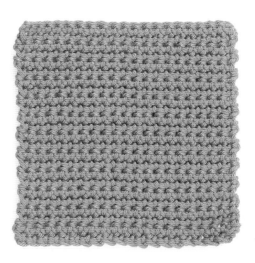

Sample in glace yarn

Sample in hand knit DK yarn

Sample in Aran yarn

choosing a yarn

When visiting a yarn shop you will probably find yourself surrounded by yarns made from an array of fibers, in an abundance of weights and an almost endless variety of shades. It is easy to get distracted by all the exciting choices and thus end up with the incorrect yarn choice for your project. If in doubt ask a store assistant for help choosing—alternatively you can use the yarn ball band as a source of information.

Ball band information

The way that yarns are packaged differs depending on the manufacturer and type of yarn. It is possible to buy yarn in a hank, which is a loosely wound coil of yarn twisted around itself. A ball or skein of yarn comes ready wound and is available in many sizes—some yarns even come on cards or cardboard tubes. Most yarns will have a paper band or tag attached to it in some way.

The main heading on the band will be the company logo, the yarn name and its weight (i.e. 4ply).

Most balls or hanks come in certain weights—usually 1¾oz (50g) or 3½oz (100g) although it is possible to get larger amounts especially in acrylic mix yarns, which can be sold in 7oz (200g) balls.

The band should give yarn constitution and yardage (meterage).

A small graph shows recommended gauge (tension), but be careful because this is usually intended to guide knitters and not crocheters. A knitted gauge (tension) is given for stockinette (stocking) stitch, and this will usually be more stitches and rows to 4in. (10cm) than for the crochet equivalent using single crochet (UK double crochet). (See yarn weight chart on page 16)

Care instructions for the yarn will be given and it is a good idea to keep one ball band as a reference to use for washing instructions in the future.

Recommended needle size for both knitting and crochet.

Shade and dye lot number: It is important that all the yarn for a project comes from the same dye lot because slight differences in color may not be apparent in certain light but could be horribly obvious in the finished piece.

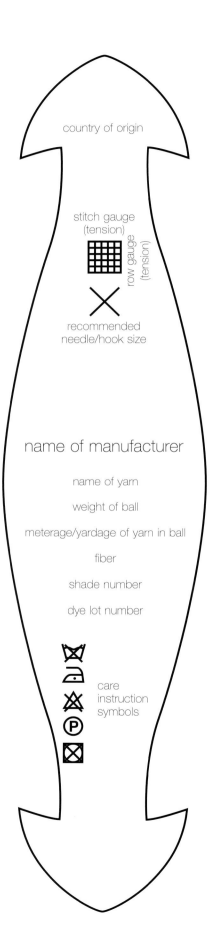

country of origin

stitch gauge (tension)

row gauge (tension)

recommended needle/hook size

name of manufacturer

name of yarn

weight of ball

meterage/yardage of yarn in ball

fiber

shade number

dye lot number

care instruction symbols

Laundering and dry cleaning symbols

Hand Washing

Do not wash by hand or machine

Hand wash only

Machine Washing

Machine washable in warm water at stated temperature

Machine washable in warm water at stated temperature, cool rinse and short spin

Machine washable in warm water at stated temperature, short spin

Bleaching

Bleaching not permitted

Bleaching permitted (with chlorine)

Pressing

Do not press

Press with a cool iron

Press with a warn iron

Press with a hot iron

Dry Cleaning

Do not dry clean

May be dry cleaned with all solutions

May be dry cleaned with perchlorethylene or fluorocarbon or petroleum-based solvents

May be dry cleaned with fluorocarbon or petroleum-based solvents only

Always check the yarn ball band for washing and pressing instructions. The standard laundering symbols that are used on most ball bands can be seen here.

Machine washing

Even if the ball band states the yarn is machine washable it is a good idea to do a test wash before putting a finished project in the washing machine. Try using your gauge (tension) swatch as a test piece in order to see how your yarn reacts when washed and dried.

substituting yarn

So long as you stick to the same yarn ply you can choose to change the type of yarn you use for your project, but there are a few things to bear in mind and few calculations that need to be made.

Evaluating drape

If you want to change the type of yarn you are going to use to make a garment, you must think about the way that the yarn is intended to behave. If (for example) the pattern you have chosen is for a floaty longer length jacket, then the chances are that the yarn used by the designer will have a fine quality to it, such as a light cotton or a silk.

To be sure you make the right yarn choice, work a good-sized gauge (tension) sample before you begin on your project. This will not only allow you to evaluate drape, but will also confirm whether or not your chosen alternative achieves the same stitch count as the intended yarn.

Calculating yarn amounts

A pattern will tell you how much yarn to buy for your project. If you change the type of yarn used, then you may also have to change the amount of yarn you purchase. This is because all yarns will achieve a different length in relation to their weight. For example, a 1¾oz (50g) ball of DK wool may have as much as 131 yards (120 meters) of yarn, whereas a 1¾oz (50g) ball of cotton may have as little as 87 yards (80 meters). To calculate how many balls of an alternative yarn to buy work out the total yardage (meterage) of the original yarn then divide this by the yardage (meterage) of one ball of your chosen alternative.

Example:
Pattern requires 15 balls of DK wool (131yd/120m a ball) = 1965yd/1800m of yarn
So if you use DK Cotton yarn (87 yds/80m a ball) = 1965 divided by 87 = 22.5 (23 balls)

how to read a pattern

Crochet patterns come in two main types: the written kind, where the rows or rounds needed to complete the project are typed in word form; and charts or graphs, which rely on the reader to follow a schematic drawing. Some patterns will provide both these options, but within the last few years charts have become more commonplace because they are printed using less paper and are less open to misinterpretation since the crocheter is better able to understand abbreviations and terminology when looking at symbols.

Reading a written pattern

So as not to take up a huge amount of space, written patterns have standardized terminology and characters such as brackets and asterisks to denote repeated instructions.

Square brackets [ ] ×

Square brackets are used when an instruction needs to be repeated or where more than one stitch needs to be worked into the same stitch or place.

Asterisks *

These are sometimes used in place of, or can be written in conjunction with, square brackets. The most common place to find an asterisk is in a command such as "rep from *," which would mean that you find the first asterisk above this instruction and repeat the section of pattern from this point. Sometimes asterisks are used in pairs, for example "rep from * until **." This would mean that the pattern is repeated from the first single asterisk above the instruction to the following double pair. Be careful to make sure you are working from the correct asterisk, because some patterns use them throughout so you could be in danger of following the repeat from the wrong one. Always search for the first asterisk before the instruction.

Round brackets ( )

Round brackets are used to give you an extra written instruction, such as (counts as a stitch) or (20 stitches made). Round brackets are also commonly used to tell you the stitch count at the end of a row or a round.

Capital letters

Capital letters are often used in place of a color name to save space, or to avoid confusion in case you have decided to make the project in an alternative colorway. Colors may be listed in alphabetical order: A B C, or you may be given the first letter of a word, such as C for "contrast" or MS for "Main shade," for example. The letter used to describe the yarn should be listed alongside the yarn name in the materials list at the beginning of the pattern.

Example:
20 × 1¾oz (50g) Mohair yarn shade 328 Pink (MS)
3 × 1¾oz (50g) Mohair yarn shade 301 Blue (C)

This could also be written as:

20 × 1¾oz (50g) Mohair yarn shade 328 Pink (A)
3 × 1¾oz (50g) Mohair yarn shade 301 Blue (B)

abbreviations

Written patterns contain many abbreviations. These can differ depending upon whether you are following a US or UK pattern and can even be personal to a pattern writer or designer, so always check the given abbreviations to make sure that you have understood the instruction. For stitch abbreviations see page 33.

alt	alternate	dec	decrease	sl	slip
approx	approximately	foll(s)	following	ss	slip stitch
beg	beginning	gr	group	st(s)	stitch(es)
ch sp	chain space	inc	increase	stch	starting chain
ch(s)	chain(s)	nxt	next	tch	turning chain
CL	cluster	rem	remaining	tog	together
cm	centimeter	rep	repeat	yo	yarn over
cont	continue	RS	right side	WS	wrong side

reading a symbol chart

Symbol charts can take a little practice to get to grips with, especially if you have got used to working from a written pattern. However, their advantage is that they take up a lot less space on the page, and also give you an immediate visual idea of how the crochet piece is destined to turn out. As with abbreviations and terminology, the symbols used can vary from pattern to pattern so check the symbol references to make sure that you have fully understood the instructions.

Most commonly used stitch symbols

Below is a chart showing the symbols for the most commonly used stitches.

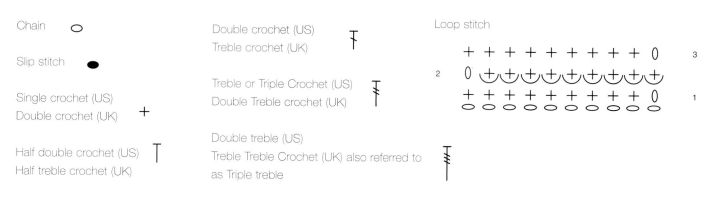

Chain

Slip stitch

Single crochet (US)
Double crochet (UK)

Half double crochet (US)
Half treble crochet (UK)

Double crochet (US)
Treble crochet (UK)

Treble or Triple Crochet (US)
Double Treble crochet (UK)

Double treble (US)
Treble Treble Crochet (UK) also referred to as Triple treble

Loop stitch

Recognizing groups of stitches

You may notice that some symbols are grouped to form "V" shapes. These indicate a group of stitches that need to be worked into the same stitch or space. They will increase the number of stitches over a given distance.

The stitch symbols below indicate that either 2, 3, 4 or 5 stitches should be worked into one stitch or space on the previous row. Some may denote a special stitch, such as a Shell Stitch.

A "tent" shaped group of symbols (∧) indicates a series of stitches that are partially worked into a range of positions and completed by drawing yarn through all the loops on the hook. The stitches are gathered together. They will decrease the number of stitches over a given distance.

The stitch symbols below indicate that either 3, 4 or 5 stitches need to be worked together. These symbols are found when working a pattern such as a chevron.

Bobbles, clusters and popcorns

The stitch symbols for these stitches portray an increase and then a decrease of stitches, and mimic the appearance of the stitches themselves. Some bobble and cluster symbols can look very similar, but a popcorn will usually have an oval shape at the top to denote its open end.

Picots

Picots are shown by a group of chain (the example below shows 4 chain) joined with a slip stitch. The number of chain can vary depending upon the pattern.

Bullion stitch

The symbol for bullion stitch is a long line with a semi-circle half way down. Do not confuse this with the symbol for raised stitches, which shows the semi circle at the bottom of the line.

Crossed stitches

Symbols that intersect indicate a pair or group of crossed stitches. The examples below show a pair of stitches crossed, one stitch crossed over a pair and a pair crossed over with a chain in between.

Spike stitches

Vertical lines traveling down from a row of stitching indicate where the hook should be placed to create the spike stitch.

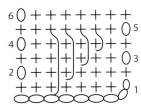

Raised stitches

Raised stitches are made by working around the post made by a previous stitch. A raised stitch is indicated by a vertical line with a curved end.

If the open end is to the left, then a raised stitch will be created on the side being worked—front post.

If the open end is to the right, then a raised stitch will be created on the reverse of the side being worked—back post.

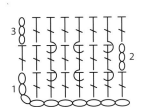

Back/front loop

The symbol for working into the back side of the chain that runs along the top of your working fabric is a dark horizontal line. The symbol for working into the front side of the chain is a lightweight line.

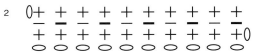

Back and front loops may also be represented by half ovals. If the open side is to the bottom, only the back loop is worked and, if the open side is to the top, only the front loop is worked.

Curved and distorted symbols

In order to achieve the shape of the finished crochet piece, the symbols often need to be distorted or drawn on a curve instead of in a straight line. In addition, sometimes a complex detail may be drawn to one side with an arrow indicating the its position.

A chart may show extra large oval chain symbols, for example, so that there is enough space for all the symbols, and therefore stitches, required by the design.

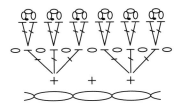

Additional symbols

Arrows and numbers may be used to indicate which direction to work and what row or round number is being worked. The chart may have a symbol for joining in a new color, or may be printed in more than one color to make the change obvious.

crochet basics

Before starting to tackle the basic crochet stitches you will need to familiarize yourself with a few essential techniques. It is worth taking plenty of time to get to grips with these so that you have the confidence to progress to the next level. Make sure that you have all the equipment needed, such as a pair of scissors and some stitch markers, and that you have a comfortable setting, with good light, and plenty of time in which to work.

first steps

First of all you need to learn how to hold the hook and the yarn correctly. When learning to crochet, choose a yarn that is smooth yet not too slippery—such as a good quality cotton—and the compatible crochet hook. Make sure your hands are clean and that your fingernails are smooth.

Holding the hook

You can choose to hold the crochet hook in one of two ways—choose whichever feels more comfortable. Be careful not to hold the hook too tightly or hold it too close to the tip.

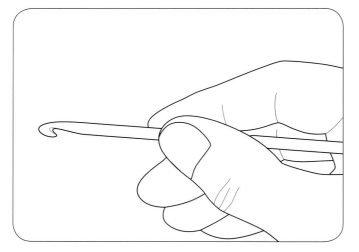

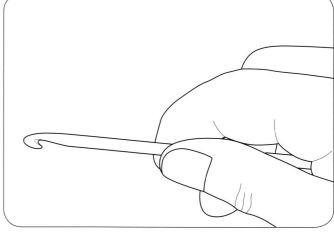

1 Some people hold the crochet hook as if it were a pencil, with their thumb resting on the flat part of the hook and their index finger also resting on the top side of the hook.

2 Some people hold the crochet hook in the palm of their hand, with their thumb resting on the flat part of the hook and their remaining fingers holding the hook from the underside.

Using both hands

The hand that holds the hook is not required to hold the yarn as well—the yarn is held in the other hand. If you are already a knitter you may be tempted to hold the hook and the yarn in the same hand, as you do when knitting. This will not make your stitches wrong, but crocheting will be a slower process than if you teach one hand to hold the hook and the other to hold the yarn.

Direction of the hook

In order to work crochet stitches the crochet hook needs to be held in different ways, or turned in numerous directions, in order to catch the yarn and produce stitches.

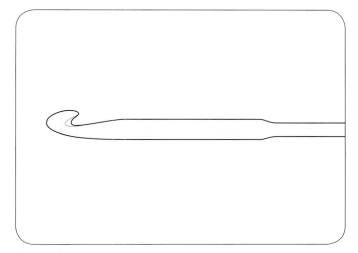

Hook facing up.

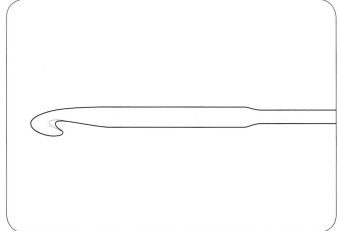

Hook facing down.

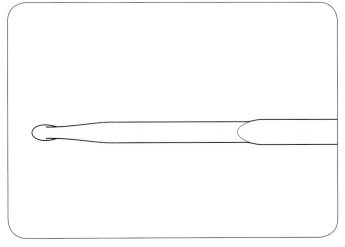

Hook facing away.

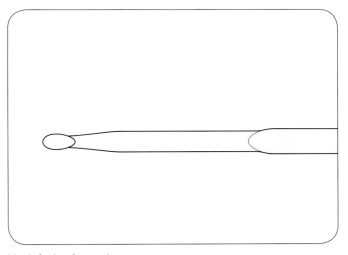

Hook facing forwards.

Making a slip knot

In order to start crocheting you need to have a starting stitch on the hook. This is made by making a slip knot.

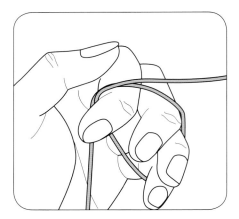

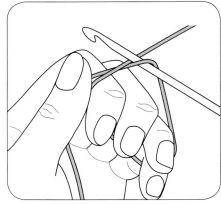

1 Leaving a tail end of approx 4in. (10cm), make a loop in the yarn by wrapping it once around the fingers of your left hand.

2 Pass the tip of the crochet hook through the loop and over the ball end of the yarn with the hook facing down.

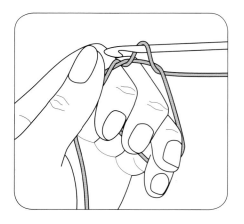

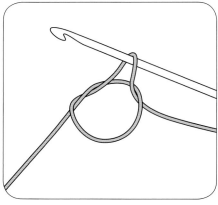

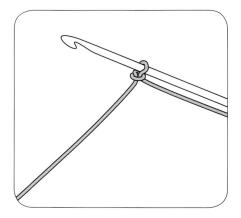

3 Use the hook to catch the ball end of yarn and pull it back through the loop.

4 Keeping the new stitch on the hook, slip the loop from your left hand.

5 Pull gently on the tail end of yarn to tighten the slip knot around the hook.

Identifying the tail end and ball end

You will find throughout this book that the yarn is referred to as either being the "tail end" or the "ball end." The tail end is the cut end of yarn, which has thus created a tail, the ball end is the working yarn that is coming from the ball.

Holding the yarn

One of the keys to producing a good crochet fabric is to achieve an even gauge (tension). Your left hand plays a vital role in this by tensioning the ball end of the yarn whilst you create your stitches. Crocheters tend to achieve this tension by holding the yarn in the left hand in various ways; in most cases the yarn is wrapped around or held between two fingers.

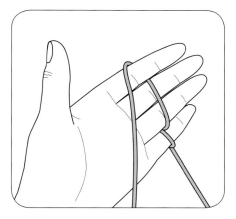

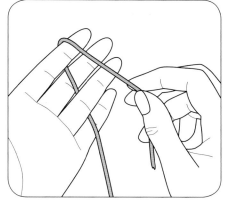

1 Leaving a length of yarn approx 4in. (10cm) from the loop on the hook, wrap the yarn around the little finger of your left hand, across the inside of your two middle fingers and then behind your index finger and to the front leaving it to rest on your index finger.

2 Leaving a length of yarn approx 4in. (10cm) from the loop on the hook, weave the yarn around the fingers of your left hand, starting with your little finger and ending with the yarn sitting behind your index finger and to the front leaving it to rest on your index finger.

Tensioning the tail

If you do not create a tension on the tail end of yarn you will find that you are attempting to crochet in mid air. The tension of the tail is regulated by the left hand.

Use the middle finger and thumb of your left hand to pull gently on the tail end of yarn by pinching it just below the hook.

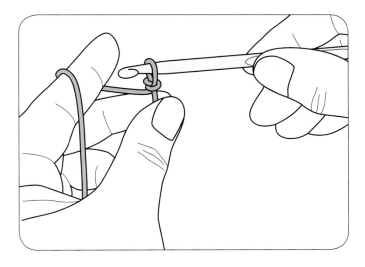

Working a foundation chain

Crochet nearly always starts with a series of chain stitches. These stitches form the basis of the work and are equivalent to the "cast on" used in knitting. Chain stitches are also used to take the hook to the correct height at the end of a row in preparation for the following row. You may find that you struggle to keep an even gauge (tension) at first, but it is important to keep the chains even and not to make them too tight or loose. With practice you should find that this becomes easier.

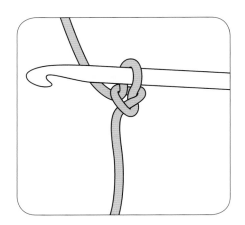

1 Place a slip knot on the hook and hold it in the right hand. Hold the yarn in the left hand, using your preferred method, and at the same time keep a good tension on the tail end of the yarn. With the yarn sitting to the reverse of the hook, turn the hook so that it is facing away from you.

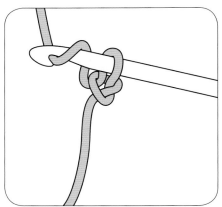

2 *Push the crochet hook against the yarn then rotate the hook in an counterclockwise direction in order to catch the yarn around the hook, finishing the step with the hook facing down.

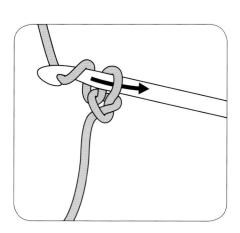

3 Draw the yarn through the slip knot or the loop on the hook. Note that the fingers tensioning the tail end of the yarn are not shown in steps 1–4 to keep the diagrams clear and simple, but the yarn should be kept under tension at all times.

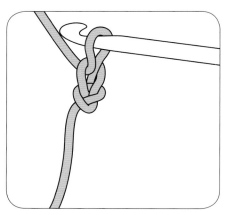

4 Rotate the hook in the opposite direction so that the hook is left facing up and the new stitch is resting on the hook.

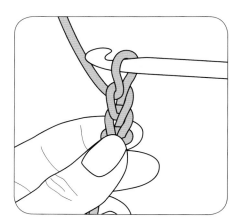

5 Continue to work from * to create more chain stitches. You will need to reposition the tensioning fingers of your left hand every couple of stitches to ensure a good tension on the yarn.

Counting chains

When working from a pattern you will be asked to work a given number of chain, so it is important that you can recognize the formation of each chain and thus count correctly.

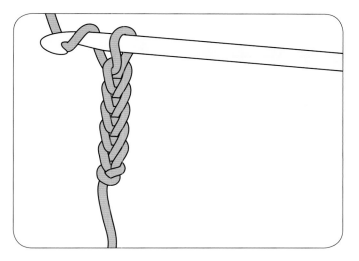

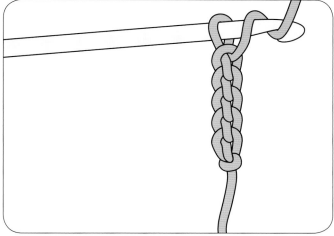

The front of the chain looks like a series of V shapes made by the yarn. Each V is a chain loop sitting between a chain loop above and a chain loop below. The first chain at the beginning will have the slip knot sitting directly underneath it. The surface of the chain is smooth on this side. Stitches should be counted from this side of the chain where possible.

The reverse of the chain has a row of bumps that have been created by the yarn. These bumps sit behind the V and run in a vertical direction from the beginning of the chain up to the hook. The surface of the reverse of the chain is more textural than the front side.

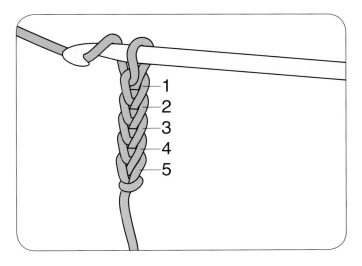

When counting the chain you do not count the stitch that sits on the hook. This is because a loop will remain on the hook up until the moment you fasten off. When creating a large number of chain it may be a good idea to use stitch markers at a predetermined interval, say every 10 or 20 stitches, to make counting easier.

Avoiding too tight chain stitches

When making chain (or subsequent stitches) you must make sure that each stitch is taken up onto the thicker part of the hook before starting the next one. If you work your stitches on the thinner part of the hook they will become tight, and you will struggle to place your hook into them on subsequent rows.

Turning chain

When creating rows or rounds of crochet in various stitches you will need to make a chain long enough to take you to the height of your next row before you commence your chosen stitches. When working on a flat piece of crochet, the chains created at the end of a row are referred to as turning chains. Each stitch has a suggested number of chains that should take your hook to the correct height for the row. However, if you find that the chain is creating either a loop, or appears to be pulling the subsequent stitches too tight, you may need to change the number of chain stitches worked.

US	UK
Single Crochet = 1 chain	Double Crochet = 1 chain
Half Double Crochet = 2 chain	Half treble crochet = 2 chain
Double Crochet = 3 chain	Treble Crochet = 3 chain
Treble Crochet = 4 chain	Double Treble Crochet = 4 chain

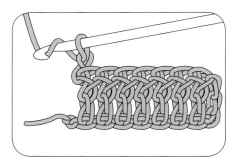 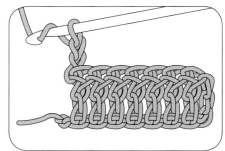

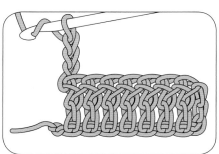 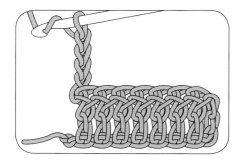

The turning chain is usually counted as the first stitch of the row. For example the written pattern may say something such as: "3ch (counts as a dc (UK tr))." This would mean that you work 3 chain to get you to the height of the row and that the 3 chain will then subsequently count as

the equivalent of one double crochet (UK treble crochet) stitch.

In some cases you may find that the chain count is longer than the stitch height. This could be because the chain has to travel not only in a vertical direction to create the height of the row, but also

in a horizontal direction to travel along the row. For example, the written pattern may say: 5ch (counts as 1dc (UK tr) and 2ch). This would mean that 3 of the chain are worked to replicate a double crochet (UK treble crochet) and the remaining 2ch are made in order to travel along the row.

At the end of the row or round you will need to work your final stitch into the top of the turning or starting chain of the previous row. The top of the chain will look different to the other stitches and will not always have a clear gap in which to place your hook. Failure to work a stitch into the top of the turning or starting chain (where required) will mean that you achieve the incorrect stitch count.

Starting or turning chains

When working in the round with always the same side facing, the chains created at the beginning of the round to get the hook to the height of the next stitch is sometimes referred to as a starting chain. In the case of a turning chain the work is turned, so alternate sides of the work face the crocheter.

basic stitches

The technique of crochet can be very relaxing and rewarding and the variation of fabrics that can be created is almost endless. There are a variety of stitches used to create the crochet fabric; sometimes these stitches are used alone to create a standard consistent fabric, other times they are used together to create a more unusual and variegated pattern or to create a motif. There are five stitches to learn in this section.

US		UK	
Single Crochet	sc	Double Crochet	dc
Double Crochet	dc	Treble Crochet	tr
Half Double Crochet	hdc	Half Treble Crochet	htr
Treble or Triple Crochet	tr	Double Treble Crochet	dtr
Slip Stitch	ss	Slip Stitch	ss

Working into the foundation chain

To create a crochet fabric, stitches are worked into the foundation chain to create the first row. Subsequent rows are then usually worked into the top of the previous row. The first row can be a little tricky because you will be working into the foundation chain and not into stitches. If you find that your foundation chain is too tight then it may be an idea to make this chain on a slightly larger hook.

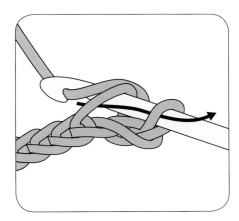

1 When working into the foundation chain, you can choose whether to place your hook into the top side of the chain, thus working over just one yarn.

2 Or you may decide to place your hook into the lower part of the chain, thus working over two yarns.

The back of the chain

To make a decorative edging you can work your foundation row into the yarn 'bumps' at the reverse of the foundation chain. This can be a little tricky, but creates a nice edge where the foundation chain is clearly visible on the right side.

Single crochet (UK double crochet)

This is probably the most commonly used crochet stitch; it is hard wearing and durable and the fabric produced has a dense, sturdy feel. It is a very good stitch to use for things for the home such as cushion covers and blankets. The abbreviation for this stitch in a pattern is sc (dc in the UK).

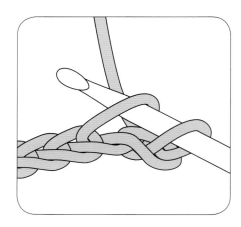

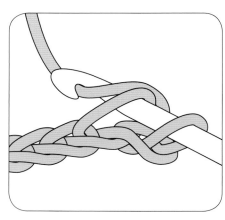

1 To work the first row, make a foundation chain to the required length, adding 1 chain to allow for turning. Insert your hook into the second chain below the hook.

2 *With the hook facing forward, pass the hook under the yarn so that this crosses over the hook.

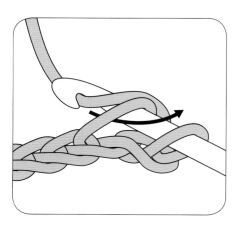

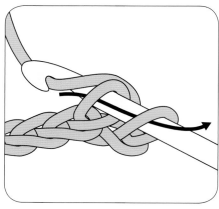

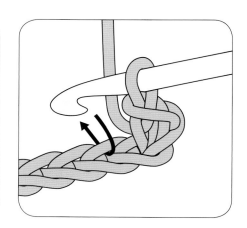

3 Rotate the hook counterclockwise until it faces down, in order to catch the yarn. Draw the yarn through the chain stitch so that there are two loops on the crochet hook.

4 By rotating the crochet hook as before, catch the yarn again and draw the yarn through both loops on the crochet hook.

5 One complete single crochet (UK double crochet) stitch has been made. To continue, place the hook into the next foundation chain and repeat from *.

Calculating yarn amounts

For every row of stitches you will use between five and six times the length of the row in yarn. For example: a row that measures 8in. (20cm) could use up to 40in. (100cm) of yarn to complete.

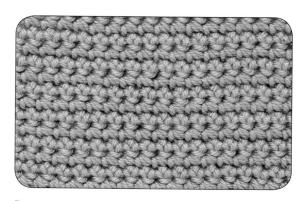

Repeated rows of single crochet (UK double crochet).

Counting stitches

With the right side facing you will see that there is the appearance of a chain running along the top of your first (or subsequent) row of double crochet. This chain looks much like the foundation chain, but it now has a series of V shaped stitches sitting underneath.

To count the stitches, count from the hook down to the end of the row, making sure that you do not count the stitch on the hook. The stitch at the very beginning of the row may be sitting in a slightly vertical direction.

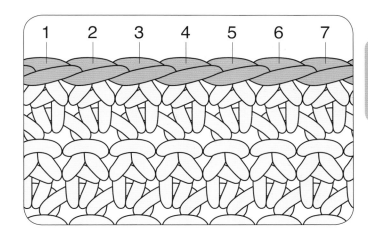

Counting stitches

To produce a good standard of crochet fabric, you must remember to count your stitches regularly. It is a good idea to count at the end of every row.

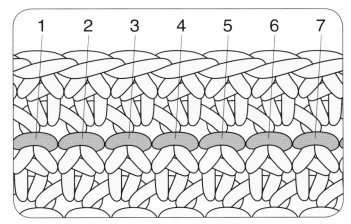

Working rows

Once you have completed your first row, you are ready to continue to work your fabric. The first row is always the hardest and subsequent rows are much easier to achieve.

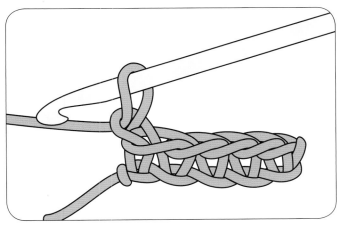

1 At the end of the first row, work 1 chain (as for foundation chain) and turn the work over so that the back is facing.

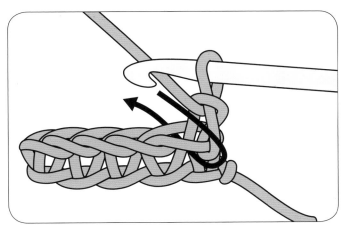

2 Insert the hook under the whole of the first stitch below the chain top loops. (This is the final stitch of the previous row and looks like a V shape running along the top of the piece of crochet) Work from * as for first row (see page 34).

Double crochet (UK treble crochet)

This stitch produces a more open and softer fabric than single crochet (UK double crochet). The stitches produced appear like posts leading up from the previous row, and because it produces these longer stitches this is quite a speedy stitch to complete once mastered. The abbreviation for this stitch in a pattern is dc (tr in the UK).

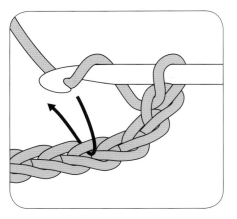

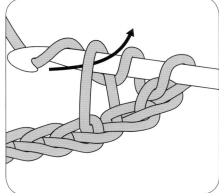

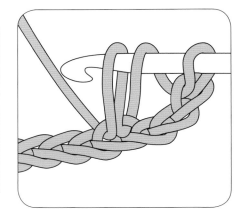

1 To work the first row, make a foundation chain to the required length, adding 3 chain to allow for turning. Wrap the yarn around the hook (from back to front) once. Insert the hook into the fourth chain below the hook.

2 *With the hook facing forward, pass the hook under the yarn so that it crosses over the hook. Rotate the hook counterclockwise until it faces down in order to catch the yarn. Draw the yarn through the chain stitch.

3 There are three loops on the crochet hook.

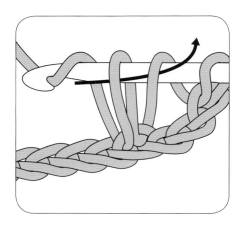

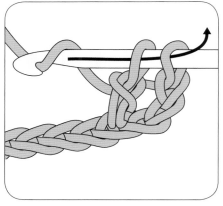

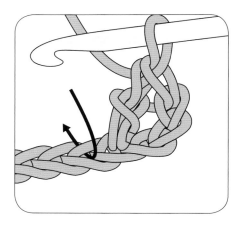

4 By rotating the crochet hook as before, catch the yarn again. Draw the yarn through two loops on the crochet hook.

5 Catch the yarn again and draw through the two remaining loops on the crochet hook.

6 One complete double crochet (UK treble crochet) stitch has been made. However, because the turning chain, in this case, is counted, two double crochet (UK treble crochet) stitches have been created. To continue, wrap the yarn around the hook, place the hook into the next foundation chain, and then repeat from *.

Counting stitches

With the right side facing you will see that there is a row of "post" stitches leading from the top of your first (or subsequent) row of stitches.

To count the stitches, count the posts from the hook down to the end of the row. The stitch at the very beginning of the row is the turning chain and is counted as a stitch.

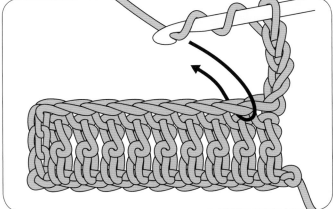

Working rows

The next row of double crochet (UK treble crochet) differs from the first in that the turning chain that leads from the last stitch of the previous row is counted as a stitch.

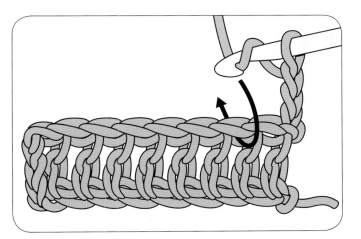

1 At the end of the first row, work 3 chain stitches (as for foundation chain) and turn the work over so that the back is facing. Wrap the yarn around the hook; insert the hook under the top two chain loops of the second stitch to the left of the turning chain. (This is the penultimate stitch of the previous row and looks like a chain running along the top of the piece of crochet.)

2 Work from * as for first row, working a double (UK treble) into every stitch. Work the final stitch into the top of the turning chain created on the previous row.

Calculating yarn amounts

For every row of stitches you will use between 13 and 14 times the length of the row in yarn. For example, a row that measures 8in. (20cm) could use up to 112in. (280cm) of yarn to complete.

Repeated rows of double crochet (UK treble crochet).

Half double crochet (UK half treble crochet)

This stitch produces a firm durable fabric and is often used in conjunction with other stitches when making variegated patterns or motifs. The abbreviation for this stitch in a pattern is hdc (htr in the UK).

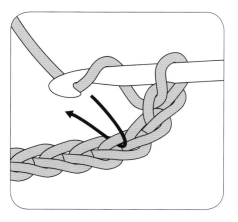

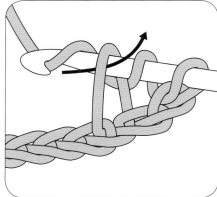

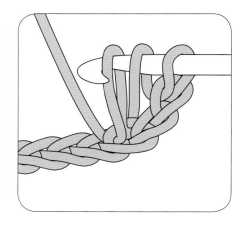

1 To work rows, make a foundation chain to the required length, adding 2 chain to allow for turning. Wrap the yarn around the hook; insert the hook into the third chain from the hook.

2 *With the hook facing forward, pass the hook under the yarn so that it crosses over the hook. Rotate the hook counterclockwise to face down and catch the yarn. Draw the yarn through the stitch.

3 There are three loops on the crochet hook.

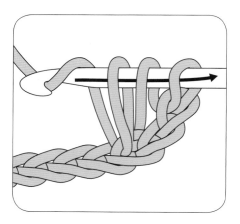

4 By rotating the crochet hook as before, catch the yarn again and draw through all the loops on the crochet hook.

5 One complete half double crochet (UK half treble crochet) stitch has been made.

6 To continue, wrap the yarn around the hook and place hook into next stitch and repeat from *.

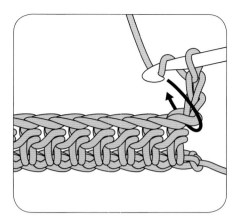 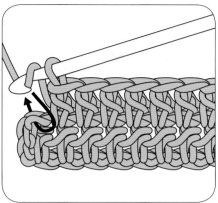

7 At the end of the row, chain 2 stitches and turn the work. For the first stitch, insert the hook into the stitch to the left of the turning chain. (This is the penultimate stitch of the previous row).

8 Work the final stitch of the row into the top of the turning chain of the previous row.

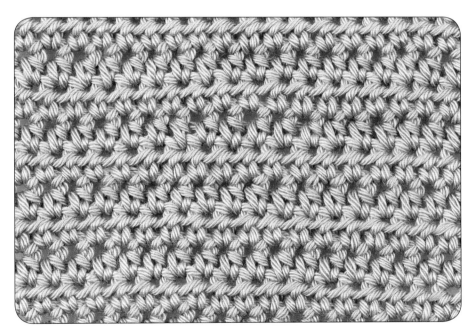

Repeated rows of half double crochet (UK half treble crochet).

Working the stitch

When drawing the yarn through three loops, take care not to split the yarn. Making sure that your hook is facing downwards and that your stitches are not too tight should make this step of the stitch easier.

Calculating yarn amounts

For every row of stitches you will use between 11 and 12 times the length of the row in yarn. For example: a row that measures 8in. (20cm) could use up to 96in. (240cm) of yarn to complete.

Treble crochet (UK double treble crochet)

This stitch is often used in conjunction with other stitches when making variegated patterns or motifs. The abbreviation for this stitch in a pattern is tr (dtr in the UK).

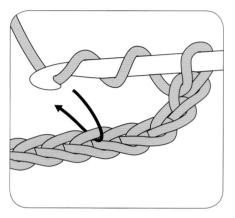

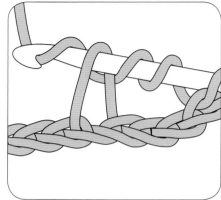

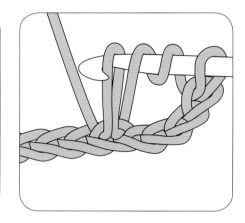

1 To work rows, make a foundation chain to the required length, adding 4 chain to allow for turning. Wrap the yarn around the hook twice; insert the hook into the 5th chain from the hook.

2 *With the hook facing forward, pass the hook under the yarn so that it crosses over the hook. Rotate the hook counterclockwise until it faces down in order to catch the yarn.

3 Draw the yarn through the stitch so that there are four loops on the crochet hook.

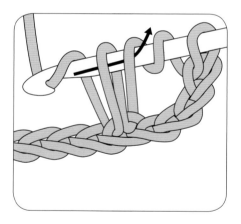

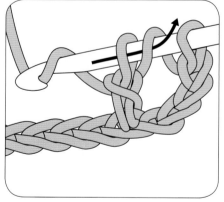

4 By rotating the crochet hook as before, catch the yarn again and draw through two of the loops on the crochet hook.

5 Catch the yarn again and draw through the next two loops on the crochet hook.

6 Catch the yarn again and draw through the remaining two loops on the crochet hook.

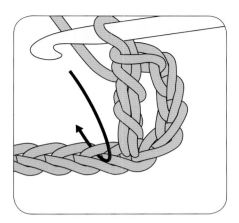

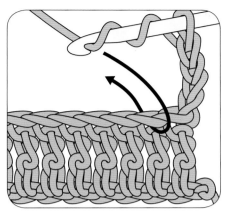

7 To continue, wrap the yarn around the hook twice, place hook into next chain, or as indicated by pattern instructions, and repeat from *.

8 At the end of the row, chain 4 stitches and turn the work. The first treble (UK double treble) is worked into the second stitch to the left of the turning chain. (This is the penultimate stitch of the previous row). At the end of the row. Work the final stitch into the top of the turning chain of the previous row.

Repeated rows of treble crochet (UK double treble crochet).

Calculating yarn amounts

For every row of stitches you will use between 20 and 21 times the length of the row in yarn. For example: a row that measures 20cm (8in) could use up to 168in. (420cm) of yarn to complete.

More stitches

Most crochet stitches produce what is referred to as a post, which is the vertical part of the stitch that leads from the previous row.

The length of the post of the stitch will vary, depending upon how many times you wrap the yarn around the hook before you begin the process of working into the previous row or chain. The more times you wrap the yarn, the more times you repeat the process of drawing the yarn through the loops on the hook.

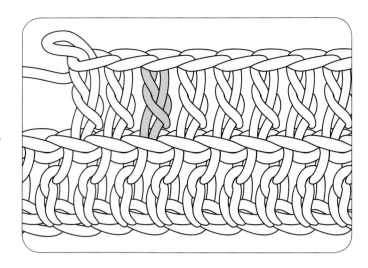

US	UK	Wrap Yarn
Double Treble Crochet (dtr)	Triple Treble Crochet (ttr)	3 Times
Triple Triple Crochet (trtr)	Quadruple Treble Crochet (quad tr)	4 Times

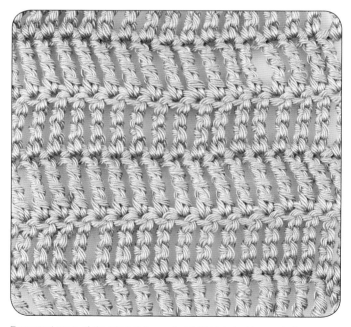

Repeated rows of double treble crochet (UK triple treble crochet).

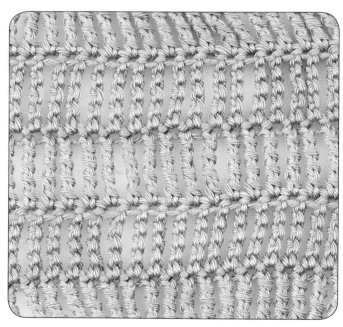

Repeated rows of triple treble crochet (UK quadruple treble crochet).

Slip stitch

Slip stitch is most commonly used in order to travel from one point in your crochet to another, or to complete a row at the end of a round. This stitch adds very little height to the work and is unlikely to be used to produce a whole fabric.

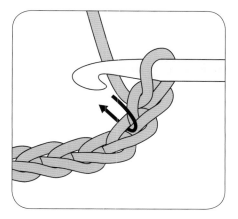
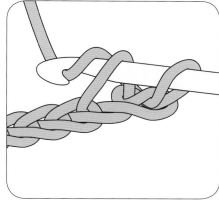
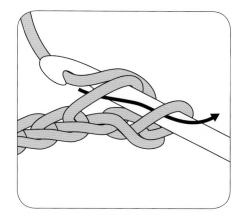

1 Make a foundation chain to the required length, adding 1 chain to allow for turning. Insert the hook into the second chain from the hook.

2 *With the hook facing forward, pass the hook under the yarn so that it crosses over the hook. Rotate the hook counterclockwise until it faces down in order to catch the yarn.

3 Draw the yarn through both the stitches on the crochet hook. To continue, insert the hook into the next chain and repeat from *.

Fastening off

Unlike a knitted fabric, crochet stitches cannot unravel in a vertical direction—but will work loose one by one across a row if the work falls from the hook, or is not fastened off once complete.

When the final stitch of the crochet piece is completed, slip the loop from the crochet hook and cut the yarn leaving a tail end of approximately 4in. (10cm). Thread the cut end of yarn through the loop from the back to front. Pull on the yarn to tighten the stitch.

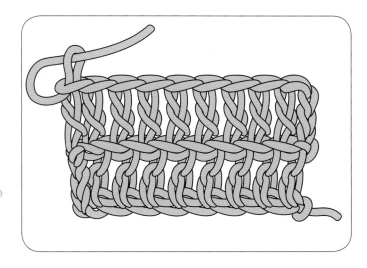

extended stitches

Extended stitches are exactly what they say they are! An extended stitch is worked in the same way as the stitches you have already learnt, except that an extra step is added in the form of an extra wrap of yarn around the hook to make the post of the stitch slightly longer.

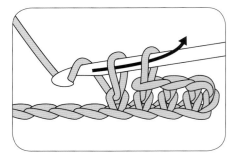

Insert the hook into the stitch. Wrap the yarn around the hook and draw through the stitch. Wrap the yarn around the hook again and draw through the first loop only on the hook. Wrap the yarn around the hook once more and draw through the remaining 2 loops on the hook.

Repeated rows of extended single crochet (UK extended double crochet).

Extended half double crochet (UK extended half treble crochet)

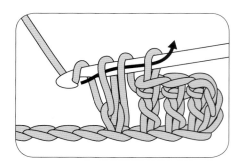

Wrap the yarn around the hook. Insert the hook into the stitch. Wrap the yarn around the hook and draw through the stitch. Wrap the yarn around the hook again and draw through the first loop only on the hook. Wrap the yarn around the hook once more and draw through the remaining 3 loops on the hook.

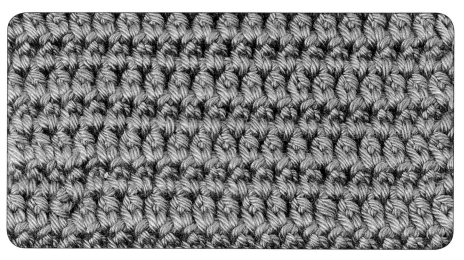

Repeated rows of extended half double crochet (UK extended half treble crochet).

Extended double crochet (UK extended treble crochet)

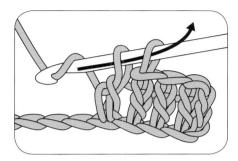

Wrap the yarn around the hook. Insert the hook into the stitch. Wrap the yarn around the hook and draw through the stitch. Wrap the yarn around the hook and draw through the first loop only on the hook. *Wrap the yarn around the hook again and draw through 2 of the remaining loops on the hook. Wrap the yarn around the hook once more and draw through the remaining 2 loops on the hook.

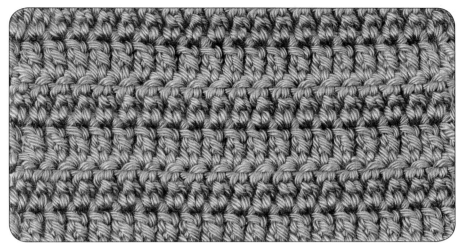

Repeated rows of extended double crochet (UK extended treble crochet).

Extended treble crochet (UK extended double treble crochet)

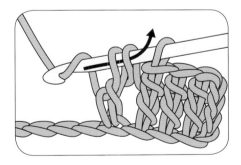

Wrap the yarn around the hook twice. Insert the hook into the stitch. Wrap the yarn around the hook and draw through the stitch. Wrap the yarn around the hook once more and draw through the first loop only on the hook. *Wrap the yarn around the hook and draw through 2 of the remaining loops on the hook. Repeat from * once more. Wrap the yarn around the hook again and draw through the remaining 2 loops on the hook.

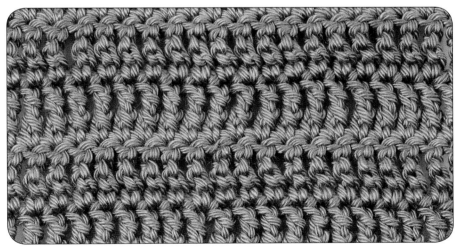

Repeated rows of extended half treble crochet (UK extended double treble crochet).

working in the correct way

Now that you have learnt the basic techniques of crochet there are some important factors that need to be taken into consideration before you launch into your first project. It is worth taking time to familiarize yourself with these, because it can save you time (and perhaps disappointment) later on. If you fail to work in the correct way you could be disheartened by the outcome of all your hard work.

Gauge (tension)

When you were a child, you were probably taught to hand write in the same way as your fellow students. However—even though the formulation of each letter was constructed and taught to you all in the same manner—the style of writing that you eventually adopted almost certainly varied from person to person within your school class. If you assume this thinking in terms of crochet it's obvious that—although everyone may all be formulating the stitches in the same way—each person will achieve a fabric that is unique to them.

One of the main reasons you end up with these distinctive fabrics is the gauge or tension. Achieving an incorrect gauge (tension) could mean that your project comes up the wrong size and that the drape/feel of the fabric created is either inconsistent, or too stiff or loose.

Working a gauge (tension) swatch

Before you start a crochet project, it is advisable to work a small swatch to measure the gauge (tension) This means the number of stitches and rows that you achieve to a pre-defined measurement—usually a 4in. (10cm) square. In some cases you may be asked to count pattern repeats within a set area rather than individual stitches, but either way the crochet pattern should give you an ideal gauge (tension). It is advisable to work a few more stitches and rows than the pattern gauge (tension) instruction suggests, so a true gauge (tension) is achieved within the square.

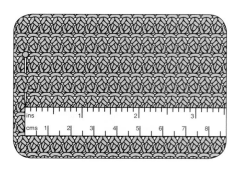

1 Using the correct hook, yarn and stitches for the project, make a gauge (tension) swatch then use a metal ruler to measure 4in. (10cm) horizontally across the square. Mark this length with a pin at each end.

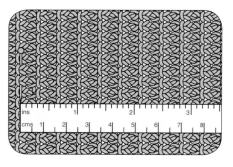

2 Do the same vertically. Count the number of stitches and rows between the pins.

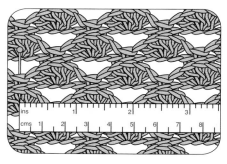

3 Measuring over a pattern follows the same principle.

This shows a crochet fabric which has been worked tighter than the ideal gauge (tension).

This shows a crochet fabric which has been worked to the ideal gauge (tension).

This shows a crochet fabric which has been worked looser than the ideal gauge (tension).

Adjusting gauge (tension)

If you find that you have more rows or stitches than the pattern suggests, then the gauge (tension) is too tight and you should switch to a larger hook. If there are fewer stitches or rows, then switch to a smaller size.

Measuring a block

The gauge (tension) of a motif or block is usually taken once the piece has been finished and blocked or steamed. Because you can achieve various motif/block shapes with crochet, you will need to be aware of how they should be measured.

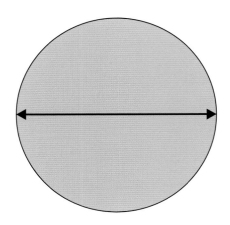

Circular block: Measure straight across the diameter.

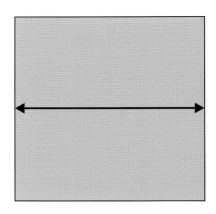

Square block: Measure straight across the center.

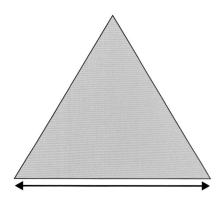

Triangular block: Measure straight across the base.

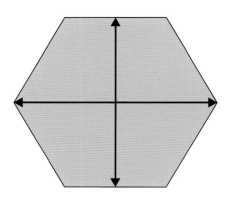

Hexagonal block (six sides): Measure across the widest point—this is point to point—or from side to side depending on which your pattern requires.

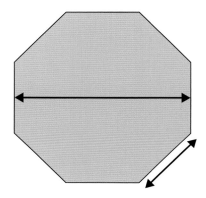

Octagonal block (eight sides): Measure from side to side, or across one edge depending on which your pattern requires.

Accurate measuring

When measuring pieces of crochet it is a good idea to block and/or steam them first. Crochet fabric has a tendency to curl up, which can make it a little tricky to measure accurately.

When measuring larger pieces try to use a metal or plastic ruler rather than a tape measure, because this will ensure that you are measuring in a straight line.

Recognizing the reverse and front side of the work

Because stitches are very similar in appearance on the reverse and the front side of a piece of crochet, it is worth taking some time to learn to recognize the formation of your stitches to avoid inconsistencies. When working on a flat piece you will have the front of a stitch showing on one row and the reverse of a stitch showing on the next, so every alternate row will look the same. However, when working in the round, without turning, you will have either the front of the stitch showing or the reverse.

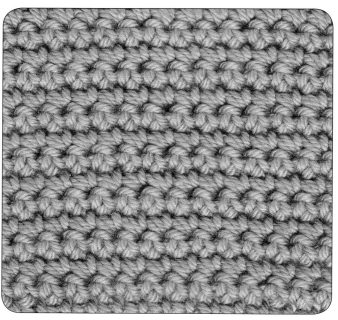

Single crochet (UK double crochet) when worked in a flat piece.

Marking the right side

In order to avoid mistakes you may want to use stitch markers or sew a small piece of waste yarn to the right side of your crochet fabric to help you distinguish one side from the other.

Front side of single crochet (UK double crochet) when worked in the round.

Reverse side of single crochet (UK double crochet) when worked in the round.

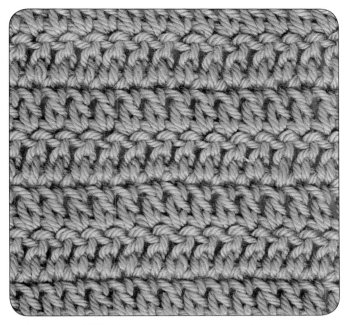

Double crochet (UK treble crochet) when worked in a flat piece.

Identifying the front side

When you get used to how stitches look you will be able to determine the front of the fabric by looking at the foundation row. The side where the chain is more visible is the front and on the back the chain is less obvious.

Front side of double crochet (UK treble crochet) when worked in the round.

Reverse side of double crochet (UK treble crochet) when worked in the round.

Joining in a new yarn

There are various ways of joining in a new yarn, depending upon which stitch you are using and whether or not you are working a flat fabric with repeated rows, or are working in the round or on a motif/block.

Joining in yarn using slip stitch

This method can be used for any stitch, but is best worked at the beginning of a row and not when working in the round.

Fasten off the yarn that has run out. Place a slip knot made from the new yarn on the hook. Place hook through the first stitch of the row, wrap the new yarn around the hook and draw it through all the loops on the hook to create a slip stitch. Continue to work with the new yarn. When the fabric is complete, undo the slip knot and sew in the yarn end.

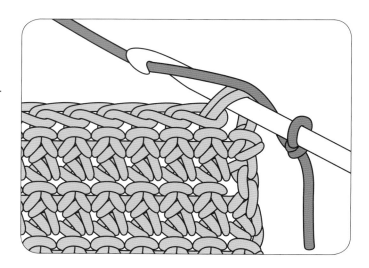

Joining in yarn using single crochet (UK double crochet)

Use these methods of joining in a new yarn at the end or the middle of a row when working on a flat piece of fabric.

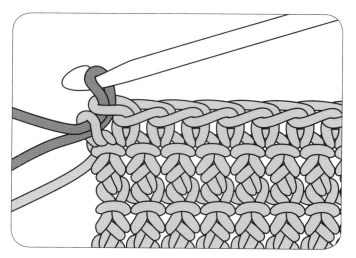

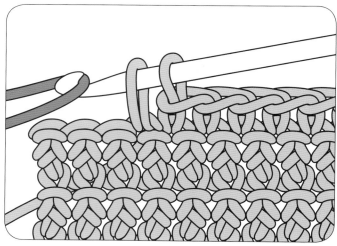

1 To join a new yarn at the end of a row, in your final stitch of the row work through the stitch until the final step of the stitch, thus leaving two loops on the hook. Wrap the new yarn around the hook and draw through the two loops.

2 When joining mid way through a row, join in the new yarn where the pattern indicates by working through the stitch until the final step of the stitch, thus leaving two loops on the hook. Wrap the new yarn around the hook and draw through the two loops. Continue to work in new yarn as required.

Joining in yarn using other stitches

When using stitches that create a post as part of their formation—such as double crochet (UK treble crochet)—use the following methods.

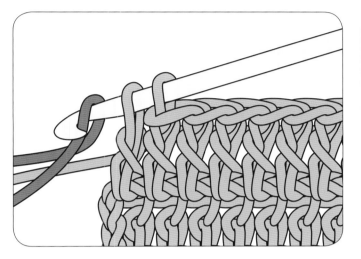

1 On your final stitch, work through the stitch until the final step of the stitch, with the last two loops on the hook. Wrap the new yarn around the hook and draw through the two loops.

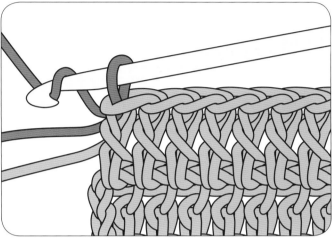

2 Turn and work the following row with the new yarn. You may want to knot the two yarn ends together to prevent them from slipping through the stitch and unraveling, but always undo the knot before sewing in the yarn ends.

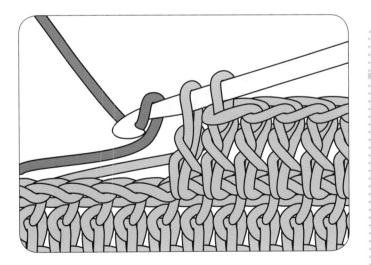

3 When joining mid row, join in the new yarn where the pattern indicates by working through the stitch until the final step of the stitch, with the last two loops on the hook. Wrap the new yarn around the hook and draw through the two loops. Continue to work in new yarn as required.

Joining a new yarn

When working on a flat piece always try and join a new yarn on the final stitch of a row in preparation for use on the first stitch of the following row.

When joining a new yarn part way through a row, it is important to create a really neat join, otherwise the yarn change could be obvious and may spoil the outcome of your piece.

Joining in a new yarn when working in the round or on a motif/block

You could choose to use any of the methods shown on pages 52–53 to join in a new yarn when working in the round or on a block or motif. However, you will get a much neater appearance if you join in the new yarn once you have fastened off the previous yarn.

Fasten off the previous yarn. Insert hook into the final stitch. Make the required number of chain to work the chosen stitch then continue to work in new yarn as required.

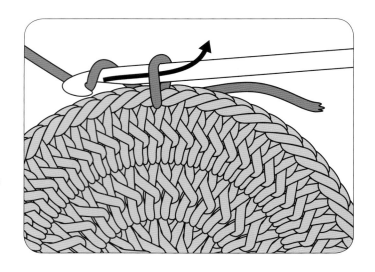

Working into spaces created by stitches or chain

You may find that you are asked to work a stitch or group of stitches into a space (abbreviation sp) created on the previous row or round, as opposed to working into a stitch.

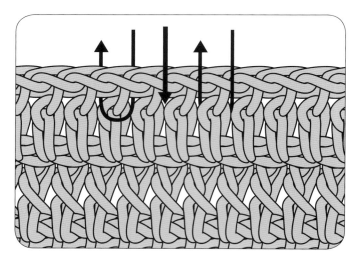

1 To work into the space between two stitches when using stitches that create a post as part of their formation—such as double crochet (UK treble crochet)—you will need to insert the hook into the gap that is formed between the two stitches, which is lower that the chain stitch that runs along the top of the piece and that joins one stitch to the next.

2 To work into a space created by a chain, insert the hook into the gap created by the chain and not into individual stitches. You will see that this causes the stitches to wrap themselves around the chain and cover it.

Skipping stitches

In some cases a pattern may ask you to skip either one or a number of stitches, either to decrease the stitch count or to make a pattern repeat work. To skip the required number of stitches you will need to count the stitches on the previous row, then work your subsequent stitch into the first stitch beyond this stitch or group of stitches. This technique is often used in lace or open work.

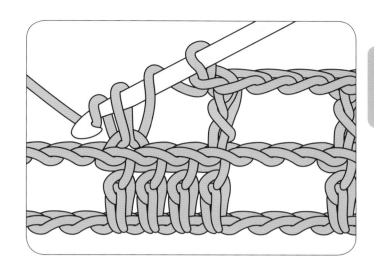

Weaving over a yarn end

To avoid the need to sew yarn ends in (page 56), you can choose to work your next row of crochet over the top of a yarn end, thus trapping it within the formation of the stitch.

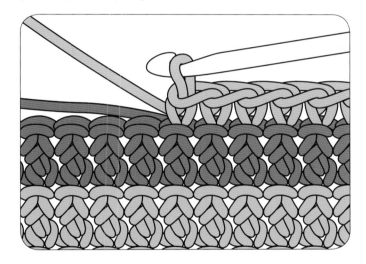

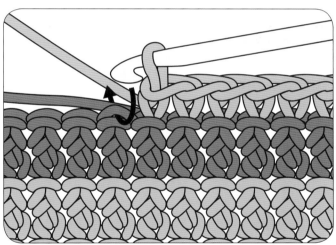

1 Work to the position of the yarn tails and prepare to work the stitch of your choice. Hold the tail end of the yarn in line with the top of the previous row, to the left of the stitches just worked.

2 Insert the hook into the following stitch position and under the tail end of yarn. Complete the stitch, trapping the yarn tail within it. Repeat for approximately 2in. (5cm) Trim the remaining yarn, being careful not to cut too close to the final stitch.

Sewing in yarn ends

If you are working on a piece that uses more than one length of yarn, you will need to either sew or weave (page 55) these in to create a neat and durable piece of crochet fabric. If you do not finish off the yarn ends then your piece may unravel.

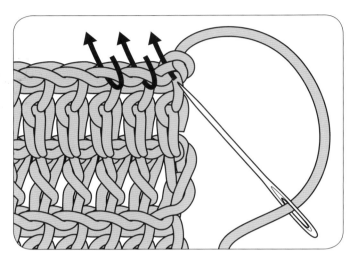

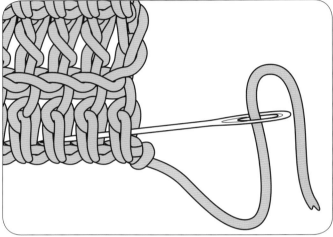

1 To sew in a yarn end at the top edge, thread a large tapestry needle with the yarn end and sew though the reverse side of each stitch of the last row of crochet. Sew for approximately 2in. (5cm) then make an extra stitch into the final back loop. Trim the remaining yarn, being careful not to cut too close to the final stitch.

2 To sew in a yarn end at the lower edge, thread a large tapestry needle with the yarn end and sew though the core of each stitch of the first row of crochet. Sew for approximately 2in. (5cm) then bring the yarn though the work and make an extra stitch into the back loop of a stitch. Trim the remaining yarn, being careful not to cut too close to the final stitch.

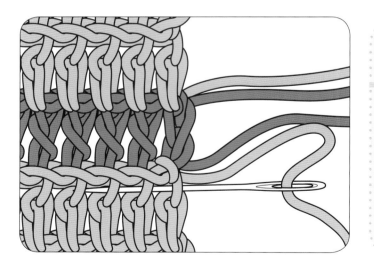

Keeping things neat and tidy

It is a really good idea to sew the yarn ends in as often as possible as you work. This will mean that your work stays neater, stitches are less likely to unravel and you will not be faced with a mammoth sewing task once your crochet is complete.

3 To sew in yarn ends on a stripe pattern work using either of the two above methods, being careful that the yarn ends are not showing through to the right side of the work.

working in the round

Many crochet motifs are created by working in the round. This often means that there is no need to turn your work at the end of each row, so that you constantly have one side of the work facing you. Working in the round is relatively easy and most of the techniques used should now be familiar to you, but some of the techniques may be used in a slightly different way when working in the round.

Making a ring using a chain

To start your circular motif, you need to create a base of chain stitches to work around.

1 Make the required number of chain; the more chain that are made at the start, the larger the hole at the center of the motif will be.

2 Join the chain using a slip stitch: to do this, insert the hook into the first chain made after the initial slip knot.

3 Wrap the yarn around the hook and bring through all loops on the hook. Tighten by pulling gently on the yarn.

Placing the hook correctly

If you are not used to working into a ring it can be tricky working out where to place the hook. Once you have joined the ring with a slip stitch—and before you start working the next row—open out the ring with your fingers to identify the center so you do not work into a chain by mistake.

Making a yarn ring

Instead of using chain to make your ring base, you can choose to make a yarn ring. This method should not be used with slippery yarns as they can loosen over time.

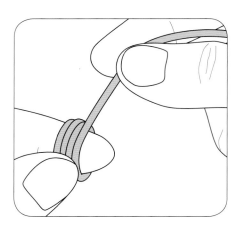

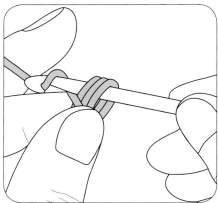

1 Wind the yarn several times around your left index finger, holding the yarn end secure between the finger and your thumb.

2 Carefully slip the yarn ring from your finger and onto the crochet hook. Wrap the yarn around the hook and draw through the center of the ring. Work the required number of chain to create the height of the chosen stitch.

Working stitches into the center of the ring

The central ring will be covered over by your first row of stitches, so it will not be visible once your piece is complete.

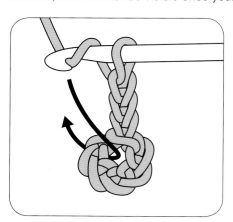

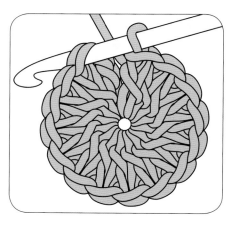

1 Make the central ring, then work the required number of chain to create the height of the stitch. The three chains shown here will count as the first double crochet (UK trebie crochet).

2 To create the next and each subsequent stitch, start by placing the hook into the center of the ring. Push the stitches around the central ring to bunch them up and make room for all the stitches required. Count the stitches at the end of the round, remembering that the chain could count as a stitch.

3 When the round is complete, join the last stitch to the top of the first stitch using a slip stitch. (For how to neaten slip stitch at end of round, see page 247.)

The magic loop method of starting a round

The magic loop (also known as the magic circle) is an alternative way of starting off a piece of crochet to be worked in the round while avoiding being left with a gap in the center circle. Rather than starting off with a length of foundation chain that is joined into a ring ready for the first row of crochet stitches, you start off with a simple loop of yarn.

The magic loop creates an adjustable ring that can be drawn up tight after the first row of crochet has been completed to close the gap. This is useful for items where you want to create a tight, dense texture—for example for toys that you will eventually fill with stuffing.

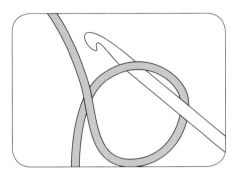

1 Start by making a loop in the working end of the yarn. Leave a fairly long tail (6–8in/15–20cm) so you have plenty to work with. Pinch the join of the loop together with the fingers of your left hand. The diameter of the loop should be about ¾–1¼in (2–3cm).

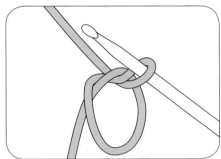

2 Insert the hook from right to left through the loop to pick up the working end of the yarn and make 1ch (this does not count as a stitch).

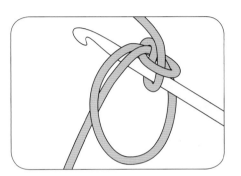

3 Make the first stitch into the loop (this example shows single crochet [UK double crochet}.) You need to insert the hook under both strands of yarn—the yarn that forms the loop and the yarn that forms the hanging tail—before picking up the working yarn and pulling it through.

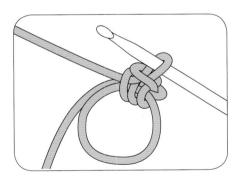

4 First single crochet (UK double crochet) stitch made.

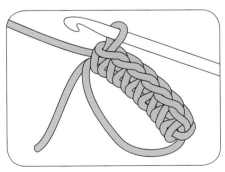

5 Continue until you have made as many stitches as are required.

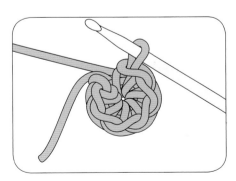

6 Pull on the tail end of the yarn to close the center gap. Join the round with a slip stitch into the first stitch.

Working the next (second) round

When working a flat motif you must create a flat and even circle, otherwise you will end up with a tube. You will need to increase the number of stitches used on every new round by working more than one new stitch into all or some stitches on the previous round. This could be done into every stitch of the round, or at set intervals around the piece. As a general rule, on the first increase row you will be asked to work 2 stitches into every stitch of the previous round.

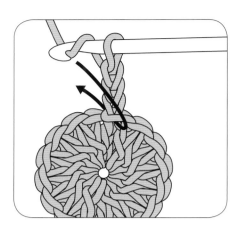

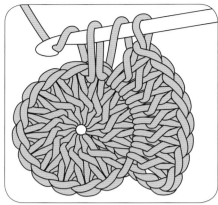

1 Work the required number of chain to create the stitch height. The three chains shown here count as the first double crochet (UK treble crochet). Work the first stitch into the base of the chain.

2 Work two stitches into every stitch of the previous round. When the round is complete, join the last stitch to the top of the first stitch using a slip stitch.

Increasing around the ring

After the first row of increasing, you will need to add new stitches less frequently. You may find that you are asked to work an increase into one stitch of the previous round and then work one or two single stitches before repeating the increase once more. Sometimes the increases are more spread out, and you may even be asked to work more than 2 stitches into a stitch on the previous round to achieve the correct stitch count.

When working from a chart, an increase is indicated by two or three stitches sitting in a V or W formation above a single stitch the row below.

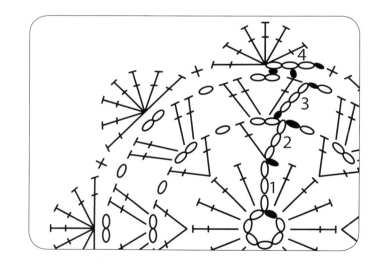

Keeping rounds flat

Keeping a piece of round crochet flat can be quite hard and success may depend on your gauge (tension). If you find that your piece is becoming "frilly" or you seem to be creating a tube instead of a flat circle then you may need to change your hook or the number of stitches by which you increase. For more information on troubleshooting see pages 246–249.

Working a spiral

Spirals are a very easy motif to achieve in crochet, because you do not have to finish the round with a slip stitch, or start a round with the required number of chain—you simply continue to work in the round increasing every so often to avoid the piece becoming a tube. It is worth using a stitch marker to pin point the start of a new round. Spirals can be worked in any stitch, but it may be an idea to start with a smaller stitch on the first round.

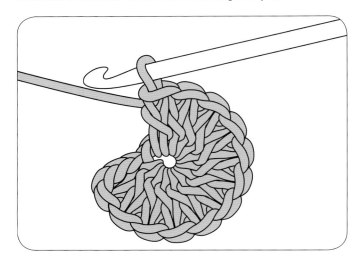

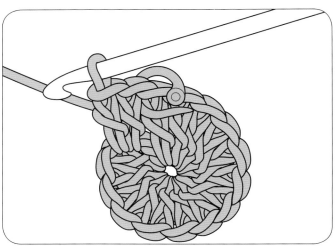

1 Begin with a central ring, then, working into the center of the ring, fill the rest of the ring with the desired number of stitches. In this sequence of diagrams the spiral is made using double crochet (UK treble crochet).

2 Work 2 stitches into the first stitch of the previous round. Mark the first of these with a small stitch marker.

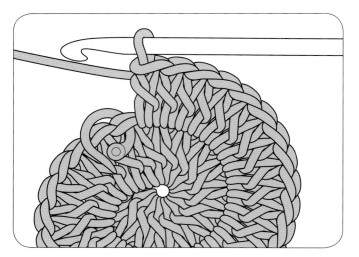

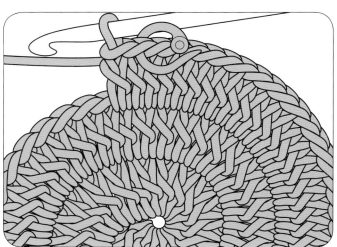

3 Work 2 stitches into every stitch of the round until you reach the marker that indicates the end of the round.

4 Remove the marker and once again work 2 stitches into the first stitch of the previous round. Mark the first of these with a small stitch marker. As the spiral increases in circumference, increase less often and maybe work one or two single stitches before increasing again. Continue in this way until the piece is the required size.

Stepped end spiral

When the spiral is complete you can fasten off your yarn and sew it in on the reverse of the motif. Because you have not completed the round with a slip stitch into a stitch on the previous round, you will be left with a stepped end.

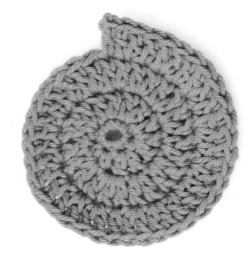

A stepped end spiral.

Tapered end spiral

You may not want the end of your spiral to be as obvious as it is with the stepped end, so you could choose to create a tapered end. To do this, work a sequence of stitches that range down in size into the next 3 or 4 stitches, so creating a tapered end.

A tapered end spiral.

Two color spiral

Spirals can be very effective when worked in more than one color. These are best worked in single crochet (UK double crochet). There is no reason to restrict yourself to just two colors—if you want to use three or even four colors, just join in the yarn at the center of the ring as described and then work each round using your chosen color.

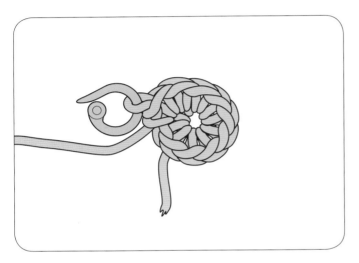

1 Begin by filling the central ring with the required number of stitches. Place the stitch left on the hook onto a stitch marker.

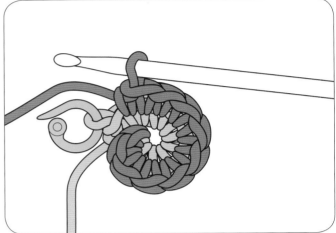

2 Using the second color of yarn, insert the hook into the center of the ring, draw the yarn through and complete a stitch. Work the second round using this color.

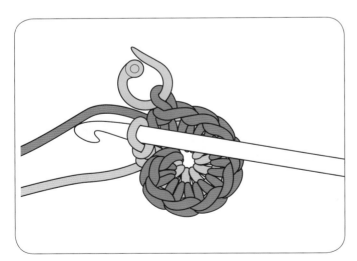

3 When the round is complete and the marker has been reached, place the stitch left on the hook onto a stitch marker.

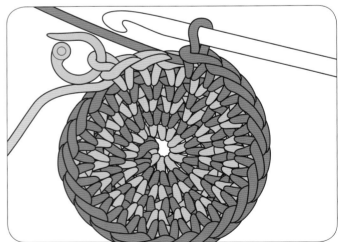

4 Return the original stitch to the hook and complete the third round making sure that you work 2 stitches into the first stitch of the previous round. Continue in this way until the piece is the required size.

Turning corners to create blocks

Many crochet motifs start off with a circle of stitches made around a central chain—even sharp edged shapes, such as squares and triangles, may have been started with a circle as a base. To create a more angular shape from a circle, you will need to learn how to create corners.

Making a square from a central chain

To work around a corner, you need to work more than one stitch into a space. In this example the classic "granny square" is made with double crochet (UK treble crochet) throughout.

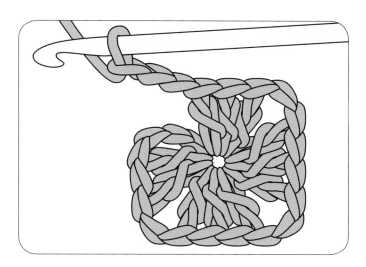

1 Make 6ch and join with a ss to form a ring. Work 3 chain to reach the height of the stitch (this will subsequently count as a stitch). Work 2 more stitches into the center of the ring. *To create a corner, work 3ch. Work 3 stitches into the center of the ring. Repeat from * until 4 corners have been created. Work a ss into the top of the 3ch.

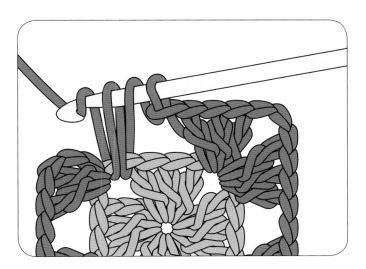

2 On the second and subsequent rounds, join the new color in at a corner space. This time, work 3 sts, 3ch, then 3 sts into the corner made on the previous round.

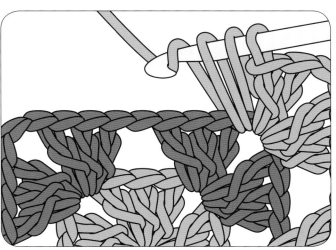

3 As the granny square gets bigger, work a single block of 3 sts into the single chain on the row below, in order to travel along the block between the corners.

Making a square from a round

In this example, an existing round motif is shown with no chain corners so the piece retains its circular shape. To make it square, you need to ensure that the number of stitches already created is divisible by 4 to guarantee that you achieve the correct number of corners at an equal spacing.

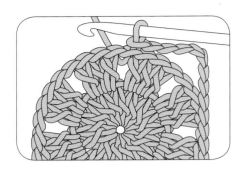

1 Work a series of chain spaces around the piece to allow the next row to be worked. Make a larger chain space at each of the 4 corners.

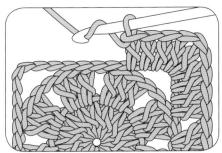

2 On the subsequent round, work small groups of stitches in line with the sides of the block then a larger multiple of stitches into the corner—it is good idea to make this an uneven number such as 3, 5 or 7 depending upon the size of the block and the depth of the post of the stitch.

Making corners on other blocks

If you are making a shape other than a square, you will need to create a different number of corners.

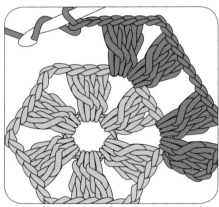

1 When working hexagonal (6 sided) or octagonal (8 sided) shapes, start with a larger central ring to allow enough room for the corners on subsequent rounds. On the classic granny hexagon, work as for the granny square repeating corners created by chain and groups of stitches around the initial ring, making sure that you achieve the correct number of corners for the shape.

2 On the subsequent rounds, join the new color in at a corner space and work 2 groups of stitches joined by a chain to create the corner for the next round.

3 When making an existing circular shape into an angular shape, work more than one round before you start to make the corners.

Creating a point

To make a more pronounced point at each corner of the motif, you can try making a stitch with a longer post as the central stitch of the corner group.

stitch directory

Abbreviations and symbols can differ depending upon whether you are following a US or a UK pattern and can even be personal to a pattern writer or designer, so it is really important that you make sure you understand all the crochet abbreviations and symbols before you start working from this Stitch Directory.

Don't be fooled by simply reading the stitch names, because some stitch references are the same yet mean very different things. For example, US and UK patterns share stitch names (such as double crochet, or treble crochet for example), yet these names do not refer to the same stitches. Single crochet in US terminology is a dense stitch with a short post, which in the UK is called double crochet. However, double crochet in the US is a longer stitch with a post, which is perhaps twice the height of the UK stitch, and is known in the UK as treble crochet.

All patterns in this section are written using US terminology only. See page 33 for stitch abbreviations.

Traditional Granny Square

Base ring: 4ch, join with a ss to form a ring.
Round 1: Ch5 (counts as 1dc and 2ch), [3dc into ring, 2ch] 3 times, 2dc into ring, ss into 3rd of 5-ch.
Round 2: Ss into next sp, 5ch (counts as 1dc and 2ch), 3dc into same sp, *1ch, skip 3 dc, [3dc, 2ch, 3dc] into next sp; rep from * twice more, 1ch, skip 3 dc sts, 2dc into same sp as 5-ch at beg of round, ss into 3rd of 5-ch.

Round 3: Ss into next sp, 5ch (counts as 1dc and 2ch) 3dc into same sp, *1ch, skip 3 dc, 3dc into next sp, 1ch, skip 3 dc **, [3dc, 2ch, 3dc] into next sp; rep from * twice more and from * to ** once more, 2dc into same sp as 5-ch, ss into 3rd of 5-ch.
Round 4: Ss into next sp, 5ch (counts as 1dc and 2ch) 3dc into same sp, *[1ch, skip 3 dc, 3dc into next sp] twice, 1ch, skip 3dc **, [3dc, 2ch, 3dc] into next sp; rep from * twice more and from * to ** once more, 2dc into same sp as 5-ch, ss into 3rd of 5-ch. Fasten off.

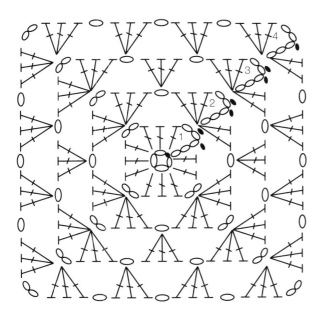

Granny Triangle

Base ring: 4ch, join with a ss to form a ring.

Round 1: Ch6 (counts as 1dc and 3ch) [3dc into ring, 3ch] twice, 2dc into ring, ss into 2nd ch of 5-ch.

Round 2: Ss into first sp, ch6 (counts as 1dc and 3ch), 3dc in same sp as ss, *2ch, [3dc, 3ch, 3dc] in next 3ch-sp; rep from * once more, 2ch, 2dc into first sp, ss into 3rd ch of 5-ch.

Round 3: Ss into first sp, ch6 (counts as 1dc and 3ch), 3dc in same sp as ss, *2ch, 3dc into next 2ch-sp, 2ch, [3dc, 3ch, 3dc] in foll 3ch-sp; rep from * once more, 2ch, 3dc into next 2ch-sp, 2ch, 2dc into first sp, ss into 3rd ch of 5-ch.

Round 4: Ss into first sp, ch6 (counts as 1dc and 3ch), 3dc in same sp as ss, *[2ch, 3dc into next 2ch sp] twice, 2ch, [3dc, 3ch, 3dc] in foll 3ch-sp; rep from * once more, [2ch, 3dc into next 2ch-sp] twice, 2ch, 2dc into first sp, ss into 3rd ch of 5-ch. Fasten off.

 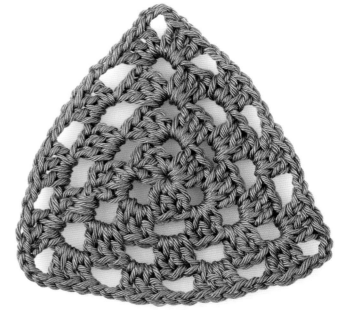

Five Point Star

Note: Pattern is worked as a spiral—do not work a ss at the end of each round.

Base chain: 2ch.

Round 1: 5sc into 2nd ch from hook.

Round 2: 3sc into each sc. (15 sts)

Round 3: [1sc into next st, 6ch, ss into 2nd ch from hook, 1sc into next ch, 1hdc into next ch, 1dc in next ch, 1tr into next ch, 1 tr into st at base of sc, skip 2sc] 5 times, ss into first sc. Fasten off.

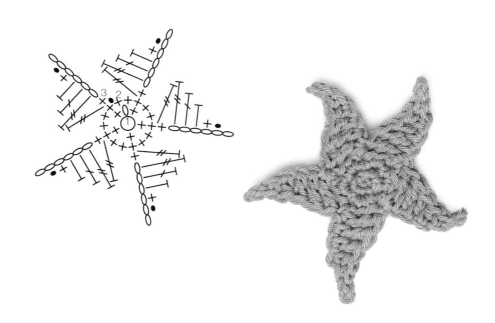

Traditional Hexagon

Note: Work 1 round each in colors A, B, C, and D.

Base ring: 4ch, join with a ss to form a ring.

Round 1: Ch3, dc2tog into ring (counts as dc3tog), [3ch, dc2tog into ring] 5 times, 1ch, 1hdc into top of 3-ch.

Round 2: Ch3, dc2tog into sp made by hdc (counts as dc3tog), *3ch, [dc3tog 3ch, dc3tog] into next sp; rep from * 4 more times, 3ch, dc3tog into last sp, 1ch, 1hdc into top of 3-ch.

Round 3: 3ch, dc2tog into sp made by hdc (counts as dc3tog), *3ch, [dc3tog 3ch, dc3tog] into next sp **, 3ch, dc3tog into next sp; rep from * 4 more times and from * to ** once more, 1ch, 1hdc into top of 3-ch.

Round 4: 3ch, 1dc into sp made by hdc, *3dc into next sp, [3dc, 2ch, 3dc] into next sp **, 3dc into next sp; rep from * 4 more times and from * to ** once more, 1dc into next sp, ss into top of 3-ch.

Round 5: 1ch, 1sc into same place, 1sc into each dc and each ch to end of round, ss into first sc.
Fasten off.

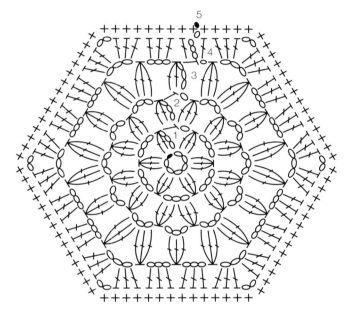

Changing colors

When working samples such as the Granny Square or Hexagon you need to start each new color in a corner space. This will make it difficult to weave the yarn tail in as you work your next row so you will have to sew it in (see page 56).
To make the piece neater try to join the yarn in at a different corner on each round.

tubular crochet

One of the exciting things about the craft of crochet is that you can choose whether or not you want to produce a flat piece of fabric or a piece that forms a tube or cylinder. Tubular crochet can be used to make garments, mittens, socks, accessories and toys. When making a tube or cylindrical shape each row of stitching is referred to as a round.

Working a spiral cylinder using single crochet (UK double crochet)

When using stitches with shallow posts—such as single crochet (UK double crochet)—you can work the cylinder in a spiral. Working in this stitch means that you do not need to complete each round with a slip stitch or start a round with a chain to reach the height of the stitch.

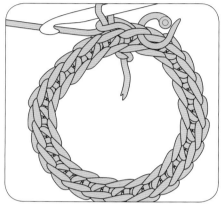

1 Make a chain to the required length, making sure it is not twisted. Work a slip stitch into the first stitch to form a ring. Work one round of stitches into each chain. Join the round by working a slip stitch into the first stitch made.

2 Insert a stitch marker into the last stitch made. Work another row, working a new stitch into every stitch of the previous round.

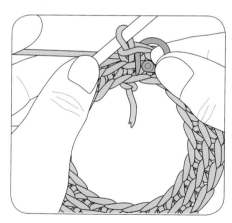

3 At the end of the round, do not work a slip stitch into the first stitch of the previous round but continue in a spiral by working into the first stitch of the round and replacing the marker in the new stitch to mark the end/beginning of the round. Continue in this way, replacing the marker at the end/beginning of each round until piece is the required length.

A cylinder in single crochet (UK double crochet).

Working a cylinder without turns using double crochet (UK treble crochet)

When using only stitches with longer posts—such as double crochet (UK treble crochet)—you cannot work the cylinder in a spiral and need to finish each round with a slip stitch and begin each round with some chain.

By working without turns you will always have the right side of the work facing outwards.

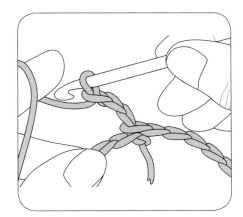

1 Make a chain to the required length, making sure it is not twisted. Work a slip stitch into the first stitch to form a ring. Work 3 chain to reach the height of the stitch (this will subsequently count as a stitch).

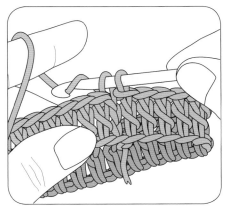

2 Work one round of stitches into each chain. Join the round by working a slip stitch into the top of the 3 chain post that was made at the beginning of the round.

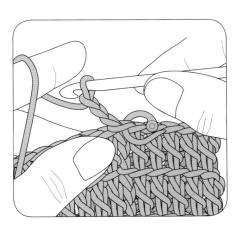

3 Insert a stitch marker into the last stitch made. Work 3 chain to reach the height of the stitch (this will subsequently count as a stitch). Work another row, working a new stitch into every stitch of the previous round. Continue to work in this way, replacing the marker at the end/beginning of each round until piece is the required length.

A cylinder without turns.

Avoiding a twisted chain

If you find that you twist the chain when trying to work the first row of stitching, you can opt to work the crochet as a flat piece for the first row then join it with a slip stitch to create the tubular piece. Once the piece is complete, you will need to sew in the yarn ends to replace the slip stitches that were omitted.

Working a cylinder with turns using double crochet (UK treble crochet)

When using only stitches with longer posts—such as double crochet (UK treble crochet)—you cannot work the cylinder in a spiral and need to finish each round with a slip stitch and begin each round with some chain. By working with turns you could have a reversible fabric, and could also add design features such as beads and sequins.

 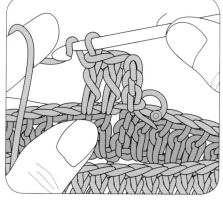 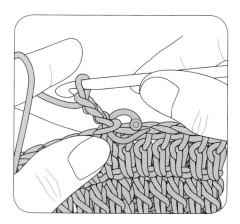

1 Make a chain to the required length, making sure it is not twisted. Work a slip stitch into the first stitch to form a ring. Work 3 chain to reach the height of the stitch (this will subsequently count as a stitch). Work one round of stitches into each chain. Join the round by working a slip stitch into the top of the 3 chain post that was made at the beginning of the round. Insert a stitch marker into the last stitch made. Work 3 chain to reach the height of the stitch (this will subsequently count as a stitch). Turn so that the reverse side of the fabric is facing.

2 Work another row, working a new stitch into every stitch of the previous round. At the end of the round, work a slip stitch into the top of the 3 chain post that was made at the beginning of the round.

3 Work 3 chain to reach the height of the next round. Turn. Continue to work in this way, replacing the marker at the end/beginning of each round until piece is the required length.

A cylinder with turns.

amigurumi

Amigurumi usually take the form of cute stylized animals with human characteristics and facial features—rabbits, monkeys, bears, and cats—although other everyday items—cakes, confectionery, flowers and foliage—are also made using this technique. The toys are on a small scale, often with hand stitching detail. They are made using single crochet (UK double crochet) using a small hook in relation to the weight of the yarn, thus creating a sturdy and durable fabric.

Making a toy

Here is the pattern for a basic toy. If you want to make it bigger or smaller, simply increase or decrease the number of stitches and rows used. Gauge (tension) is not important so long as your crochet is tight enough to prevent the stuffing from poking through the fabric. The toy is worked using single crochet (UK double crochet) throughout.

Head

Make 2 chain.

Round 1: Work 6 stitches into the first chain to make a ring. Do not finish the round with a slip stitch; instead, continue to work in a spiral.

Round 2: Work 2 stitches into each stitch. (12 sts)

Round 3: [1sc into the next sc, 2sc into the next st] 6 times. (18 sts)

Round 4: [2sc into the next sc, 1sc into the next 2 sts] 6 times. (24 sts)

Cont to increase the number of sts by 6 sts on each round by working 2sc into one stitch at evenly spaced intervals until there are 36 sts.

Work 10 rounds without increasing.

Round 17: [sc2tog into the next 2 sts, 1sc into the next 4 sts] 6 times. (30 sts)

Cont to decrease the number of sts by 6 sts across the next round and subsequent rounds by working 2sctog at evenly spaced intervals until there are 12 sts.

Work a slip stitch into the next st and fasten off leaving a tail end of yarn approximately 12in (30cm) long.

Body

Work this piece as for the Head but cont to increase the number of stitches until there are 42 sts.

Work 16 rows without increasing.

Decrease as for the head.

Arms, legs, tails and ears

Make 2 chain.

Round 1: Work 6 stitches into the first chain to make a ring. Do not finish the round with a slip stitch; instead, continue to work in a spiral.

Round 2: Work 2 stitches into every stitch. (12 sts)

Work straight to the required length.

Work a slip stitch into the next st and fasten off leaving a tail end of yarn approximately 12in (30cm) long.

Finishing

Amigurumi toys need to be stuffed very firmly, so make sure you use plenty of filling. To give the toy a little more weight at the base of the body, add some plastic beads or dried beans or lentils (but not if the toy is for a very young child).

Where possible, sew up using one of the tail ends of yarn that were left attached to the crochet pieces. Line up the slip stitches from the head and the body and sew the two pieces together using a tail end of yarn, making sure you sew stitch-for-stitch tightly around the whole join. Sew on the limbs and other features.

To sew the face detail, use a sharp sewing needle to embroider eyes, nose, and any othe rfeature. You may want to use pieces of cut felt and small beads to add more detail.

The finished amigurumi toy.

texture and lace stitches

The craft of crochet lends itself beautifully to the production of lace and textural designs. Indeed, the craft's popularity historically reflected the fashion for handmade bobbin lace; crochet lace was a cheaper and more practical copy—even Queen Victoria, who often purchased Irish-made crochet lace, learned to crochet herself. The variation of stitch formations and effects is staggering, and perhaps endless, but none are beyond the reach of a home-based crocheter—as long as you are confident in using a combination of various stitches.

ridge stitches

Create a line of yarn, or a ridge, by crocheting into one side of the chain along the top of a row using any stitch or combination of stitches. The ridge will be on either the right side or wrong side every alternate row if you work continuously into one side of the stitch. If you want a ridge on just one side of the fabric on every row, alternate which side of the stitch you work through.

Working into the front of a stitch using single crochet (UK double crochet)

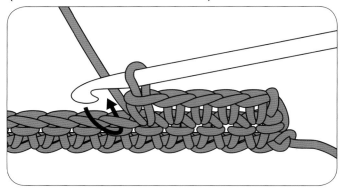

Hold the crochet flat so that the chain that runs along the top of the previous row is clearly visible. Insert the hook through the front side of the chain stitch on the previous row.

Working into the front of a stitch using double crochet (UK treble crochet)

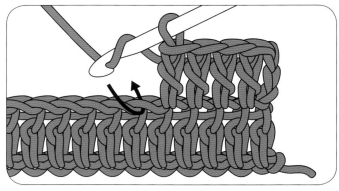

Hold the crochet flat so that the chain that runs along the top of the previous row is clearly visible. Insert the hook through the front side of the chain stitch on the previous row.

Working into the back of a stitch using single crochet (UK double crochet)

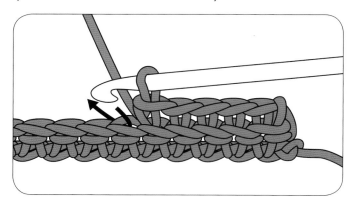

Hold the crochet flat so that the chain that runs along the top of the previous row is clearly visible. Insert the hook through the far side of the chain stitch on the previous row.

Working into the back of a stitch using double crochet (UK treble crochet)

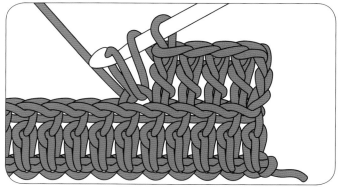

Hold the crochet flat so that the chain that runs along the top of the previous row is clearly visible. Insert the hook through the far side of the chain stitch on the previous row.

stitch directory

Abbreviations and symbols can differ depending upon whether you are following a US or a UK pattern and can even be personal to a pattern writer or designer, so it is really important that you make sure you understand all the crochet abbreviations and symbols before you start working from this Stitch Directory.

Don't be fooled by simply reading the stitch names, because some stitch references are the same yet mean very different things. For example, US and UK patterns share stitch names (such as double crochet, or treble crochet for example), yet these names do not refer to the same stitches. Single crochet in US terminology is a dense stitch with a short post, which in the UK is called double crochet. However, double crochet in the US is a longer stitch with a post, which is perhaps twice the height of the UK stitch, and is known in the UK as treble crochet.

All patterns in this section are written using US terminology only. See page 33 for stitch abbreviations.

Irregular Ridges

Foundation chain: multiples of 1 + 3

Foundation row: 1dc into 4th ch from hook, 1dc into each ch to end, turn.
Row 1: Ch3, (counts as 1dc), 1dc into front loop only of every st, finish with 1dc into top of tch, turn.
Row 2: Ch1, 1sc into back loop only of every st, finish with 1sc into top of tch, turn.
Row 3: Ch1, 1sc into front loop only of every st to end of row, turn.
Row 4: Ch3, (counts as 1dc), 1dc into back loop only of every st to end of row, turn.
Repeat Rows 1–4 to required length.

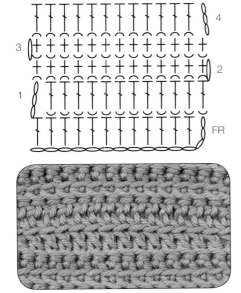

Faux Ribbing

Foundation chain: multiples of 1 + 1

Foundation row: 1sc into 2nd ch from hook, 1sc into each ch to end, turn.
Row 1: Ch1, 1sc into back loop only of every st to end of row, turn.
Repeat Row 1 to required length.

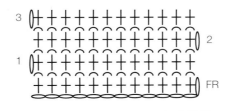

Back Loop Half Double Crochet

Foundation chain: multiples of 1 + 2

Foundation row: 1hdc into 3rd ch from hook, 1hdc into each ch to end, turn.
Row 1: Ch2, 1hdc into back loop only of every st to end of row, turn.
Repeat Row 1 to required length.

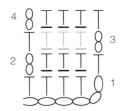

Crochet ribbing

Faux ribbing is often used on its side as shown in the sample above center, so it looks more like knitted ribbing.

raised stitches

This technique is also often referred to as making "post" stitches or "relief" stitches and the fabric produced by this method is heavily textured and sturdy. It is made by inserting the hook between the posts of stitches on the previous row and working the subsequent stitch around the post of a stitch. The hook can be inserted between the stitches either from the front of the work or from the back, thus producing two different stitches.

Working a raised stitch from the front

When working into the front of the fabric, insert the hook as described here.

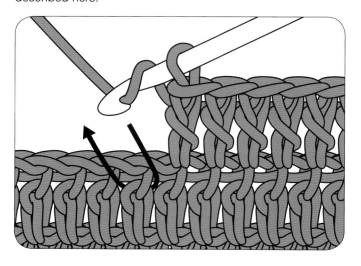

Insert the hook into the gap between two stitches from front to back, then out to the front side of the work through the gap between the following two stitches as the arrow shows.

Making the stitch

It is wise to use a stitch that produces a long post. Here we show double crochet (UK treble crochet).

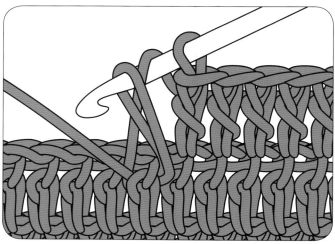

Wrap the yarn around the hook. Place the hook through the work from the front as described left. Wrap the yarn around the hook once more and draw it around the stitch to the front of the work to form a loop on the hook. Complete the stitch.

Splitting stitches

When inserting the hook into the gap between the posts of the stitch take care not to split the yarn with your hook. Splitting the yarn can create a messy stitch and can alter the appearance and gauge (tension) of the following stitches.

Working a raised stitch from the back

When working into the back of the fabric, insert the hook as described here.

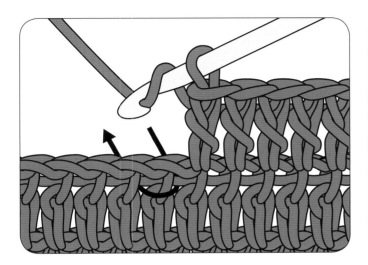

Insert the hook into the gap between two stitches from back to front, then out to the reverse side of the work through the gap between the following two stitches as the arrow shows.

Making the stitch

Again it is wise to use a stitch that produces a long post. Here we show double crochet (UK treble crochet).

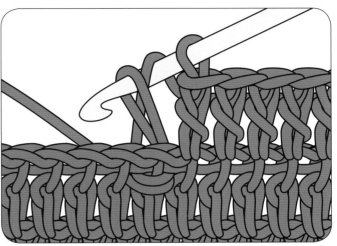

Wrap the yarn around the hook. Place the hook through the work from the back as described left. Wrap the yarn around the hook once more and draw it around the stitch to the reverse of the work to form a loop on the hook. Complete the stitch.

spike stitches

These stitches are sometimes referred to as "dropped" stitches and are made by working over the top of stitches made on a previous row. This technique can be particularly effective when working in contrasting colors in a stripe formation, but is also attractive as a plain colored fabric.

Working a spike stitch using single crochet (UK double crochet)

This technique is the best method for working this stitch.
Work to where a spike stitch is required.

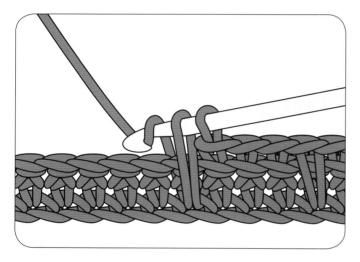

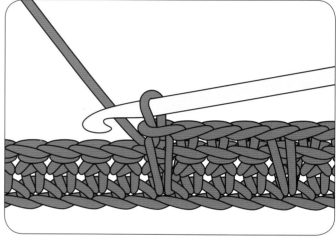

1 From the front count down a few rows (depending upon how deep the spike stitch needs to be) then push the hook through the fabric to the reverse of the work being careful not to split the yarn. Wrap the yarn around the hook then draw through to the front of the work to form another loop on the hook.

2 Do not pull the loop tight, because this will cause the crochet to pucker. Wrap the yarn around the hook and complete the stitch.

Perfect spike stitches

It can be quite difficult to identify where to insert the hook into the crochet fabric in order to make a spike stitch sit perfectly. It is a little difficult to achieve a perfect vertical spike stitch so take your time and practice. Undo stitches that look skewed if need be.

stitch directory

Abbreviations and symbols can differ depending upon whether you are following a US or a UK pattern and can even be personal to a pattern writer or designer, so it is really important that you make sure you understand all the crochet abbreviations and symbols before you start working from this Stitch Directory.

Don't be fooled by simply reading the stitch names, because some stitch references are the same yet mean very different things. For example, US and UK patterns share stitch names (such as double crochet, or treble crochet for example), yet these names do not refer to the same stitches. Single crochet in US terminology is a dense stitch with a short post, which in the UK is called double crochet. However, double crochet in the US is a longer stitch with a post, which is perhaps twice the height of the UK stitch, and is known in the UK as treble crochet.

All patterns in this section are written using US terminology only. See page 33 for stitch abbreviations.

Basket Weave Stitch

Foundation chain: multiples of 8 + 4
Special Abbreviations: FP = raised double crochet stitch worked around Front Post
BP = raised double crochet stitch worked around Back Post
Note: In this case the FP symbol on the chart means create a raised stitch so it appears raised on the right side of the work. BP symbol on the chart means create a raised stitch so it appears raised on the wrong side of the work. The copy decsribes the stitch to be worked as it will appear on the side you are working.

Foundation row: 1dc into 4th ch from hook, 1dc into each ch to end, turn.
Row 1: Ch2 (counts as 1dc), skip next st, *1FP around each of next 4 sts, 1BP around each of next 4 sts; rep from * finishing with 1dc into top of tch, turn.
Rows 2–4: Repeat Row 1.
Row 5: Ch2 (counts as 1dc), skip next st, *1BP around each of next 4 sts, 1FP around each of next 4 sts; rep from * finishing with 1dc into top of tch, turn.
Rows 6–8: Repeat Row 5.
Repeat Rows 1–8 to required length.

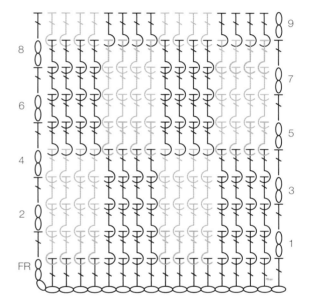

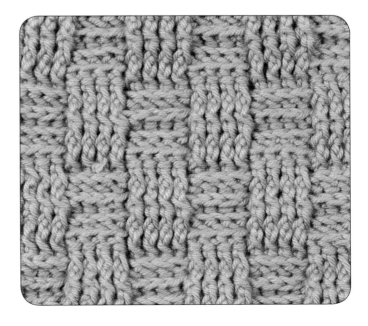

Raised Columns

Foundation chain: multiples of 8 + 2

Special Abbreviations: FP = raised double crochet stitch worked around Front Post; BP = raised double crochet stitch worked around Back Post

Foundation row: 2dc into 6th ch from hook, *2ch, 2dc into next ch, skip 2 ch, 1hdc into each of next 2 ch, skip 2 ch, 2dc into next ch; rep from * to last 3 ch, skip 2ch, 1hdc into final ch, turn.

Row 1: Ch2 (counts as 1dc), skip hdc and next 2dc, *[2dc, 2ch, 2dc] into next ch-sp, 1FP around each of next 2 hdc; rep from * until 1 2ch-sp rem, [2dc, 2ch, 2dc] into the next ch-sp, 1dc into top of tch, turn.

Row 2: Ch2 (counts as 1dc), skip 3 dc, *[2dc, 2ch, 2dc] into next ch-sp, 1BP around each of next 2 dc; rep from * until 1 2ch-sp rem, [2dc, 2ch, 2dc] into the next ch-sp, 1dc into top of tch, turn.

Row 3: Ch2 (counts as 1dc), skip 3 dc, *[2dc, 2ch, 2dc] into next ch-sp, 1FP around each of next 2dc; rep from * until 1 2ch-sp rem, [2dc, 2ch, 2dc] into the next ch-sp, 1dc into top of tch, turn.

Repeat Rows 2 and 3 to required length.

Alternating Spike Stitch

Foundation chain: multiples of 2

Special Abbreviation: SP = spike stitch made by working 1sc into st one row below next st

Note: Work in two colors, working alternate rows in alternate colors throughout.

Foundation row: 1sc into 2nd ch from hook, 1sc into each ch to end, turn.

Row 1: 1ch, 1sc into next st, *SP over next sc, 1sc into next st; rep from * to end of row, turn.

Row 2: 1ch, 1sc into next st, *SP over next sc, 1sc into next st; rep from * to final st, 1sc, turn.

Repeat Rows 1 and 2 to required length.

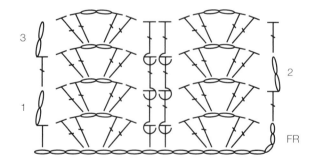

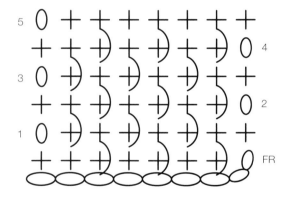

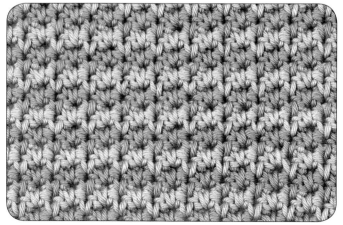

Spike Cluster Stitch

Foundation chain: multiples of 8 + 6

Special Abbreviation: SPC (spike cluster) = Pick up 5 spike loops over the top of the next st by inserting hook into work as follows: 2 sts to the right and 1 row down; 1 st to the right and 2 rows down; directly below and 3 rows down; 1 st to the left and 2 rows down; 2 sts to the left and 1 row down (6 loops on hook). To complete stitch, insert hook into top of next st, yarn over hook, draw through first loop on hook, yarn over hook, draw through all loops

Note: Work in two colors, working four rows in alternate colors throughout.

Foundation row: 1sc into 2nd ch from hook, 1sc into each ch to end, turn.

Row 1: Ch1, 1sc into each st to end, skip tch, turn.

Rows 2–3: Repeat Row 1.

Row 4: Ch1, 1sc into next 4 sts, *1SPC over next st, 1sc into next 7 sts; rep from * finishing with 1sc into final st, skip tch, turn.

Rows 5–7: Repeat Row 1.

Row 8: Ch1, 1sc into next 8 sts, *1SPC over next st, 1sc into next 7 sts; rep from * to last 5 sts, 1SPC over next st, 1sc into next 4 sts, skip tch, turn.

Repeat Rows 1–8 to required length.

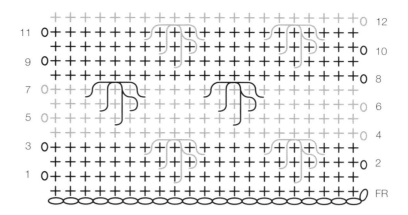

Colored spikes

Spike stitches can create some fantastic effects when worked in different colors and on varying rows. They can look especially effective when worked in the round and can act as a good definition stitch between the petals on a crochet flower, for example.

crossed stitches

As the name suggests this technique is worked by making stitches cross over each other, with one stitch sitting in front of the other once complete. It is similar to the technique of cabling in the craft of knitting. The technique works best when used with stitches that make a long post. The crochet fabric produced using this method is neater in appearance and easier to work if a row of plain stitching is worked between each crossover row.

Working a crossed stitch in front using double crochet (UK treble crochet)

Work to where the crossed stitch is required, then follow this technique.

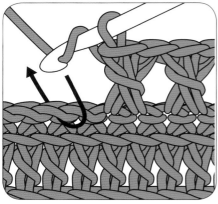

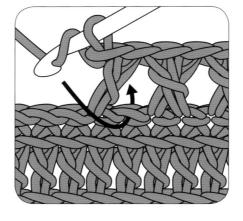

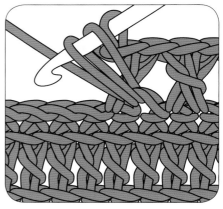

1 Miss one stitch from the previous row and work a stitch into the following stitch in the usual way.

2 Wrap the yarn around the hook. From the front insert the hook into the missed stitch on the previous row.

3 Wrap the yarn around the hook and draw it through to form another loop on the hook.

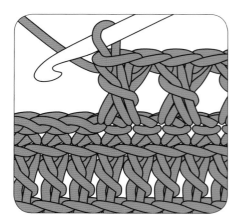

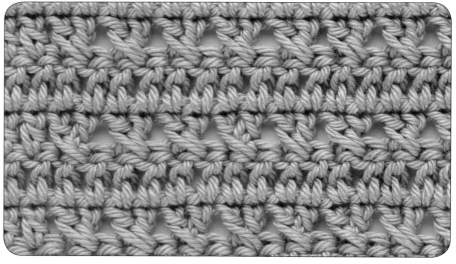

4 Wrap the yarn around the hook and draw it through to form another loop on the hook. Complete the stitch so that it is crossed in front the first stitch.

Crossed stitch in double crochet (UK treble crochet).

Working a crossed stitch behind using treble crochet (UK double treble crochet)

Work to where the crossed stitch is required, then follow this technique.

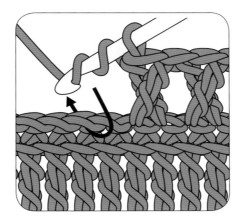

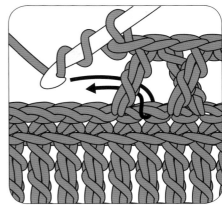

1 Work to where the crossed stitch is required. Miss one stitch from the previous row and work a stitch into the following stitch in the usual way.

2 Wrap the yarn around the hook twice. Working behind the first stitch, from the front insert the hook into the missed stitch on the previous row.

Base fabric

The illustrations show crossed stitches being made on a background fabric where ridge stitches have been worked previous rows, but you can choose to make crossed stitches using any base fabric.

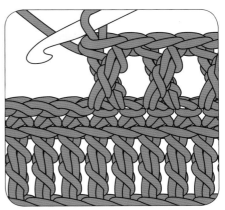

3 Wrap the yarn around the hook and draw it through to form another loop on the hook.

4 Complete the stitch so that it is crossed behind the first stitch.

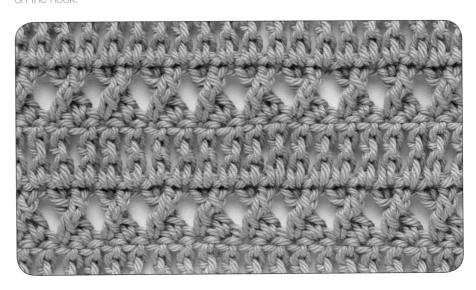

Crossed stitch in treble crochet (UK double treble crochet).

cables

Cables can be made using a variety of stitches, but are most effective when made in conjunction with a rib effect base stitch worked into the front of a post. To create the cross over required by the cable, a stitch is worked several stitches either in advance of or in arrear of the current stitch.

Making a cable

Here we show a base fabric made using half double crochet (UK half treble crochet) with the cables made using treble crochet (UK double treble crochet).

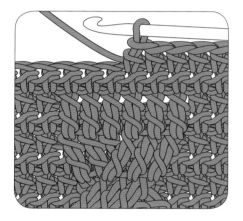

1 Work the base fabric to where the cable is required.

2 Miss 3 stitches along to the left. Work one tr (UK dtr) into the front posts of the next 3 stitches.

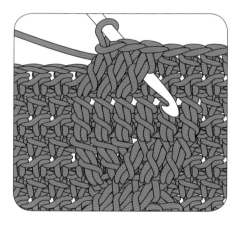

3 Working behind these 3 stitches, work 3 more into the missed stitches, starting with the one furthest to the right.

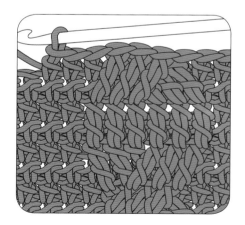

4 Complete the row using hdc (UK htr) placing other cables where required. Work the subsequent rows to form the base fabric cabling when required.

It is possible to work a cable which crosses the stitches over in the other direction by wiorking infront of the set of raised stitches instead of behind them.

clusters

A cluster is made by working a series of incomplete stitches into either a sequence of single stitches or into a chain space to form a group of close sitting stitches. On the final step of the stitch all the stitches are joined together to form one stitch.

2-stitch cluster made over 2 stitches using double crochet (UK treble crochet)

Clusters are most effective when made using stitches with long posts.

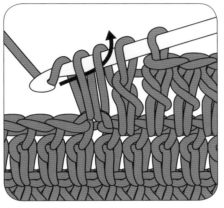

1 Wrap the yarn around the hook and work a stitch into the next stitch on the row, stopping before the last step of the stitch so that two loops remain on the hook.

2 Work another stitch in the same way into the next stitch, or as directed, so that 3 loops remain on the hook.

3 Wrap the yarn around the hook and draw through all the loops remaining on the hook to produce just one stitch.

Working a cluster into a chain space

Work a series of incomplete stitches into the space created by a chain on the previous row. Finish by drawing the yarn through the stitches as seen right—here a four-stitch cluster is being shown.

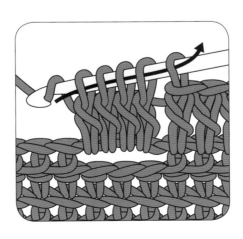

puff stitch

Puff stitches are similar in appearance to both bobbles and popcorns, but they are a little softer with less definition than either. A puff stitch is made by working 3 or more stitches into the same stitch or space.

A puff stitch made using double crochet (UK treble crochet)

Work to where a puff stitch is required, then follow this technique.

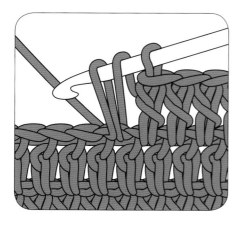 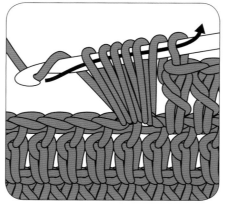 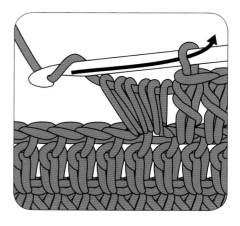

1 *Wrap the yarn around the hook and draw through the stitch leaving 3 loops on the hook.

2 Repeat from * twice more, inserting the hook into the same stitch each time. (There are 7 loops on the hook). Wrap the yarn around the hook and draw through all the loops left on the hook.

3 Wrap the yarn around the hook once more and draw through the stitch that remains on the hook, thus securing all the loops in place.

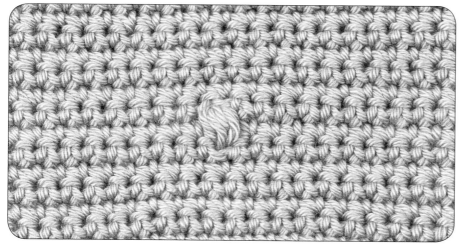

A puff stitch in double crochet (UK treble crochet) on a single crochet (UK double crochet) base fabric.

popcorn

A popcorn is made by working a group of stitches into one stitch or space, as for a puff stitch or bobble, but it differs to both in that it is made from complete groups of stitches that are then joined together on the final step of the stitch. A popcorn is a relief stitch that works best when made using a stitch with a long post; it looks rather like a small pouch.

Basic 5-stitch popcorn

Here we show a popcorn made using double crochet
(UK treble crochet).

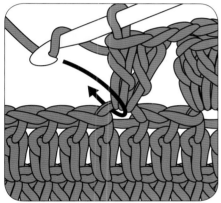
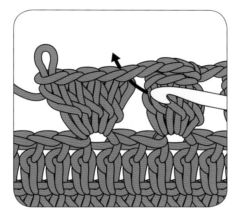
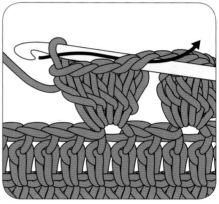

1 Work to where a popcorn is required. Miss two stitches on the previous row. Work a group of 5 stitches into the next stitch.

2 Remove the hook from the working stitch. Making sure that this stitch does not unravel, insert the hook into the top chain of the first stitch of the group of 5.

3 Place the working stitch back on the hook and draw it through the top of the first stitch of the group of 5. Wrap the yarn around the hook a final time and draw through the final stitch, thus securing the popcorn.

The finished 5-stitch popcorn on a single crochet (UK double crochet) base fabric.

bobbles

A bobble is a very sturdy stitch, which is made by working a group of stitches into one stitch or space—as for a puff stitch, or popcorn stitch—at the end of the stitch the group of stitches are worked together to form just one stitch.

Basic 5-stitch bobble

Double crochet (UK treble crochet) bobbles on a base of single crochet (UK double crochet) worked into the back of the stitch.

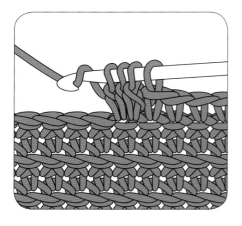

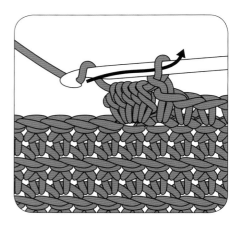

1 With the wrong side of the work facing, work to where a bobble is required. Work 3 incomplete stitches by leaving the last loop of each stitch on the crochet hook, so that 4 loops remain on the hook.

2 Work 2 more incomplete stitches, to leave 6 loops on the hook. Wrap the yarn around the hook and draw through all the loops on the hook.

3 Wrap the yarn around the hook a final time and draw through the loop on the hook. Gently push the group of stitches through to the right side of the work.

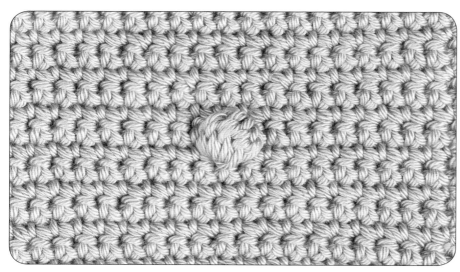

A 5-stitch bobble.

Multicolored bobble

This technique is the ideal one for multicolored bobbles.

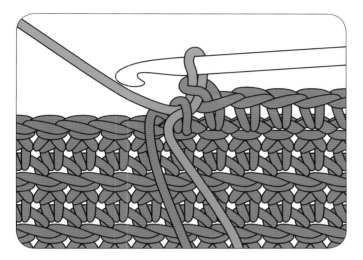

1 With the wrong side of the work facing, work to where a bobble is required, changing yarn color on the final step of the last stitch.

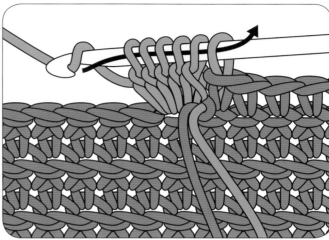

2 Using this new color, work 5 incomplete stitches by leaving the last loop of each stitch on the crochet hook so that 6 loops are on the hook. Wrap the yarn around the hook and draw through all the loops on the hook.

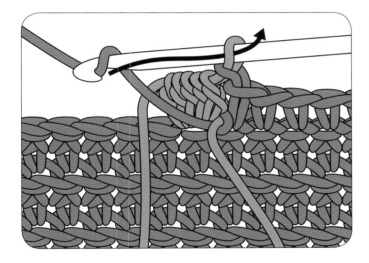

3 Pick up the original color and strand it across the back of the bobble. Wrap the yarn around the hook a final time and draw through the loop on the hook. Gently push the group of stitches through to the right side of the work.

A series of multicolored bobbles.

stitch directory

Abbreviations and symbols can differ depending upon whether you are following a US or a UK pattern and can even be personal to a pattern writer or designer, so it is really important that you make sure you understand all the crochet abbreviations and symbols before you start working from this Stitch Directory.

Don't be fooled by simply reading the stitch names, because some stitch references are the same yet mean very different things. For example, US and UK patterns share stitch names (such as double crochet, or treble crochet for example), yet these names do not refer to the same stitches. Single crochet in US terminology is a dense stitch with a short post, which in the UK is called double crochet. However, double crochet in the US is a longer stitch with a post, which is perhaps twice the height of the UK stitch, and is known in the UK as treble crochet.

All patterns in this section are written using US terminology only. See page 33 for stitch abbreviations.

Trinity Stitch

Foundation chain: multiples of 2

Foundation row: 1sc into 2nd ch from hook, work sc3tog by inserting hook into same ch as prev sc, then into each of next 2 ch, *1ch, sc3tog by inserting hook into same ch as 3rd st of previous sc3tog, then into each of next 2 ch; rep from * to last ch, 1sc into same ch as 3rd st of previous sc3tog, turn.
Row 1: Ch1, 1sc into next st, sc3tog by inserting hook into same st as prev sc, then into top of next sc3tog, then into next ch-sp, *1ch, sc3tog by inserting hook into same ch-sp as 3rd st of prev sc3tog, then into top of next sc3tog, then into next ch-sp; rep from * to end, 1sc into same ch as 3rd st of previous sc3tog, turn, skip tch, turn.
Repeat Row 1 to required length.

Making bobbles and clusters

Making stitches such as bobbles and clusters is good fun and relatively easy. When working multiple stitches together it is important that you try and achieve a nice even gauge (tension) on every stitch as you need each one to be uniform and not stand proud.

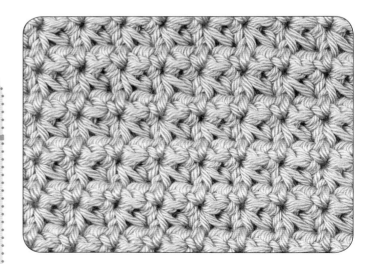

Lacy Popcorns

Foundation chain: multiples of 8 + 2
Special Abbreviations: Popcorn = Popcorn made from 5dc

Foundation row: 1sc into 2nd ch from hook, *1ch, skip 3 ch, [1dc, 1ch, 1dc, 1ch, 1dc] into next ch, skip 3 ch, 1sc into next ch; rep from * to end, turn.
Row 1: Ch6 (counts as 1dc and 3ch), skip 1dc, 1sc into next dc, *3ch, Popcorn into next sc, 3ch, skip 1dc, 1sc into next dc; rep from * to final sc, 3ch, 1dc into last sc, turn.
Row 2: Ch1, 1sc into the first dc, *1ch, [1dc, 1ch, 1dc, 1ch, 1dc] into next sc, 1ch, 1sc into top of next Popcorn; rep from * to end working final sc into 3rd of 6-ch, turn.
Repeat Rows 1 and 2 to required length.

Wavy Puff Sprays

Foundation chain: multiples of 17 + 2

Foundation row: 1dc into 4th ch from hook (counts as dc2tog), [dc2tog over next 2 ch] twice, *[1ch, hdc4tog into next ch] 5 times, 1ch **, [dc2tog over next 2 ch] 6 times; rep from * finishing last rep at ** (6 ch remain) [dc2tog over next 2 ch] 3 times, turn.
Row 1: Ch1, 1sc into each st and each ch sp to end. Do not work a sc into tch, turn.
Row 2: Ch3, skip 1st, 1dc into next st (counts as dc2tog), [dc2tog over next 2 sts] twice, *[1ch, hdc4tog into next st] 5 times, 1ch **, [dc2tog over next 2 sts] 6 times; rep from * finishing last rep at ** (6 sts remain), [dc2tog over next 2 sts] 3 times, skip tch, turn.
Repeat Rows 1 and 2 to required length.

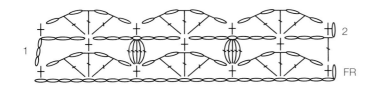

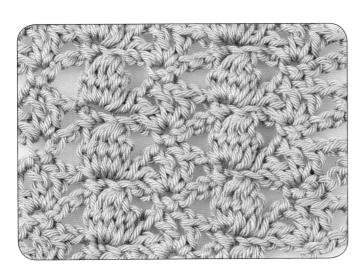

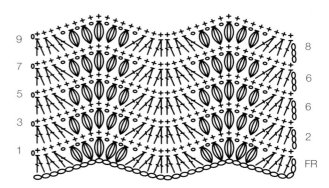

Side Saddle Cluster Stitch

Foundation chain: multiples of 5 + 2
Special Abbreviation: Cluster = made by working dc4tog

Foundation row: 1sc into 2nd ch from hook, *3ch, cluster over next 4 ch, 1ch, 1sc into next ch; rep from * to end, turn.
Row 1: Ch5 (counts as 1dc and 2ch), 1sc into next cluster, *3ch, cluster into next 3ch-sp, 1ch, 1sc into next cluster; rep from * finishing by working 3ch and cluster into next 3ch-sp, 1dc into final sc, skip tch, turn.
Row 2: Ch1, skip 1st, 1sc into next cluster, *3ch, cluster into next 3ch-sp, 1ch, 1sc into next cluster; rep from * finishing last rep with 1sc into tch-sp, turn.
Repeat Rows 1 and 2 to required length.

Alternate Bobbles

Foundation chain: multiples of 4 + 3
Special Abbreviation: MB = Bobble made from 4dc

Foundation row: 1dc into 4th ch from hook, 1dc into each ch to end, turn.
Row 1: Ch1, 1sc into next 2 dc, *MB, 1sc into next 3 dc; rep from * to final 3 sts, MB, 1sc into next dc, 1sc into 3rd ch of 3-ch of tch, turn.
Rows 2 and 4: Ch3 (counts as 1dc), skip 1st, 1dc into each st to end, turn.
Row 3: Ch1, 1sc into next 4 dc, *MB, 1sc into next 3 dc; rep from * finishing by working 1dc into top of tch, turn.
Row 5: Ch1, 1sc into next 2 dc, *MB, 1sc into next 3 dc; rep from * to final 3 sts, MB, 1sc into next dc, 1sc into into top of 3ch-tch, turn.
Repeat Rows 2–5 to required length.

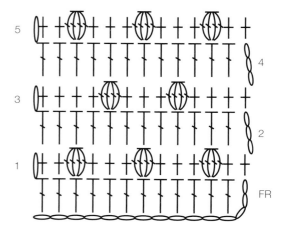

bullion stitch

This is a nifty little stitch, although it can take quite a lot of practice to perfect. It is a popular stitch with freeform crocheters and works well in chunky yarns.

Working the stitch

Work to where a bullion stitch is required.

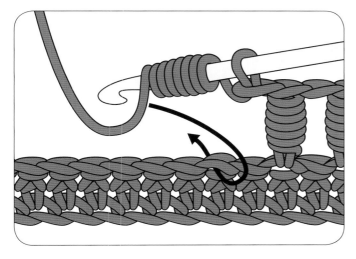

1 Wrap the yarn around the hook seven times, making sure that the yarn is resting on the thickest part of the hook.

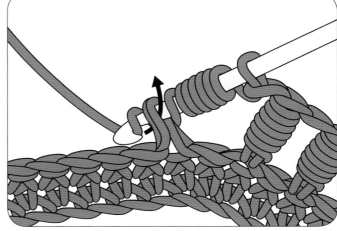

2 Insert the hook into the next stitch. Wrap the yarn around the hook once more. Draw through the stitch.

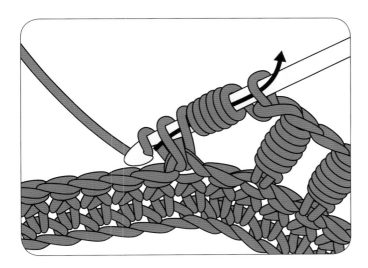

3 Wrap the yarn around the hook once more. Draw through the yarn through all 9 loops on the hook.

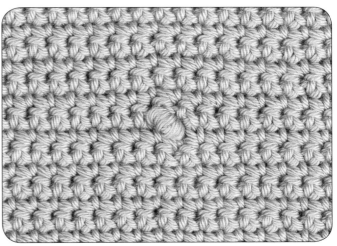

A finished bullion stitch.

loop stitches

Loops are a fun way to add texture to your crochet, although they can be time consuming and do tend to use quite a lot of yarn. Crochet loops can be really effective as an edging to a fabric or as an all over pattern. Loop stitches are worked on a wrong side row and are best worked within a dense stitch, such as single crochet (UK double crochet).

Basic loop stitch

It is worthwhile spending some time practicing this stitch because you may have difficulty making all the loops an even length. It is a good idea to work one or two plain stitches at the beginning and end of the row to make sewing up easier.

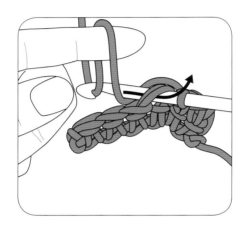

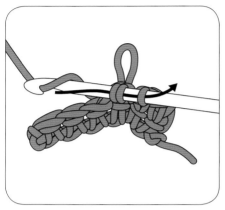

1 With the wrong side of the work facing, work to where a loop is required. Insert the hook into the next stitch. Loop the yarn around either the index or middle finger of the left hand and use the hook to draw the two strands of yarn at the base of the loop through the stitch.

2 Allow the loop to drop from the finger. Wrap the yarn around the hook once more.

3 Carefully draw the yarn through all the loops on the hook. Tug the made loop gently, to tighten.

Basic loop stitch.

Loop stitch worked over a card

Using a piece of stiff card cut to the required size can help you to ensure that your loops are consistent.

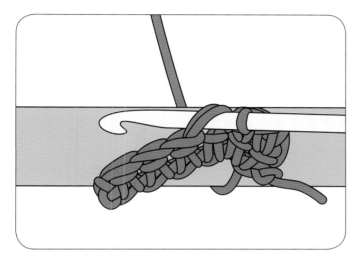

1 With the wrong side of the work facing, work to where a loop is required. Insert the hook into the next stitch. Hold the crochet piece against the card using the right hand. Wrap the yarn around the card so that the yarn sits to the reverse.

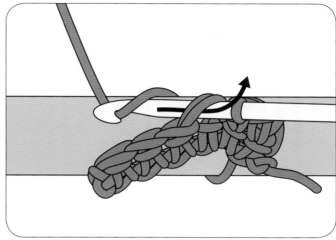

2 Transfer the crochet and the card to the left hand. Wrap the yarn around the hook and draw through the stitch.

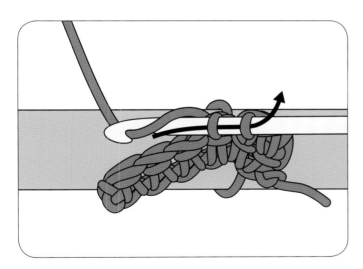

3 Wrap the yarn around the hook once more and draw through all the loops on the hook. Continue to work in this way to the end of the row. Remove card.

Loop stitch worked over a card.

stitch directory

Abbreviations and symbols can differ depending upon whether you are following a US or a UK pattern and can even be personal to a pattern writer or designer, so it is really important that you make sure you understand all the crochet abbreviations and symbols before you start working from this Stitch Directory.

Don't be fooled by simply reading the stitch names, because some stitch references are the same yet mean very different things. For example, US and UK patterns share stitch names (such as double crochet, or treble crochet for example), yet these names do not refer to the same stitches. Single crochet in US terminology is a dense stitch with a short post, which in the UK is called double crochet. However, double crochet in the US is a longer stitch with a post, which is perhaps twice the height of the UK stitch, and is known in the UK as treble crochet.

All patterns in this section are written using US terminology only. See page 33 for stitch abbreviations.

Fur Stitch

Foundation chain: multiples of 8 + 2
Special Abbreviation: Loop Stitch (WS facing) = wrap yarn around left index finger to make a loop, insert hook into next st, draw through both threads of the loop; yarn over hook and draw through all loops to complete the stitch
Note: Yarn loops are cut once completed.

Foundation row: 1dc into 4th ch from hook, 1dc into each ch to end, turn.
Row 1: Ch1, 1sc into next 2 dc, *Loop Stitch into each of next 4 sts **, 1sc into next 4 sts; rep from * finishing last rep at **, 1sc into next st and the top of the tch, turn.
Row 2: Ch3 (counts as 1dc), skip 1 st, 1dc into each st to end, skip tch, turn.
Repeat Rows 1 and 2 to required length.

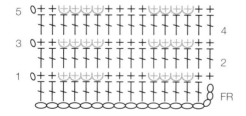

Loop Stitch With Bead

Foundation chain: multiples of 1 + 1
Special Abbreviation: Loop Stitch (WS facing) = wrap yarn around left index finger to make a loop, insert hook into next st, draw through both threads of the loop; yarn over hook, draw through all loops to complete stitch
Note: Beads need to be threaded onto the yarn before starting the pattern and should be incorporated into each loop.

Foundation row: 1sc into 3rd ch from hook, 1sc into each ch to end, turn.
Row 1: Ch1 (counts as 1sc), skip 1 st, Loop Stitch into each st to end, 1sc into top of tch, turn.
Row 2: Ch1 (counts as 1sc), skip 1 st, 1sc into each st to end, 1sc into top of tch, turn.
Repeat Rows 1 and 2 to required length.

chevron stitches

Chevron stitches are sometimes referred to as "ripple" stitches. You can create a range of effective chevron designs in crochet and the pattern is often set on the foundation row then repeated throughout. Chevrons are made by working corners at two repeated points in the piece; if you imagine a hill and a valley then the top of the hill is the point of the stitch where a corner is made by increasing, the bottom of the hill (or the valley) is where a point is made by decreasing stitches. The number of stitches between each point varies, but the stitch count usually remains constant throughout—in order to keep the stitch count correct it is a good idea to count at the end of every row. If you find you have lost stitches then you may need to increase into the first or last stitch of the row.

A chevron made using single crochet (UK double crochet)

This technique is for a basic chevron stitch.

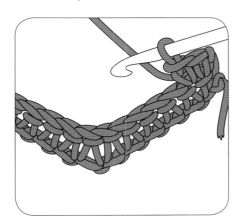 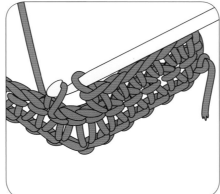 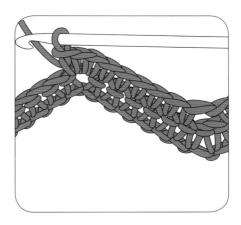

1 Make a chain to the required length, work a row of stitches into the chain. Work 2 stitches into the first stitch of the row.

2 Work to where the decrease is required, *miss the next 2 stitches. Continue to work stitches into each stitch on the previous row.

3 Work to where the increase is required, work 3 stitches into the next stitch. Continue to work stitches into each stitch on the previous row. Repeat from * to the end of the row. Work 2 stitches into the final stitch before turning to work the next row. Repeat on the next row.

A chevron in single crochet (UK double crochet).

A chevron made using double crochet (UK treble crochet)

In order to keep the sides of the work neat and the stitch count correct, the chevron pattern made with stitches with a longer post may require a decrease or a slip stitch to be worked at the beginning of the row.

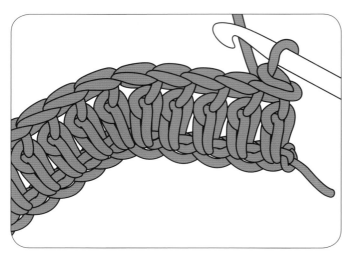

1 Work the first row, turn and work a slip stitch into the second stitch of the previous row. Work the turning chain.

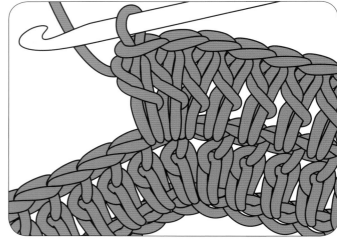

2 *Work to where the increase is required, work 3 stitches into the next stitch.

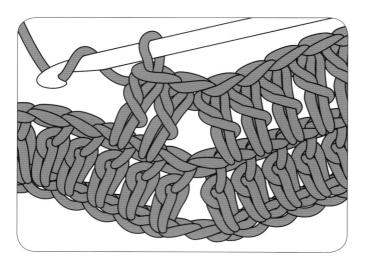

3 Work to where the decrease is required, miss the next 2 stitches. Continue to work stitches into the next sequence of stitches on the previous row. Repeat from * to the end of the row.

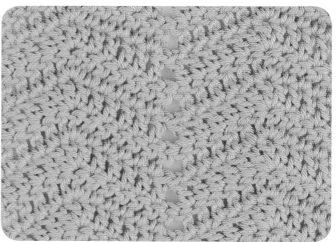

Chevron in double crochet (UK treble crochet).

A wave stitch made using double crochet (UK treble crochet)

A wave stitch is similar to a chevron in that stitches are increased to make a "hill" top and decreased to make a "valley." However, a wave is less angular, with the decreases and increases made over more stitches.

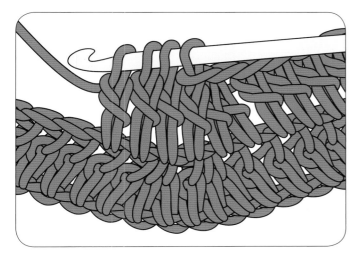

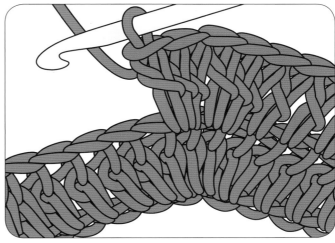

1 Work to where the decrease is required, (this is the 6 stitches at the base of the valley, 3 either side of the central point). *Into the next 3 stitches work 3 incomplete stitches, leaving one loop remaining on the hook for each stitch as if working a cluster. Work the 3 stitches together by drawing the yarn through the final loops. Repeat from * once more.

2 Work to where the increase is required, (this is central pair of stitches at the top of the previous wave). Work 3 stitches into each of these stitches.

Wave stitch in double crochet (UK treble crochet).

Using stitch markers

It can be difficult to keep track of where you should be decreasing and increasing your stitches. To make this easier, use stitch markers to identify the points of the chevron.

stitch directory

Abbreviations and symbols can differ depending upon whether you are following a US or a UK pattern and can even be personal to a pattern writer or designer, so it is really important that you make sure you understand all the crochet abbreviations and symbols before you start working from this Stitch Directory.

Don't be fooled by simply reading the stitch names, because some stitch references are the same yet mean very different things. For example, US and UK patterns share stitch names (such as double crochet, or treble crochet for example), yet these names do not refer to the same stitches. Single crochet in US terminology is a dense stitch with a short post, which in the UK is called double crochet. However, double crochet in the US is a longer stitch with a post, which is perhaps twice the height of the UK stitch, and is known in the UK as treble crochet.

All patterns in this section are written using US terminology only. See page 33 for stitch abbreviations.

Wave and Chevron Stitch

Foundation chain: multiples of 6 + 2
Note: Work 2 rows in colors A, B, C & D throughout.

Foundation row: 1sc into 3rd ch from hook, *1sc into each st to end, turn.
Row 1: Ch1 (counts as 1sc), skip 1 st, *1hdc into next st, 1dc into next st, 3tr into next st, 1dc into next st, 1hdc into next st, 1sc into next st; rep from * to end, turn.
Rows 2–3: Ch1 (counts as 1sc), skip 1 st, 1sc into next st 3 sts, *3sc into next st, 1sc into next 2 sts, over next 3 sts work sc3tog, 1sc into next 2 sts; rep from * to last 5 sts, 3sc into next st, 1sc into next 2 sts, over final 2 sts work sc2tog, turn.
Row 4: Ch4 (counts as 1tr), skip 1 st, 1tr into next st, *1dc into next st, 1hdc into next st, 1sc into next st, 1hdc into next st, 1dc into next st, **over next 3 sts work tr3tog; rep from * finishing last rep at **, over final 3 sts, tr2tog into the next st and the tch, turn.
Rows 5–6: Ch1 (counts as 1sc), skip 1 st, 1sc into each st to end, turn.
Repeat Rows 1–6 to required length.

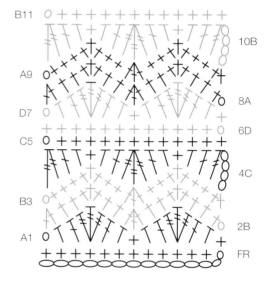

Chevron Stitch 1

Foundation chain: multiples of 16 + 2

Foundation row: 2sc into 2nd ch from hook, *1sc into next 7 ch, skip 1ch, 1sc into next 7 ch, 3sc into next ch; rep from * to last st, 2sc into final ch, turn.
Row 1: 1ch, 2sc into next sc, *1sc into next 7 sts, sk 2 sc, 1sc into next 7 sts, 3sc into next sc; rep from * to last st, 2sc into final st, turn.
Repeat Row 1 to required length.

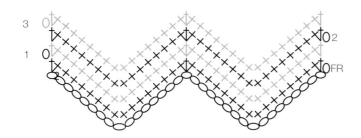

Chevron Stitch 1 from the front.

Chevron Stitch 1 from the reverse.

Double Crochet Chevron

Foundation chain: multiples of 23 + 3
Note: Work 2 rows in colors A and B throughout.

Foundation row: 1dc into 4th ch from hook, 1dc into next 3 ch, *3dc into next ch, 1dc into next 5 ch, skip 2 ch, 1dc into next 5 ch; rep from * to final 6 ch, 3dc into next ch, 1dc into next 5 ch, turn.
Row 1: Ss into 2nd dc, 3ch (counts as 1dc), 1dc into next 4 sts, *3dc into next st, 1dc into next 5 sts, skip 2 dc, 1dc into next 5 sts; rep from * to final 6 sts, 3dc into next st, 1dc into next 5 sts, turn.
Repeat Row 1 to required length.

Double Crochet Chevron from the front.

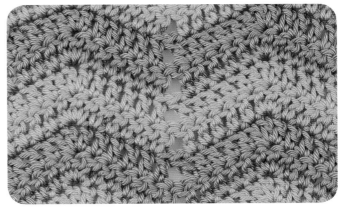

Double Crochet Chevron from the reverse.

mesh stitches

A mesh fabric can be used as a background fabric for more textural stitches—and as it is a very open fabric, it works very well in lace patterns. It can be tricky to keep the stitch count correct so make sure that you count your stitches at the end of a row.

Basic mesh

To make a mesh you will need to use stitches with a long post.
For a basic mesh, work your stitches into the stitch itself.

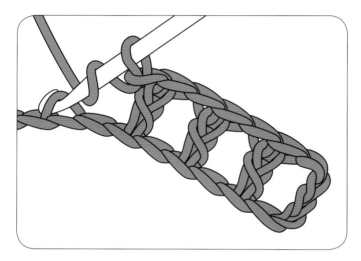

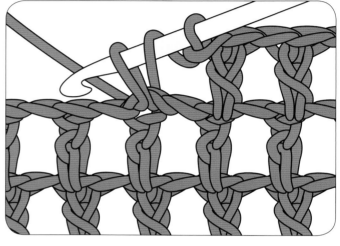

1 Work a row of stitches into the foundation chain, skipping 1ch and working 1ch between each stitch.

2 Insert the hook into the top of the stitch on the previous row. This will create a mesh where the stitches line up on every row.

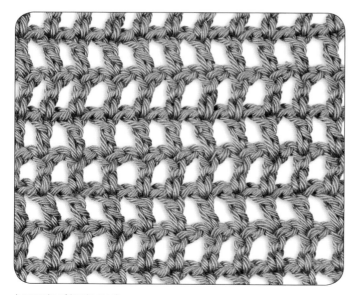

A sample of basic mesh.

Off-set mesh

For a basic off-set mesh, work your stitches into the gap between stitches.

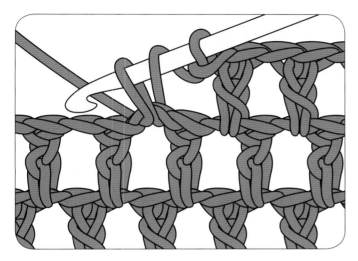

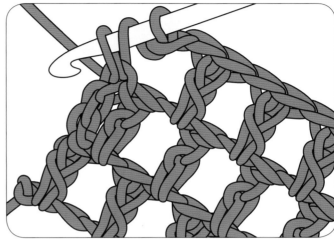

1 Work a row of stitches into the foundation chain, skipping 1ch and working 1ch between each stitch. On the subsequent row, insert the hook into the space made by the mesh pattern on the previous row.

2 The mesh pattern becomes off set and there are fewer spaces into which to work stitches. Make an extra stitch at the end of the row into the top of the first stitch on the previous row to correct the stitch count.

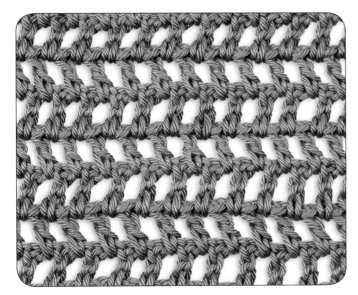

A sample of off-set mesh.

Using mesh stitch

Making a mesh stitch fabric is an incredibly quick way to create really fast finished projects. Why not try making a basic wrap or a scarf? You may even want to try making an eco friendly shopping bag using string or garden twine.

trellis stitches

Trellis stitch also works really effectively as a background for textural stitches and can look especially attractive when used in conjunction with a lace edging, for example.

Trellis pattern

The trellis is created by working a series of chain stitches into the space created by chain on the previous row. This is a really good stitch for beginners.

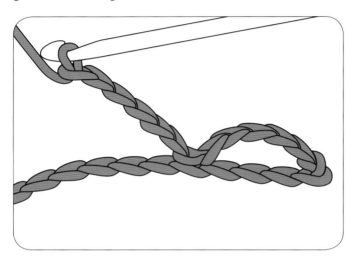

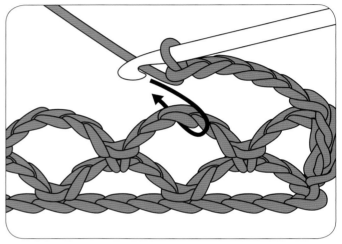

1 Chain spaces are created by working a series of chain loops that are about a third longer than the number of skipped chain stitches. The chain length can vary from pattern to pattern.

2 The last chain loop of the row is slightly shorter. The chain at the beginning of the row is then anchored into the space made by the chain on the previous row, using a slip stitch or other short post stitch.

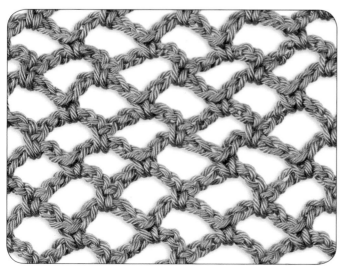

A sample of trellis.

Varying the trellis

When working a trellis you can choose how many chain you wish to use between securing your stitches—the more chain you make the larger the gaps in the trellis will be. You may also want to try some experiments to create irregular sized spaces thus working in a more freeform way.

shell and fan stitches

Shell and fan stitches are made by working a group of stitches into one space or stitch. Because a group of stitches can take up more space than a single stitch, the stitches spread themselves out to create the appearance of a shell or a fan. Shells and fans are often used in conjunction with a mesh or trellis background to make intricate lace patterns.

Basic 3-stitch shell using double crochet (UK treble crochet)

A small group of stitches, such as 3 or 4, are referred to as a shell.

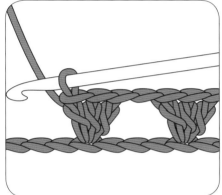

1 Work to where the shell is required, miss the number of chains/stitches stated in the pattern, (here a skip of 3 chain). Work a stitch into the next chain/stitch.

2 Work another 2 stitches into the same chain/stitch, thus completing a shell.

3 In order to keep the stitch count correct it may be necessary to work a half shell at the beginning or end of the row. To do this at the beginning of the row, work 2 stitches into the first stitch.

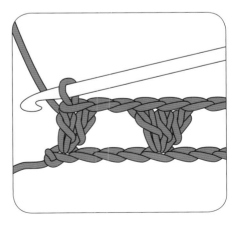

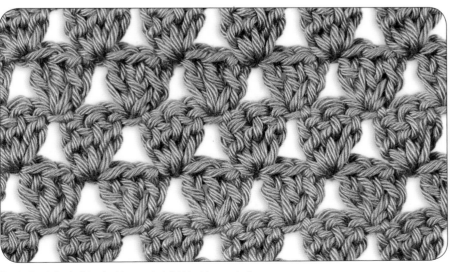

4 To do this at the end of the row, work 2 stitches into the final stitch of the row.

Basic 3-stitch shell in double crochet (UK treble crochet).

Working a wide fan stitch over more than one row

A large group of stitches, say 5 or 7, is referred to as a fan because they take up more space than a shell.

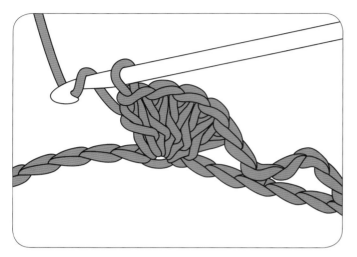

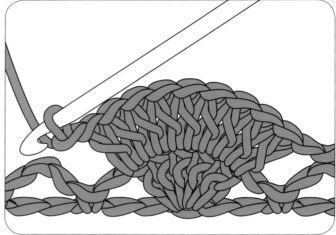

1 The fan stitch may begin on the very first row after the foundation chain, or it could be made on subsequent rows. Keep a tally of the stitches as they are made. Fans are often made from an uneven multiple of stitches, such as 5 or 7. Getting the number wrong on the first row could throw the pattern on the subsequent rows.

2 To make a fan that increases in width over a few rows, increase as the pattern suggests into the top of the fan made on the previous row. Once again, keep a tally of the stitch count.

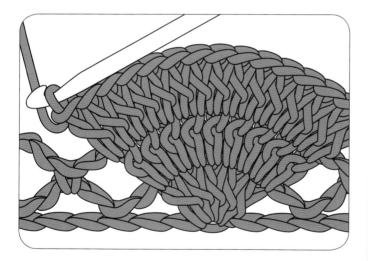

3 On the final row of a pattern repeat, increase as the pattern suggests into the top of the fan made on the previous row. Once again, keep a tally of the stitch count.

Wide fan stitch worked over more than one row.

Working fan stitch into a chain space

The pattern may ask that the group of stitches that form the fan are worked into the space created by a chain on the previous row.

To work in this way, insert the hook into the gap formed by the chain on the previous round and work the stitches over the top of the chain thus encasing it within the stitches.

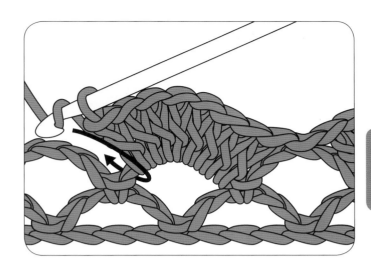

Fan stitch worked into a chain space.

stitch directory

Abbreviations and symbols can differ depending upon whether you are following a US or a UK pattern and can even be personal to a pattern writer or designer, so it is really important that you make sure you understand all the crochet abbreviations and symbols before you start working from this Stitch Directory.

Don't be fooled by simply reading the stitch names, because some stitch references are the same yet mean very different things. For example, US and UK patterns share stitch names (such as double crochet, or treble crochet for example), yet these names do not refer to the same stitches. Single crochet in US terminology is a dense stitch with a short post, which in the UK is called double crochet. However, double crochet in the US is a longer stitch with a post, which is perhaps twice the height of the UK stitch, and is known in the UK as treble crochet.

All patterns in this section are written using US terminology only. See page 33 for stitch abbreviations.

Shell Trellis Stitch

Foundation chain: multiples of 12 + 3

Foundation row: 2dc into 3rd ch from hook, *skip 2 ch, 1sc into next ch, 5ch, skip 5 ch, 1sc into next ch, skip 2 ch, 5dc into next ch; rep from * finishing final rep with 3dc into final ch, turn.
Row 1: Ch1, 1sc into next st, *5ch, 1sc into next 5ch-sp, 5ch, 1sc into 3rd dc of 5dc; rep from * finishing final rep with 1sc into top of tch, turn.
Row 2: *Ch5, 1sc into next 5ch-sp, 5dc into next sc, 1sc into next 5ch-sp; rep from * finishing with 2ch, 1dc into final sc, skip tch, turn.
Row 3: Ch1, 1sc into next st, *5ch, 1sc into 3rd dc of next 5dc, 5ch, 1sc into next 5ch-sp; rep from * to end, turn.
Row 4: Ch3 (counts as 1dc), 2dc into the base of the ch, *1sc into next 5ch-sp, 5ch, 1sc into next 5ch-sp, 5dc into next sc; rep from * finishing final rep with 3dc into final sc, skip tch, turn.
Repeat Rows 1–4 to required length.

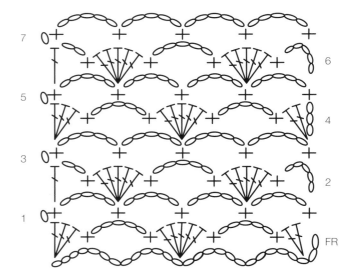

Working fans

Fans are an effective way of making crochet fabric and work well when combined with a background trellis. Fans can be made from any number of stitches, but try to keep an uneven number so that you have a central stitch to work fans into on subsequent rows.

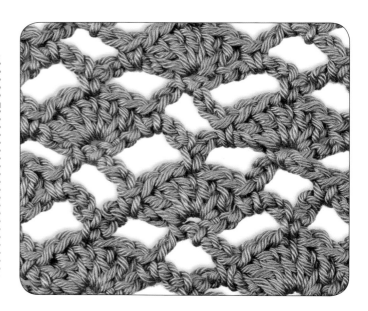

Mesh Ground 1

Foundation chain: multiples of 2 + 6

Foundation row: 1dc into 6th ch from hook, *1ch, skip next ch, 1dc into next ch; rep from * to end, turn.
Row 1: Ch4 (counts as 1dc and 1ch), *1dc into next dc, 1ch; rep from * to end, working last dc into 2nd tch, turn.
Row 2: Ch4 (counts as 1dc, 1ch), *1dc into next dc, 1ch; rep from * to end, working last dc into 3rd tch, turn.
Repeat Row 2 to required length.

Plain Trellis

Foundation chain: multiples of 4 + 2

Foundation row: 1sc into 6th ch from hook, *5ch, skip 3 ch, 1sc into next ch; rep from * to end, turn.
Row 1: *Ch5, 1sc into next 5ch-sp; rep from * to end, working final sc into 3rd tch, turn.
Row 2: *Ch5, 1sc into next 5ch-sp; rep from * to end, working final sc into sc on prev row, turn.
Repeat Row 2 to required length.

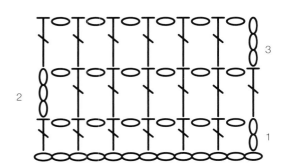

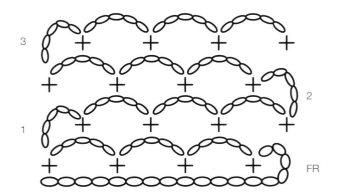

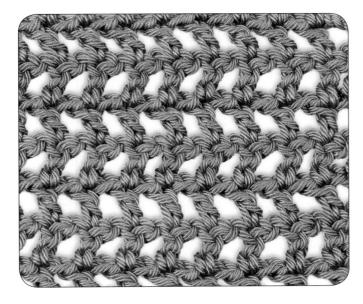

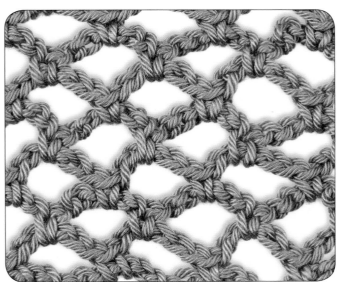

freeform crochet

The pieces made using this technique are unique and the craft has been described as being like painting—with the hook as a brush and the yarn as paint. The results can be abstract or realistic. Freeform is original design, and thus goes beyond the realm of patterns and the restrictions that usually apply. Freeform differs from traditional crochet in that fabric is created in pieces and then either sewn or crocheted together.

Scrumbling

The most common technique for freeform crochet is called scrumbling; a name coined by Sylvia Cosh and James Walters in the 1970s. Scrumbling is a method of creating fabric pieces that are joined together to create wearable art—they are usually created about palm sized and moved around within a template to create the fabric. This form of crocheting is rather like creating a jigsaw, with all the pieces of crochet joining together to form the desired effect.

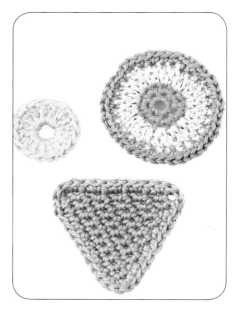  

Make a few crochet pieces. Don't worry about following a pattern—just use what you have learnt so far to make a few various shapes and sizes. Use a variety of yarns; eyelash and textural yarns work especially well.

Join the pieces, using either a sewn stitch or with a crochet stitch using a yarn tail end.

Add on more pieces, either by sewing or crocheting.

Embellish and add to the piece by working bullion stitches, chain stitches, picot edges, bobbles and even by adding beads, sequins and features such as Dorset buttons (see page 231), which you can hand make to match. Freeform crochet is by nature a very textural thing, so don't worry if your pieces create ripples and waves—these can be incorporated to add to the beauty of the design.

Working freeform crochet

Working freeform crochet is the ideal way to try out unusual yarns that may be hard to use in more conventional forms of crochet.

Designs can be completely random, like abstract art, or create more pictorial images.

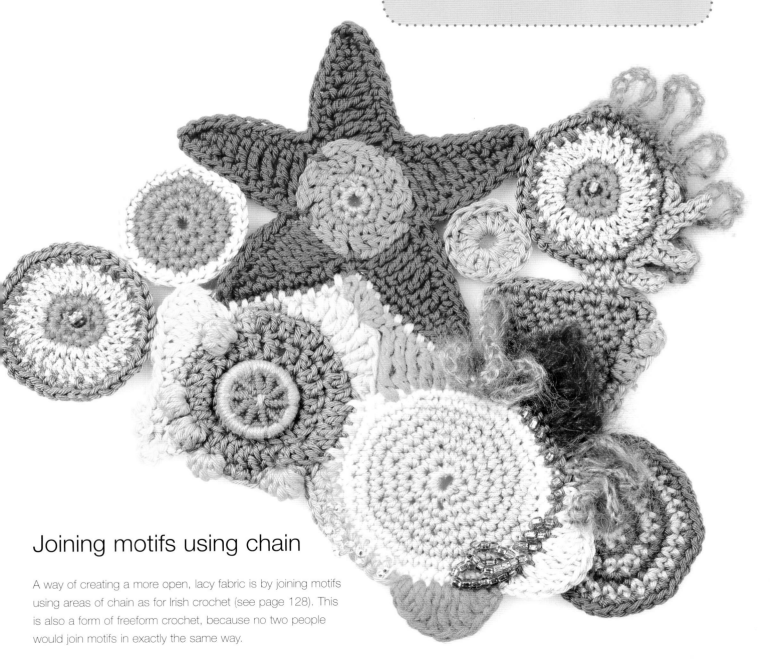

Joining motifs using chain

A way of creating a more open, lacy fabric is by joining motifs using areas of chain as for Irish crochet (see page 128). This is also a form of freeform crochet, because no two people would join motifs in exactly the same way.

thread crochet

Thread crochet is the term given to traditionally made fine lace weight crochet. The type of yarn used for this method tends to be very fine and the hooks used are also very small—the smaller the yarn and hook, the more detail you will be able to put into a piece of work. The stitches made are tiny and a single piece can take many hours to make. Both Filet and Irish crochet are forms of thread crochet. Contemporary pieces tend to be made in thicker threads with larger hooks, but the overall effect remains and some very beautiful pieces can be made.

filet crochet

Filet crochet uses stitches with a long post and areas of chain in a grid type formation. It often depicts letters and pictures and is sometimes used for table runners and lace effect window dressings. When creating a filet crochet pattern you will be required to follow a graph, which is shown in the form of a grid that differs to standard crochet charts. To make a piece of filet crochet you work a sequence of either blocks of stitches or create a space by working a chain.

Reading a traditional filet crochet chart

The traditional filet chart is shown center right. Each square represents either the number of stitches to be worked to form one block of crochet stitches or the number of chain that you need to make to create a space. The shaded square in the grid represents the block of stitches and the empty square represents the space made by the chain. The pattern will tell you at the beginning how many stitches need to be made to form a block—it could range from 2 stitches to as many as 4 or 5. The pattern will also tell you how many chain to work to form the space. Where two shaded blocks on the grid are shown next to each other this means that more than one block of stitches is worked in succession.

In the grid shown right, row 1 is read from right to left and has two spaces followed by two blocks of stitches followed by another two spaces. Row 2 is worked from left to right and has the same formation. Row 3 is read from right to left and has two blocks of stitches followed by 2 spaces, followed by another two blocks. Row 4 is read from left to right and is a repeat of row 3.

Contemporary filet chart

You may find a filet crochet chart is given in the form immediately below instead, using symbols to represent the stitches instead of a grid formation.

The two charts below both illustrate the same design as in the sample in the photograph at the bottom of the page.

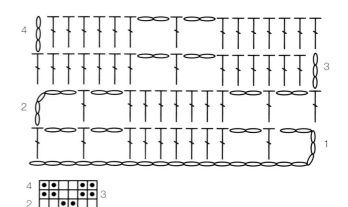

A section of filet crochet that would be created by following either of the charts above right.

Starting the first row with a space

If you are starting the filet crochet with a space then you will need to make a foundation chain, a chain long enough to be equivalent to the height of the stitch used, plus the length of the chain needed to travel along the top of the piece and thus form the framework for the next row.

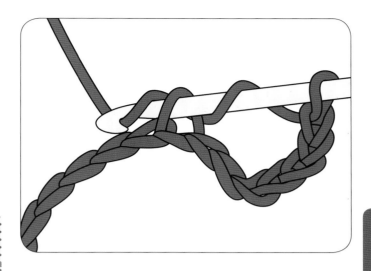

Making the chain

When making a space at the start of a row it may seem you are making too many chain so the space will be too big. However, once you work the next stitch and begin the row, it should become obvious that the box formed is the correct size.

For example, double crochet (UK treble crochet) requires 3 chain to reach the same height as a stitch. If the space is then made by missing 2 of the foundation chains, then an extra 2 chain need to be added to the existing 3 chain to be equivalent to the stitch plus the chain. When working from an existing pattern it should tell you how many chain to make. Make a chain to the required length. Insert the hook into the next stitch and work one stitch.

Starting the first row with a block

Here we show a block made from 3 stitches.

1 Add the correct number of stitches to the foundation chain to accommodate the height of the chosen stitch. Work the first stitch into the next chain.

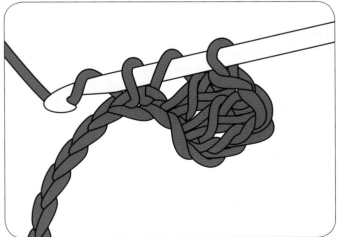

2 Work 2 further stitches into the subsequent stitches.

Working a space over a space

At some point you will need to work a space over a space.

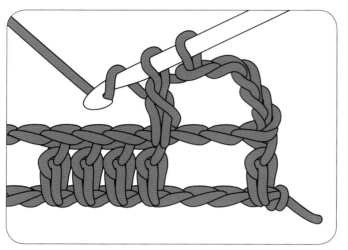

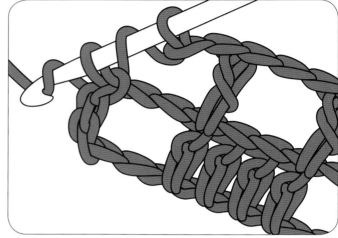

1 At the beginning of the row, work the required number of chain. Work a stitch into the top of the corresponding stitch on the row below. Continue to work to the end of the row.

2 At the end of the row, work the final stitch into the top of the turning chain on the previous row.

Working a space over a block

This is the technique for working a space over a block.

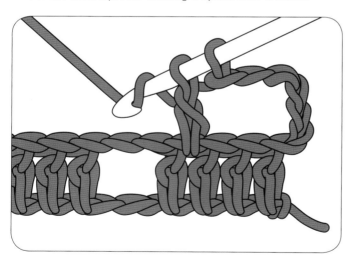

1 At the beginning of the row, work the required number of chain. Miss the block of stitches on the previous row. Work a stitch into the top of the corresponding stitch on the row below. Continue to work to the end of the row.

2 At the end of the row, work up to the last block of stitches made on the previous row. Work the final stitch into the top of the turning chain on the previous row.

Working a block over a space

This is the technique for working a block over a space.

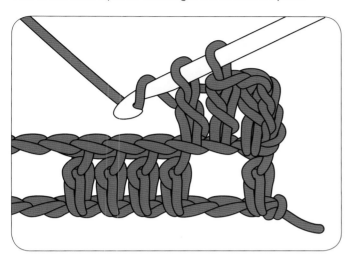 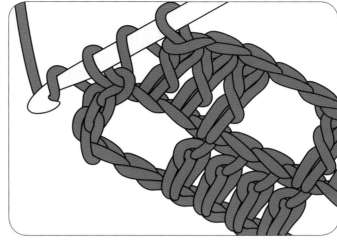

1 At the beginning of the row, work the required number of chain to reach the height of the stitch. Miss one chain at the base of the turning chain. Work into the next chain, then subsequent chain to form a block.

2 At the end of the row, work up to the last space made on the previous row. Work the final block of stitches into the top of the chain on the previous row.

Working a block over a block

This is the technique for working a block over a block.

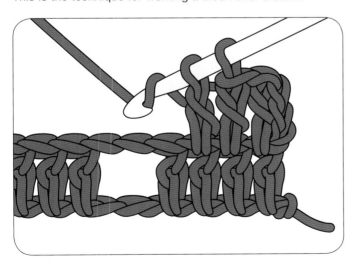 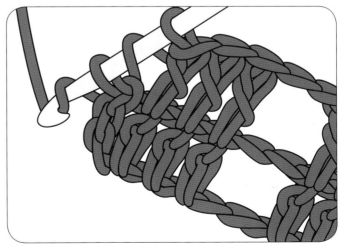

1 At the beginning of the row, work the required number of chain to reach the height of the stitch. Miss one stitch at the base of the turning chain. Work into the next stitch, then subsequent stitches to form a block.

2 At the end of the row, work up to the last block of stitches made on the previous row. Work the final block of stitches into the top of the stitches on the previous row.

Bars and lacets

It may be necessary to create a longer length of chain in order to create a bigger space, which is referred to as a bar. Using a longer bar of chain stitches can make a more intricate filet crochet design. Lacets also add detail and are used whena more angular design (such as a V shape or a slope) is required.

Working a bar over a pair of blocks

Work one stitch into the first corresponding stitch at the beginning of the block of stitches on the previous row. Work the required number of chain.

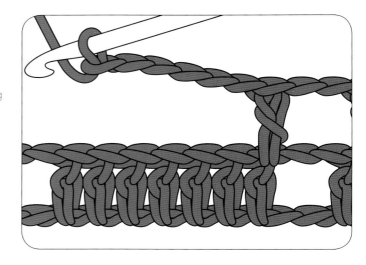

Working a pair of blocks into a bar

Work one stitch into the first corresponding stitch at the beginning of the chain bar created on the previous row. Work the required number of stitches into the chain.

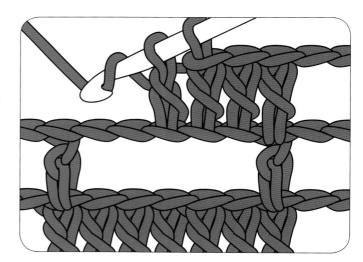

Working a bar over a pair of spaces

Work one stitch into the first corresponding stitch at the beginning of the space on the previous row. Work the required number of chain, work a stitch into the corresponding stitch at the beginning of the block on the previous row.

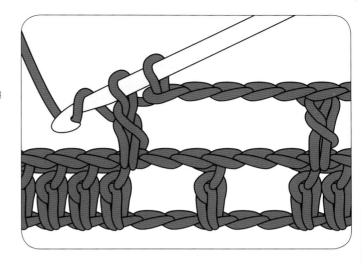

Working two spaces over a bar

Work one stitch into the first corresponding stitch at the beginning of the space on the previous row. Work the required number of chain, work a stitch into the center of the chain made on the previous row to form a space. Work the required number of chain once more, work a stitch into the corresponding stitch at the beginning of the block on the previous row.

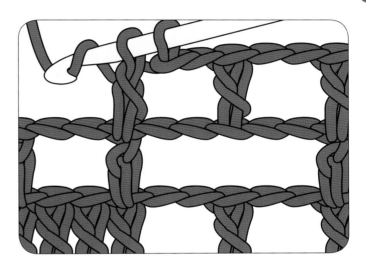

Using the light

Filet crochet pieces are very effective when displayed with light behind them, which is why they are often used as panels to dress windows. When working your piece, be sure to hold it up to the light at frequent intervals to get an idea of the effect the design is creating.

Working a lacet over a pair of blocks

Work to where the lacet is required. Work one stitch into the first corresponding stitch at the beginning of the block of stitches on the previous row. Work the required number of chain to form half the lacet. Secure with a slip stitch or sc (UK dc) at the center of the block on the previous row. Work the required number of chain to complete the lacet. Work a stitch into the corresponding stitch at the end of the block on the previous row.

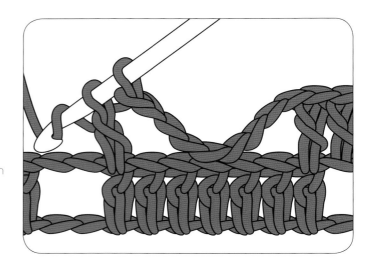

Working a bar over a lacet

Work to where the lacet was made on the previous row. Work the required number of chain to form the bar. Work a stitch into the corresponding stitch after the lacet on the previous row.

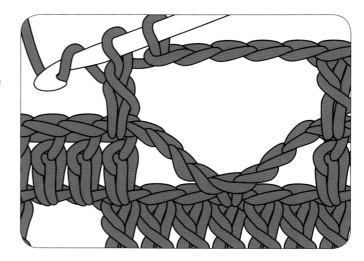

Working a lacet over a pair of spaces

Work to where the lacet is required. Work one stitch into the first corresponding stitch at the beginning of the space created on the previous row. Work the required number of chain to form half the lacet. Secure with a slip stitch or sc (UK dc) at the top of central stitch on the previous row. Work the required number of chain to complete the lacet. Work a stitch into the corresponding stitch at the end of the block on the previous row.

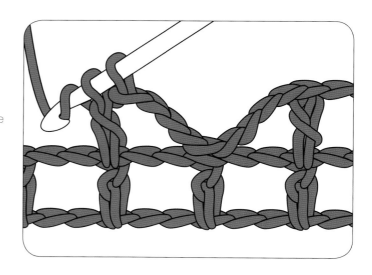

Shaping filet crochet

When shaping filet crochet you will probably need to increase or decrease by adding or subtracting either whole blocks or spaces from the piece. Shaping in filet crochet thus often creates a stepped appearance on the side edges, rather than a gradual sloped appearance.

Increasing by a space at the end of a row

Work to the end of the row. Work a turning chain equivalent to the height of the stitch. Work a stitch with a long post such as a dtr (UK tr tr) into the base of the stitch at the base of the chain. Work another turning chain. Turn and work the next row according to the pattern.

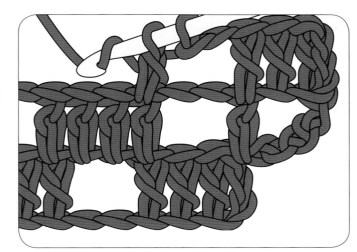

Increasing by a space at the beginning of a row

Work enough chain to equal the equivalent of the height of a stitch and twice the width of the space. Work a stitch into the top of the corresponding stitch on the row below.

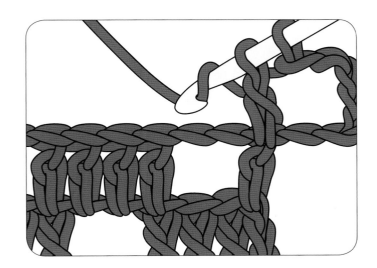

Increasing by a block at the end of the row

When making a block at the end of a row, the final group of stitches need to be worked one step higher than the row. So if for example the row has been made using double crochet (UK treble crochet) then the final block of stitches will need to be made using treble crochet (UK double treble crochet).

Work the final stitch of the row into the top of the corresponding stitch on the previous row. Work the next stitch (one step higher) into the base of the last stitch. Work the next and subsequent stitches into back of the first cross stitch on the post of the previous stitch.

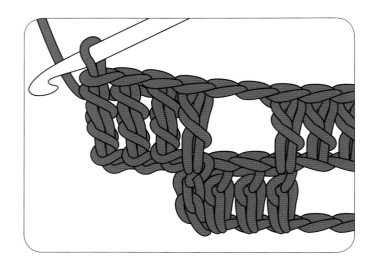

Increasing a block at the beginning of a row

Work enough chain to equal the equivalent of the height of a stitch and the width of the space. Work a stitch into the chain, counting along enough chain to equal the height of the stitch. Work subsequent stitches into the chain to create a block.

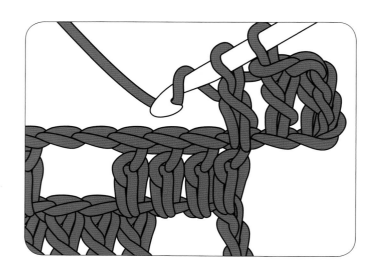

Using stitch markers

Stitch markers are very useful once again when shaping filet crochet. You can use them to mark the position of the shaping and also to make a note of your stitch count as you go along, to avoid increasing or decreasing incorrectly.

Decreasing a space at the beginning of a row

At the end of the row work one chain, turn. Work a slip stitch into the next stitch. Work slip stitches along the top of the previous row until the first block of stitches is reached. Work enough chain to start the next row and work in pattern to end.

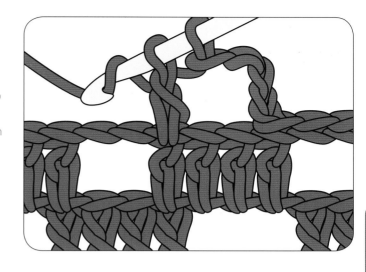

Decreasing a block at the beginning of a row

At the end of the row work one chain, turn. Work a slip stitch into the next stitch. Work slip stitches along the top of the previous row until the first space is reached. Work enough chain to start the next row and work in pattern to end.

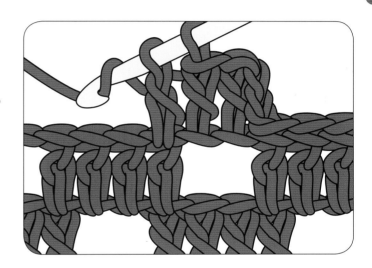

Decreasing over two rows

Work the row to the point where the decrease is needed. Work one stitch into the corresponding stitch on the previous row. Turn. Work enough chain to start the next row and work in pattern to end.

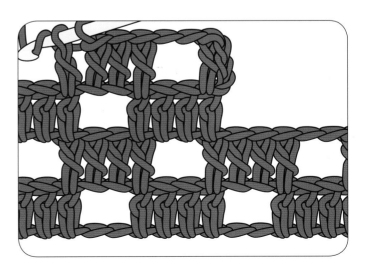

stitch directory

These three patterns will introduce you gently to the practice of filet crochet and are the ideal samplers to try out before embarking on a bigger project. Remember that when you follow a filet chart you will be working more than one stitch for each square on the chart, so it is essential that you make the correct number of stitches in your foundation chain. The length of the foundation chain is also governed by whether or not you are starting with a space or a block. Read the chart from right to left when the right side of the work is facing you and from left to right when the wrong side is facing. Use a ruler to help you remember which row you are on, or you could put a pencil line through each row as you complete it. If you struggle to see small graphs, then you could always scan the chart to make a larger copy.

Filet Diamond

In order to achieve a pictorial effect, filet crochet designs often have large blocks of dense work within a frame of open spaces. Thus pieces tend to be quite large and require a large number of stitches. However, a nice effect can be achieved over a much smaller area as this sampler shows well.

This pattern starts with a foundation chain of 44 stitches and each square of the graph represents 3 stitches. Start by working a double crochet (UK treble crochet) into the 8th chain from the hook in order to create the first space. Work across the row to the end. On the subsequent rows you will need to work 5 chain to create the first space of each row. Where you see a shaded square you need to work a group of stitches.

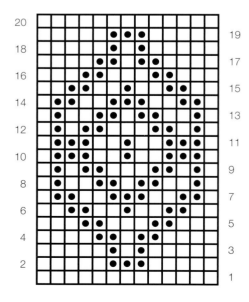

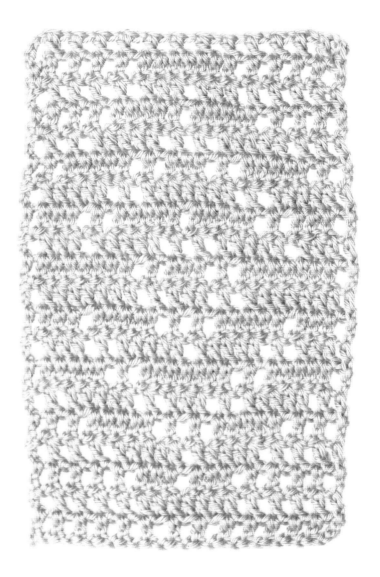

Filet Square

Filet crochet tends to be worked in straight pieces and traditionally lends itself well to the production of place mats and table runners, for example. This sample may work well as a coaster for a drink, or you could combine it with other squares to make a blanket or throw perhaps.

This pattern starts with a row of filled squares so you will not need to allow for stitches to make up a space when working the foundation chain. This pattern starts with a foundation chain of 66 stitches and each square on the chart represents 3 stitches. Start by working a double crochet (UK treble crochet) into the 4th chain from the hook. Work across the row to the end. On the subsequent rows you will need to work 3 chain to count as the first stitch. Where you see an empty square you need to work a space.

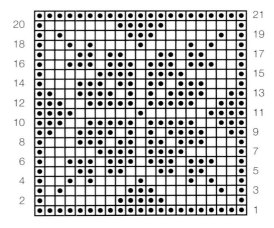

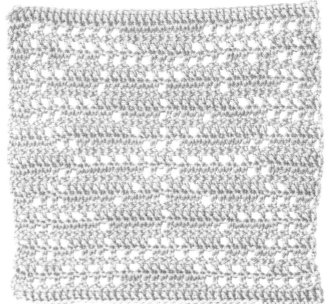

Clover Leaves

Filet crochet designs are often best seen from a distance, in order to realize the full effect of the pattern. This sample shows two clover leaves curling in alternate directions. You could repeat the pattern several times to create a nice border.

This pattern starts with a foundation chain of 39 stitches and each square of the graph represents 3 stitches. Start by working a double crochet (UK treble crochet) into the 8th chain from the hook in order to create the first space. Work across the row to the end. On the subsequent rows you will need to work 5 chain to create the first space of each row. Where you see a shaded square you need to work a group of stitches.

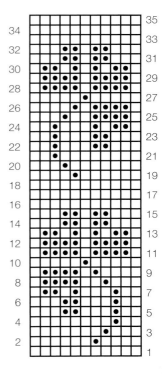

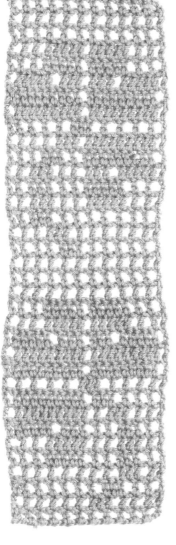

irish crochet

Irish crochet is another form of thread crochet, traditionally made using very fine threads to make stylized motifs that are then pieced together within a mesh or lace back ground. Irish crochet is often worked over a piece of cord instead of over a crochet chain, which creates a more embossed fabric.

Working over a foundation cord

To make a foundation cord for Irish crochet, use the following technique.

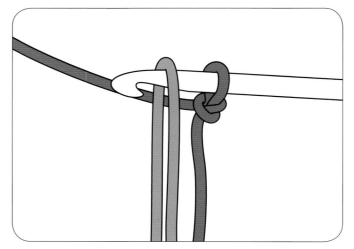

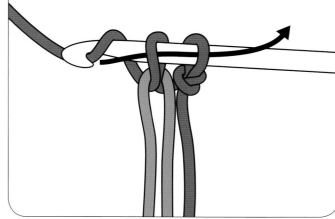

1 Using the yarn of choice, make a slip knot and place it on the hook. Hold the cord over the hook.

2 Wrap the yarn around the hook and draw through the cord. Complete a single crochet (UK double crochet) stitch to anchor the yarn to the cord.

Choosing a foundation cord

When selecting a foundation cord it is a good idea to source cord made from a slightly slippery yarn, such as nylon for example. Working over the top of such a cord will be much easier than working over a coarse thread such as twine and you will achieve a much neater final appearance. You could choose to work over a length of foundation cord, although this could mean that you will use quite a lot of yarn.

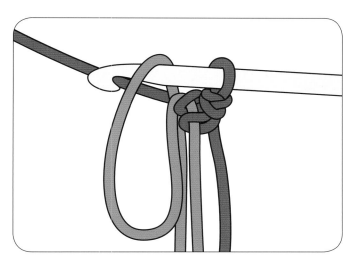

3 Wrap the cord to make a loop the required size for the motif.

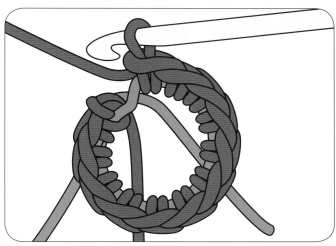

4 Work the required number of stitches over the cord. Gently pull one end of the cord to close the circle. Work a slip stitch into the first stitch to finish the row.

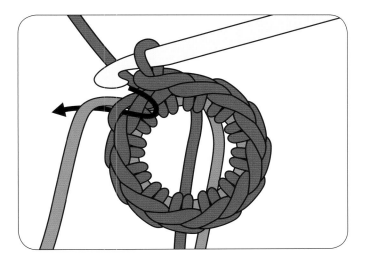

5 To work subsequent rows, hold the cord in line with the top of the crochet and enclose it within the piece, by working subsequent stitches around it.

Irish crochet worked over a foundation cord.

Working in a line

The following explains the technique of working in a line.

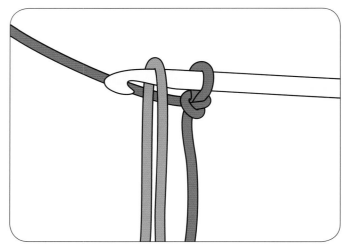

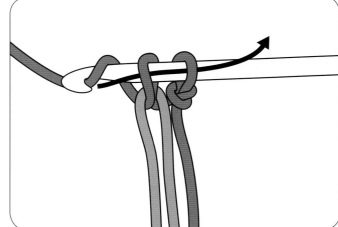

1 Using the yarn of choice, make a slip knot and place it on the hook. Hold the cord over the hook.

2 Wrap the yarn around the hook and draw through the cord. Complete a single crochet (UK double crochet) stitch to anchor the yarn to the cord.

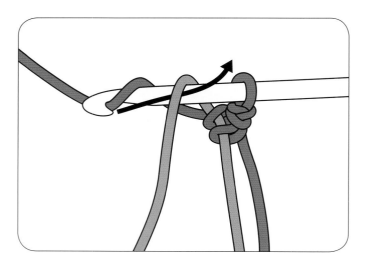

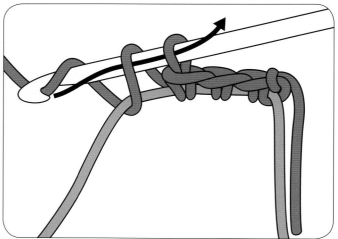

3 Take the hook under the cord from front to back. Wrap the yarn around the hook. Bring the hook back under the cord to the front. Complete the stitch.

4 Continue to work over the top of the cord, making sure that the stitches encase the cord and do not overlap each other.

Irish crochet worked in a line.

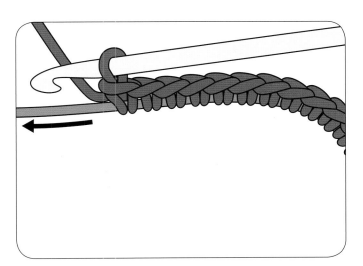

Combining pieces and joining motifs

Irish crochet motifs are made as individual pieces. These motifs are often worked in the round and are joined to each other either by making linking pieces of chain, working pieces in a line or by sewing them together. These three joining methods are often used in conjunction with each other. See pages 214–226 for details of some different methods of joining pieces together.

5 At the end of the row gently pull on one end of the cord to tighten.

Working a background mesh

Working areas of chain around a motif is a traditional Irish crochet technique. It is pretty intricate work, but can produce stunning fabrics.

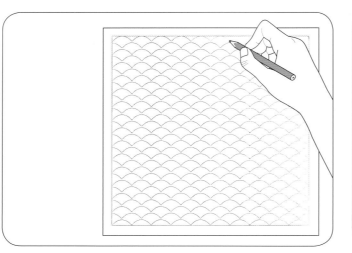

1 On a light piece of fabric draw out the background design that the motif will be worked into using a pencil.

2 Stitch the motif to the fabric using a few tacking stitches making sure that the right side is facing.

3 Work a foundation chain and subsequent background mesh in line with the drawn grid pattern.

4 Keeping the pattern correct incorporate the motif by working slip stitches into the piece where it makes contact with the background mesh.

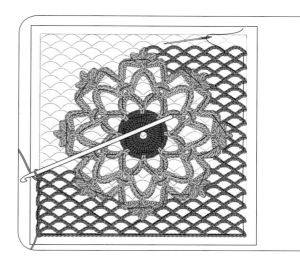

Working Irish crochet

Working Irish crochet can be a rather time consuming project and it also takes a lot of skill and practice to work effectively. Try not to be too ambitious with your first project and don't choose a really tiny hook and fine yarn as this will only make things more difficult.

5 As the piece gets bigger you may need to tack the background mesh to the fabric in order to stop it from slipping as you work.

A piece of Irish crochet on a background mesh.

tunisian and entrelac crochet

Tunisian crochet is also referred to as Afghan crochet, tricot crochet and "shepherds knitting." The technique uses a slightly different hook to traditional crochet and the technique combines elements of both crochet and knitting. Entrelac is a technique used by both crocheters and knitters alike and is a method of creating a sequence of square shapes in order to make a textured fabric that resembles a basket weave.

tunisian crochet

Tunisian crochet produces a durable and slightly elastic fabric and is worked without turns so that the front of the piece is always facing. As with standard crochet, you can create a few different fabrics using the Tunisian crochet method. There is basic stitch, which is also referred to as simple stitch, Tunisian stocking stitch, Tunisian purl stitch and Tunisian crossed stitch. These various stitches are made by inserting the hook into different parts of the stitch, thus creating a different yarn formation. The first row of Tunisian crochet is made by working a foundation row of stitches along a base chain, which is followed by a return row—almost like a cast off row in the craft of knitting. Subsequent rows are made by alternating a pick up row and a return row.

Tunisian crochet hook

The Tunisian crochet hook has a longer shaft than a standard hook, rather like a knitting needle with a hook at one end. The length of the hook determines the possible maximum width of the fabric.

Tunisian crochet patterns

Tunisian crochet patterns sometimes show a chart such as this one, which will also have a stitch key.

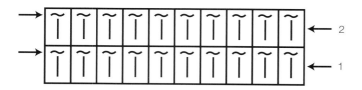

= Tunisian simple stitch (Tss)

= Tunisian knit stitch

= Tunisian mesh stitch

← = Loop row

→ = Return row

Using Tunisian crochet

Tunisian crochet uses a relatively large amount of yarn, and because Tunisian crochet stitches can be very dense and would make the ideal stitch for use in projects such as pan holders for example.

A section of Tunisian crochet.

The foundation row

To work the foundation, or base row of Tunisian crochet, use the following technique.

1 Make a foundation chain to the required length using the Tunisian crochet hook. Insert the hook into the back loop of the second chain from the hook. Wrap the yarn around the hook and draw through the back of the chain to form a loop on the hook. (2 loops are now on the hook).

2 Insert the hook into the back loop of the next stitch and draw through in the same way as before, leaving the loop on the hook. (3 loops are now on the hook).

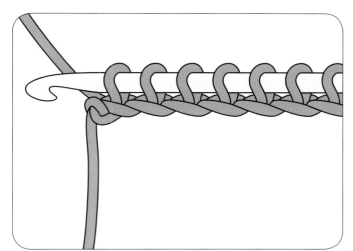

The return row

Wrap the yarn around the hook and draw through the first stitch on the hook. *Wrap the yarn around the hook again and draw it through the next two stitches. Repeat from * to the end of the row, drawing the yarn through two stitches each time until one stitch remains on the hook. Do not turn.

3 Continue to work in this way, leaving one loop on the hook after each stitch, until the required number of stitches has been made. Be careful not to over fill the hook and do not turn.

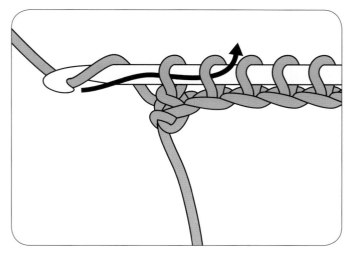

The pick up row

The last row produced a series of vertical bars of yarn leading up from the foundation row. These bars will be referred to as the stitch.

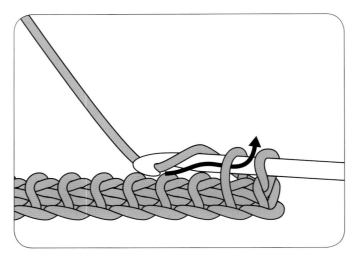

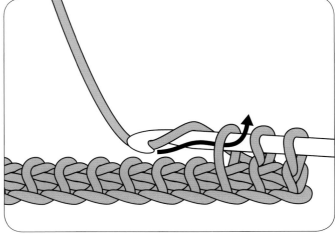

1 Miss one stitch, insert the hook into the next stitch from right to left. Wrap the yarn around the hook and draw through to make a loop on the hook. (2 loops are now on the hook).

2 Insert the hook into the next stitch, wrap the yarn around the hook and draw through the stitch to form another loop on the hook. (3 loops are now on the hook) Repeat to the end of the row, leaving one loop on the hook for every stitch worked.

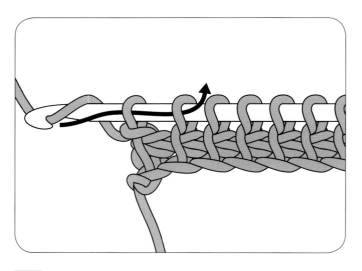

3 Repeat the return row as before.

Working the stitch

Tunisian crochet can be very therapeutic as it is made by working a repeated stitch action along complete rows each time. It is easy to get into a speedy rhythm and have some completed fabric in next to no time!

Finishing the top edge

Once you have finished your piece of Tunisian crochet it is a good idea to neaten and strengthen the top edge with a row of single crochet (UK double crochet).

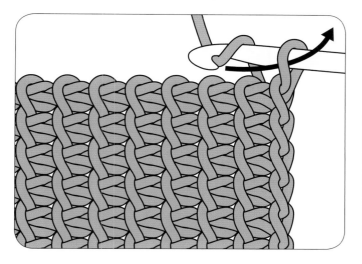

1 Make one chain to reach the height of the next row.

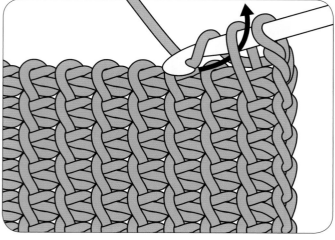

2 Insert the hook into the next stitch. Wrap the yarn around the hook and draw through the stitch.

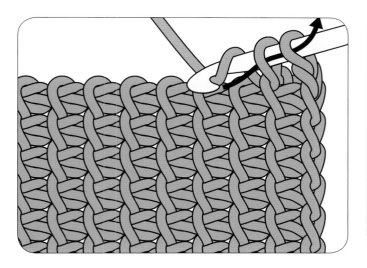

3 Wrap the yarn around the hook and draw through the two remaining loops to complete the stitch.

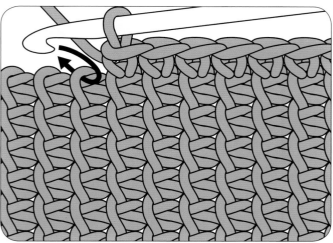

4 Continue to the end of the row, working a stitch into each corresponding stitch on the previous row.

stitch directory

Abbreviations and symbols can differ depending upon whether you are following a US or a UK pattern and can even be personal to a pattern writer or designer, so it is really important that you make sure you understand all the crochet abbreviations and symbols before you start working from this Stitch Directory.

Don't be fooled by simply reading the stitch names, because some stitch references are the same yet mean very different things. For example, US and UK patterns share stitch names (such as double crochet, or treble crochet for example), yet these names do not refer to the same stitches. Single crochet in US terminology is a dense stitch with a short post, which in the UK is called double crochet. However, double crochet in the US is a longer stitch with a post, which is perhaps twice the height of the UK stitch, and is known in the UK as treble crochet.

All patterns in this section are written using US terminology only. See page 33 for stitch abbreviations.

Tunisian Stockinette Stitch

Foundation chain: Multiples of 1 + 1

Foundation Row (RS): Insert hook into 2nd chain from hook, pick up a loop into each chain to end of row, 1ch. Do not turn.

Return Row: *Yo, draw yarn through 2 loops; rep from * to end of row, 1ch. Do not turn.

Row 1 (RS): Insert hook into center of 2nd vertical bar formed by stitch on previous row, yo, draw yarn through stitch. Rep by working a stitch into the center of each vertical bar across complete row, 1ch. Do not turn.

Row 2: Work as for return row.
Repeat Rows 1 and 2 to required length.

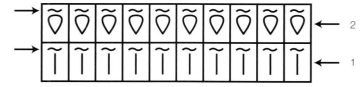

Tunisian Mesh Stitch

Foundation chain: Multiples of 1 + 1

Foundation Row (RS): Insert hook into 3rd chain from hook, yo, draw loop through st, 1ch. *Insert hook into next ch, yo, draw loop through ch, 1ch; rep from * to end of row, 1ch. Do not turn.

Return Row: *Yo, draw yarn through 2 loops; rep from * to end of row, 1ch. Do not turn.

Row 1 (RS): Skip 1 st, *insert hook into back of next horizontal ch that runs along top of previous row, yo, draw yarn through st, 1ch; rep from * to end of row, 1ch. Do not turn.

Row 2: Work as for return row.

Repeat Rows 1 and 2 to required length.

Tunisian Purl Stitch

Foundation chain: Multiples of 1 + 1

Foundation Row (RS): Yfwd, insert hook into 2nd chain from hook, yo, draw loop through ch, *yfwd, insert hook into next ch, yo, draw loop through ch; rep from * to end of row, 1ch. Do not turn.

Return Row: *Yo, draw yarn through 2 loops; rep from * to end of row, 1ch. Do not turn.

Row 1 (RS): Yfwd, insert hook into 2nd vertical bar formed on previous row, yo, draw loop through st, *yfwd, insert hook into next vertical bar, yo, draw loop through ch; rep from * to end of row, 1ch. Do not turn.

Row 2: Work as for return row.

Repeat Rows 1 and 2 to required length.

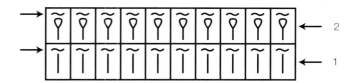

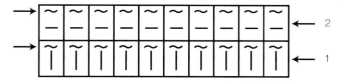

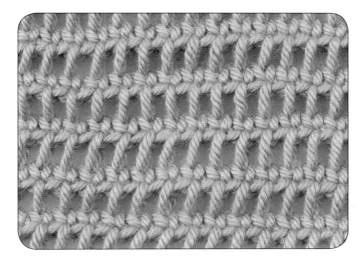

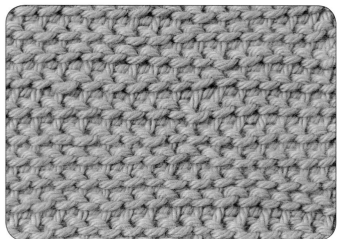

entrelac crochet

Knitted entrelac is made up of interconnected squares that sit in two orientations, whereas in the crochet entrelac technique the squares run in the same direction. This is because it is worked with the front side facing only and does not involve having to turn the work. To understand this method fully it is a good idea to first read the Tunisian crochet section on pages 136–139.

Crochet entrelac is a relatively simple technique and is a good way to work with lots of color— there is no reason why you shouldn't make every block a different shade, or you could get a great effect by using a variegated yarn.

Calculating the foundation chain

You must first calculate the number of stitches that will be required by the foundation chain. For the base row the foundation chain is used along the lower edge of the first row of squares and along the side edge of each.

Decide how many stitches wide you would like the squares to be. Then decide how many rows high the squares need to be and add the two together.

For example:

A square 6 stitches wide and 5 rows high will use 11 foundation chain. This calculation is then multiplied by the number of squares you wish to make.

For example:

The fabric is to be 4 squares wide, so the calculation is 4 x 11 = 44 Then add one chain to allow for the turning chain = 45 chain

Sample square

It is a good idea to work just one square using the Tunisian crochet method. Once this is completed to the size that you require, you can calculate how many stitches wide and how many rows high your entrelac squares needs to be.

Working the base row

Because your square is unlikely to be bigger than a few inches (centimeters) wide it is not essential that you use a Tunisian crochet hook. However, do make sure that the shaft of the hook you use is long enough to accommodate the number of stitches required.

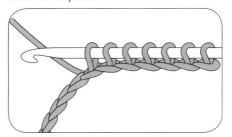

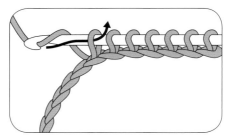

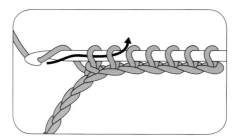

1 Make the required number of chain. Using the Tunisian crochet method as described on page 137 pick up the number of stitches needed by the first square.

2 Wrap the yarn around the hook and draw through the first stitch only.

3 *Wrap the yarn around the hook again and draw through two of the loops on the hook. Repeat from * to the end of the row, leaving one stitch on the hook—this is the same as the return row as described on page 137.

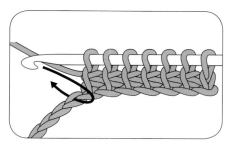

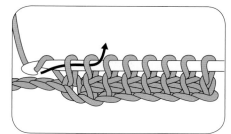

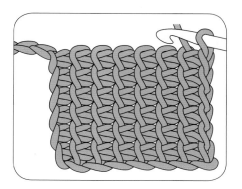

4 Make one chain, then pick up each vertical bar along the row leaving the stitches on the hook as you do so, as described for the pick up row on page 138. At the end of the row, insert the hook into the next foundation chain, wrap the yarn around the hook and draw through the stitch.

5 *Wrap the yarn around the hook again and draw through two of the loops on the hook. Repeat from * to the end of the row, leaving one stitch on the hook. This is the same as the return row as described on page 137.

6 Continue in this way until you have made a square shape.

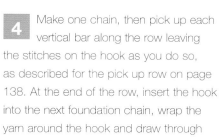

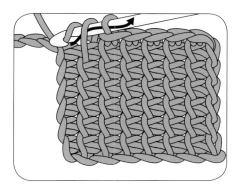

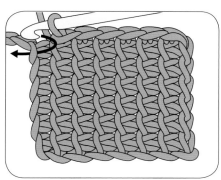

7 Work a row of slip stitch along the top edge of the square, working each slip stitch into the vertical bar made on the previous row.

8 When you reach the end of the square, work the last slip stitch into the same foundation chain as the last row was worked into.

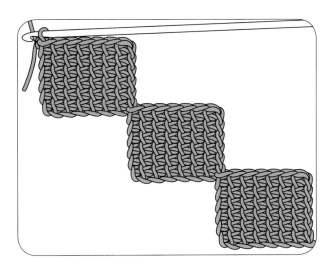

9 To make subsequent squares, insert the hook into the next foundation chain and pick up the number of stitches required by the square, then repeat all the steps until the required number of squares has been completed. Fasten off.

The second row

You can choose whether or not to change color at this point.

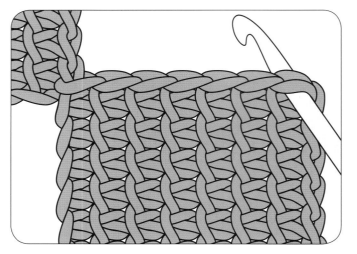

1 With the right side facing, insert the hook through the uppermost corner of the first square made on the base row.

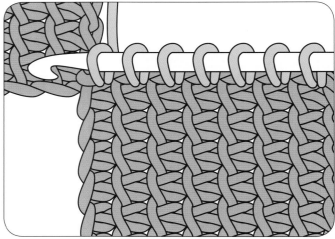

2 Pick up a stitch through this stitch and every following slip stitch at the top of the square.

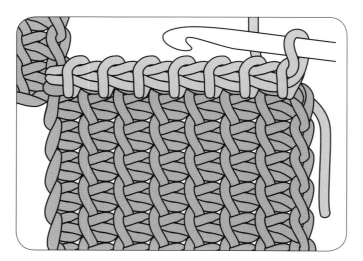

3 Wrap the yarn around the hook and draw through the first stitch only. *Wrap the yarn around the hook again and draw through two of the loops on the hook. Repeat from * to the end of the row, leaving one stitch on the hook. This is the same as the return row as described on page 137.

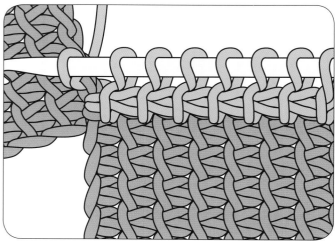

4 Make one chain, then pick up each vertical bar along the row leaving the stitches on the hook as you do so, as described for the pick up row on page 138). At the end of the row, insert the hook into the first stitch at the side of the second square on the base row, wrap the yarn around the hook and draw through the stitch.

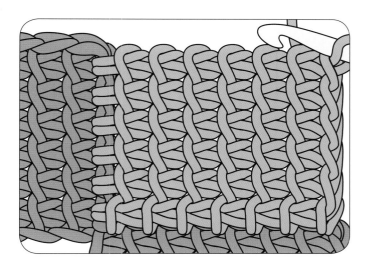

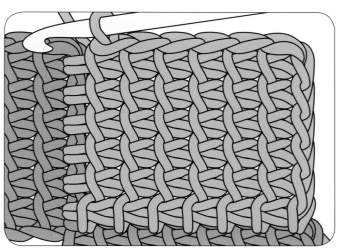

5 *Wrap the yarn around the hook and draw through two loops on the hook. Repeat from * until the square is complete.

6 Work a row of slip stitches along the top edge of the square. Insert the hook through the last stitch on the previous row, work a slip stitch.

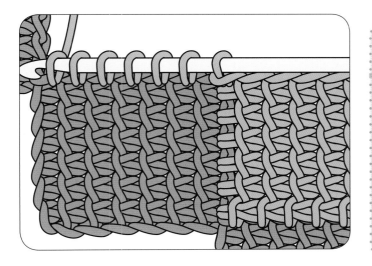

7 To make the next square pick up a row of stitches along the top edge of the next square of the base row. Work as set until you have completed the whole row of squares. Fasten off.

Filling in the sides

Because Entrelac is made by working repeated rows of complete squares you will find that the fabric produced has stepped edges. If you wish to fill these gaps to create a straight sided fabric then you will need to work some triangles at the beginning and end of certain rows.

The third row

You can choose whether or not to change color at this point.

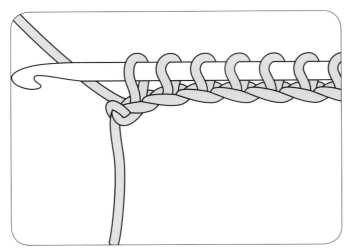

1 In the chosen color yarn make a foundation row of enough chain for the width of one square, plus one extra chain to allow for turning. Using the Tunisian crochet method as described on page 137 pick up the number of stitches needed by the first square.

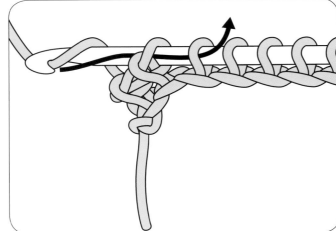

2 Wrap the yarn around the hook and draw through the first stitch only. *Wrap the yarn around the hook again and draw through two of the loops on the hook. Repeat from * to the end of the row, leaving one stitch on the hook. This is the same as the return row as described on page 137.

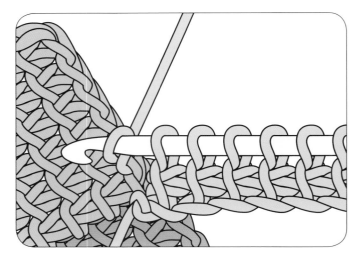

3 Make one chain, then pick up each vertical bar along the row leaving the stitches on the hook as you do so, as described for the pick up row on page 138. At the end of the row, insert the hook into the first stitch at the side of the first square on the second row, wrap the yarn around the hook and draw through the stitch.

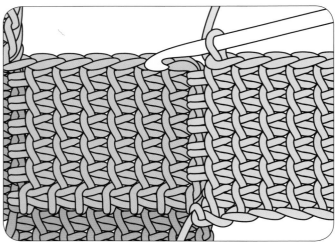

4 *Wrap the yarn around the hook again and draw through two of the loops on the hook. Repeat from * to the end of the row, leaving one stitch on the hook. This is the same as the return row as described on page 137. Work all the squares in the same way as the second row of squares until you are ready to make the final square.

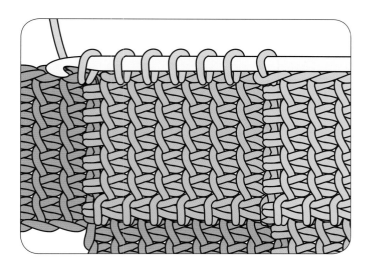

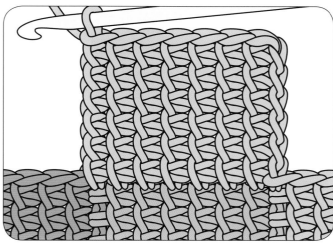

5 The final square does not have a foundation chain or a square from the previous row to work the final stitch of the row into. To work the final square, pick up along the top of the square in the same way as before. At the end of the row, pick up the final loop through the first slip stitch of the last square of the base row.

6 Work a return row as before. Continue to pick up a row and fasten off a row as described for Tunisian crochet on pages 137–138 until the final square is complete. Fasten off. Repeat the second and third rows until piece is required size.

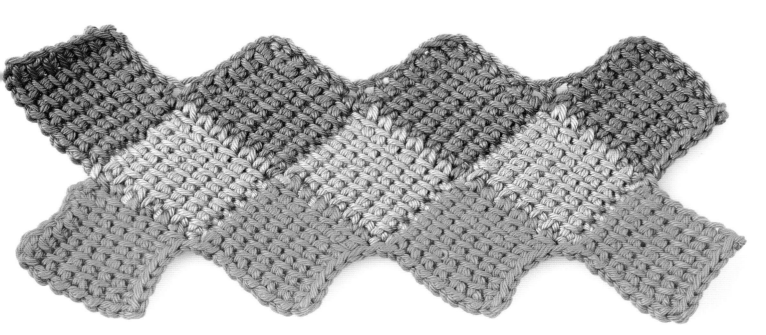

A piece of entrelac crochet in three colors.

working with color

There are two main ways to add color within a piece of crochet or knitting. Intarsia is a technique in which areas of color can be added using separate ends of yarn, which creates a single weight of fabric and in which many colors can be used in the same row. Jacquard crochet is a method in which smaller areas of color are created, with subsequent colors carried at the reverse of the work to create a double weight of fabric, this is similar to the technique of Fair Isle in the craft of knitting.

choosing colors

Although there are just three primary colors (red, yellow, and blue) there are, of course, thousands of—if not endless—permutations that result from mixing them together or by adding either white or black (which are both not officially classed as colors). Colors can be classified as belonging to different palettes: pastel shades; cool colors; warm colors; accent or bright colors; neutrals. In the world of fashion, all colors are believed to belong to one of four groups, which are often referred to in relation to seasons: Spring; Summer; Autumn; Winter. When choosing a color that you will wear, it is your skin tone that determines which colors are best suited to you.

Establishing your skin tone

First take careful analysis of your skin tone, natural hair color and eye color. To help find the undertone color of your skin, look at the inside of your arm in natural daylight. The skin in this area is at its most natural color and you should also have a clear view of your veins.

If your skin is more blue than yellow, and your veins are more blue in appearance than green, then you will be either a "Summer" or a "Winter."

If your skin tone is more yellow than blue, and your veins are more green in appearance than blue, then you will either be a "Spring" or an "Autumn."

Accent and complementary colors

This is a group of colors that you overlook at your peril! They are often used in small amounts, but can totally transform the appearance of your piece of work. An accent color is often a bright, clear shade, such as candy pink or citrus green, that—when worked in conjunction with another color palette—lifts the design and gives it a clear focus. If you want to get involved with color it is worth investing in a good color wheel, which you can get from an art shop. Try and find one that shows the complementary harmonies of a color, because this can give you a really good idea of what yarn colors will work in your piece of crochet. Color wheels are also useful if you are thinking of changing colors in an existing design.

For an example of the information a color wheel will give you, study the one shown left.

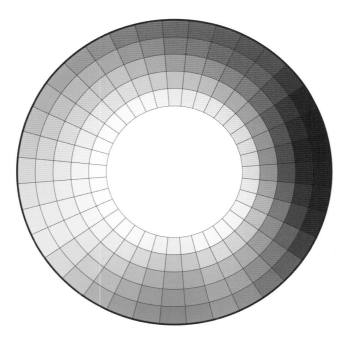

Accent colors   Complementary colors

Working from a chart

Most crochet patterns that rely on the use of color will include a graph of stitches. These graphs not only save space, but also give the crocheter a visual idea of how their project should progress. If you have never tackled graph knitting before, then intarsia is the ideal starting place. Each square or rectangle on the graph represents a stitch (horizontally) and a row (vertically). You may have a graph filled with color, or maybe one that has symbols—such as stars, dots and crosses—to represent the color used. It is always a good idea to photocopy your graph; you may even want to enlarge it slightly to make it easier to read. You may also want to use a ruler or Post-it notes to make each line clearer to read. Make sure that you line the ruler up under the row you have completed and do not block from sight the next row up the graph; this will help you to see what needs to be done on the next row and whether or not you need to carry or weave in any yarn to a certain place in preparation for it.

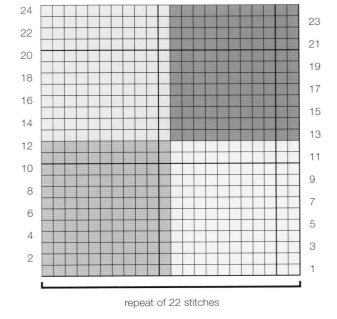

repeat of 22 stitches

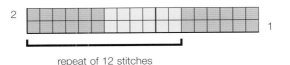

repeat of 12 stitches

The striped crochet fabric worked from the chart above.

The checked crochet fabric worked from the chart above.

Choosing between intarsia and jacquard

Choosing which method to use for adding color when crocheting is often a matter of personal taste, but as a general rule, the larger the area of alternative color used, the more advisable it is to use the intarsia method as opposed to the jacquard method. Most color work patterns will ask you to proceed in a certain way and may ask you to use the intarsia or jacquard technique or a mixture of both. Indeed, without an idea of how to work both techniques you may have a problem, because some of the techniques transpose between both methods.

intarsia

Using the intarsia method within the crochet piece creates separate areas of color. A length of yarn is used for each section of colored crochet according to the pattern, and the yarns are crossed where they meet to create a single piece. Intarsia is best worked over a shallow stitch where the post of the stitch is not too long, although areas of more textural and open stitching can look very effective when used in conjunction.

Read through the pattern carefully and confirm how much yarn you require of each color—make a note of how much of each you use for one motif and multiply by the number of motifs in the project. Intarsia patterns are usually in graph form; cross off the rows as you work and always check where colors need to be on the row above that being worked, so that you can carry yarns to the correct position if need be. Practice the basic intarsia techniques: bobbin winding; joining in new colors; changing from one color to another on both a right side and wrong side row.

Bobbins

Bobbins are used when you do not wish to have a whole ball of yarn attached to the crochet piece whilst working the intarsia method. For larger areas of color you can keep the yarn tidy in small plastic bags, secured with elastic bands. For smaller areas you can use a plastic bobbin, or make your own.

Using a plastic bobbin

These are commonly available in yarn stores and can be used for crochet and knitting alike. A plastic bobbin will only hold a relatively small amount of yarn—overloading the bobbin can cause it to unravel and may make it a little cumbersome to use.

Making a bobbin

These are quick and easy to make and you can make them as big as your hand allows!

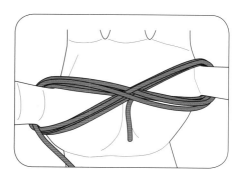
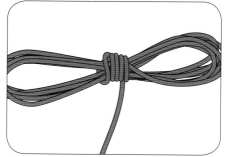
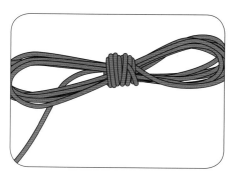

1 Wrap the yarn around the thumb and little finger of your right hand in the form of a figure eight, leaving the tail end of yarn resting in your palm.

2 Carefully remove the yarn from the fingers and cut it off the ball. Wind this yarn end around the center of the figure of eight and secure tightly with a small knot.

3 When using the bobbin, pull the yarn from the center a little at a time and keep it as close to the work as possible to avoid tangling.

Working the first row

In most cases the first row of a graph will be a right side row. If this is the case, read the chart from right to left. Just underneath the first graph row use a pencil to write down the number of stitches needed by each color on the first row.

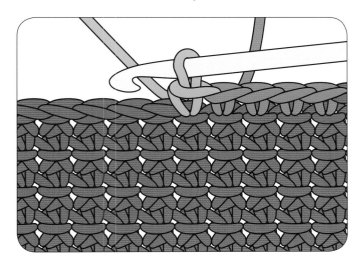

1 Leaving a tail end of yarn approx 6in. (15cm) long work the first piece of color. *Change to the next color on the final step of the last stitch, leaving a similar tail end of yarn. Work one stitch in this color.

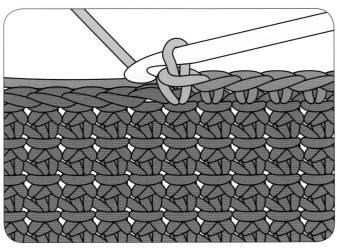

2 To catch in the tail end of yarn and thus avoid a hole in the fabric, cross the first color used over the tail end of the second color. Hold the tail end in line with the top edge of your crochet piece. Work the next stitch around the tail, as for weaving in on page 158.

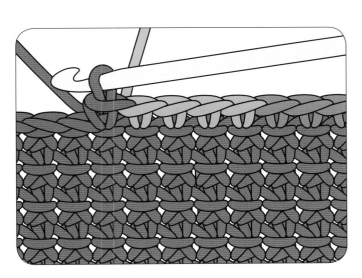

3 Work the next stitches according to the graph, repeating from * at each color change. Let the yarn drop in place at the back of the work once it has been used. At the end of the row (and each subsequent row) untangle the yarns.

Working the next row

In most cases the next row of a graph will be a wrong side row. If this is the case, read the chart from left to right.

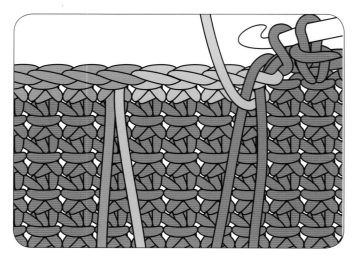

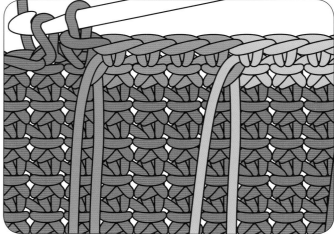

1 Work along the row to the point where the color change is needed. Bring the yarn that you have finished with forwards and hold it on this side of the work. *Change to the next color on the final step of the last stitch.

2 At the end of a wrong side row, check that all yarns are on the same side of the work and that the stitches next to the color change are not saggy.

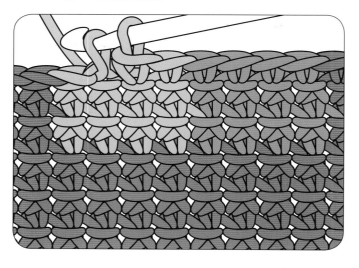

3 Continue to work in this way for subsequent right side and wrong side rows, making sure that yarns are crossed over on the reverse side of the work.

Working over yarn

Sometimes a very dark strand of yarn that has been crocheted over will show up through a much lighter color on top. In this case it might be better to sew the dark ends in around the dark color motif instead.

jacquard crochet

Using the jacquard method within the crochet piece creates small areas of color that are repeated across the row. Traditionally jacquard patterns tend to be small motifs repeated across a row, with only two colors carried at the back of the fabric between stitches, thus creating a double thickness fabric. Always crochet a gauge (tension) sample first. Jacquard crochet tends to create a slightly bulky fabric and if the yarns are carried across the back too tightly the piece will start to pucker. If the yarns are carried loosely you will have baggy stitches and holes in your fabric.

Stranding

The first technique to learn is stranding, which is where the yarns are carried across the back of the work over only a couple of stitches. It is best not to leave more than three stitches between a change in color, because the yarn can create loops on the reverse of the fabric and get caught or snagged when the piece is in use. To strand the colors, one yarn is carried over the top of the other—there is no need to catch or weave in the yarn at the back, because if it is worked properly there should not be any tangling of yarns across the row.

Strands of yarn

Keep the strands of yarn across the reverse of the work as short as possible (see page 157). In multicolored work the many strands of yarn across the back of the work do make the crochet fabric a layer thicker and so a little stiffer, but this should not cause any problem in most projects.

Working the first row

In most cases the first row of a graph will be a right side row. If this is the case, read the chart from right to left. Just underneath the first graph row use a pencil to write down the number of stitches needed by each color on the first row.

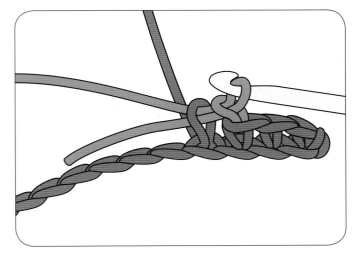

1 Leaving a tail end of yarn approx 6in. (15cm) long, work the first piece of color along the foundation chain.

2 *Change to the next color on the final step of the last stitch, leaving a similar tail end of yarn. Work one stitch in this color.

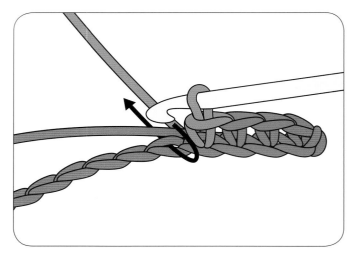

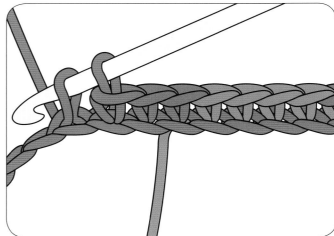

3 To catch in the tail end of yarn and thus avoid a hole in the fabric, cross the first color used over the tail end of the second color. Hold the tail end in line with the top edge of your crochet piece. Work the next stitch over the top of the tail, as for weaving in on page 158.

4 *Work the next stitches according to the graph. Drop the yarn and pick up the original color, carrying it over the reverse of the second color, being careful not to pull too tightly. Repeat from *.

Working the next row

In most cases the next row of a graph will be a wrong side row. If this is the case, read the chart from left to right.

Work along the row to the point where the color change is needed. Bring the yarn that is finished with forwards and hold it on this side of the work. *Change to the next color on the final step of the last stitch. Work the next stitches according to the graph. Drop the yarn and pick up the original color, carrying it over the reverse of the second color and being careful not to pull too tightly. Repeat from *.

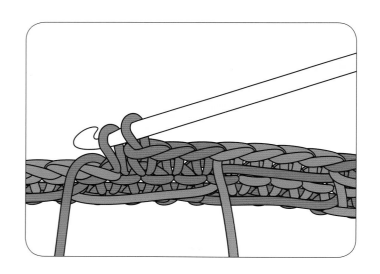

working in the correct way

To avoid your yarns ending up in a tangled mess, try to carry each yarn in the same way across the reverse of the work on each color change. Make a note at the beginning of the row which color is being carried underneath the other and which is carried over the top of the other. This will ensure that the reverse of the work is neat and tidy and all color changes are regular and uniform.

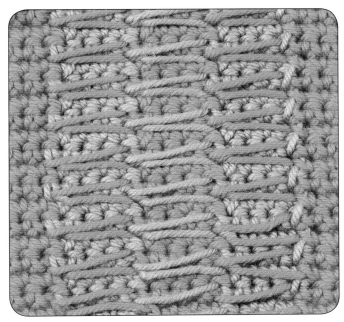

Stranding: This sample shows the reverse of a fabric where the yarns have been stranded across the reverse side of the work.

Weaving in: This sample shows the reverse of a fabric where the yarns have been woven in across the reverse side of the work.

Floats

The strands across the reverse of the work are known as floats. They are not a problem with items where the back will not be exposed, such as in a double-layered pan holder with the wrong sides stitched together facing one another.

Weaving in

You may find that your graph or pattern asks you to work more than 3 stitches between a color change. If this is the case then you will need to weave in the yarn that is traveling across the back of the work every few stitches. This is done in the same way as catching in the tail on the first row, but you may be required to do it more than once.

Once you have worked 2 or 3 stitches according to your chart, hold the yarn that is to be woven in line with the top edge of your crochet piece. Work the next stitch over the top of the tail. Continue working from the chart, stranding the yarn across the following stitches.

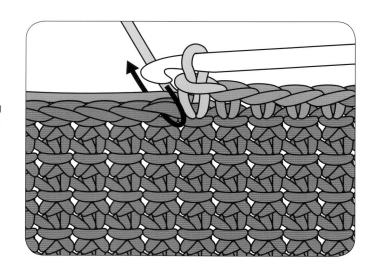

Sewing in the ends

Where yarn colors have been added in or finished with, you will be left with ends of yarn attached to the crochet piece. In the case of jacquard crochet it may be preferable—and certainly quicker—to weave these ends in as you work, using the weaving in technique as described above. However, for the intarsia technique a neater and safer alternative is to sew in the ends. It is a really good idea to sew your ends in as you go along—perhaps sew them in after every pattern repeat or allow 15 minutes towards the end of each of your crochet sessions.

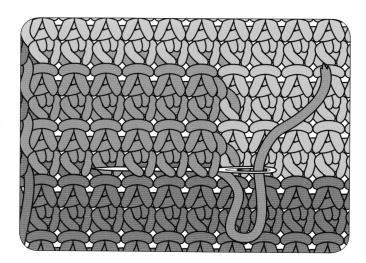

Thread a slightly sharp sewing needle (such as a large tapestry needle) with the end of yarn and sew around the outside of the shape it has created. Do this by weaving the yarn in and out of the points where the colors have been crossed over, making sure that you sew in the direction that closes gaps and doesn't enlarge any holes. Pull the crochet fabric slightly to ensure that the sewn stitches have not been worked too tightly and secure by sewing the yarn over itself a few times. Do not cut the yarn too close to your final stitch and leave an end a couple of in (cm) long. This will prevent the end from coming undone during wearing or washing of the finished item.

stitch directory

By working with more than one color you can achieve a really stunning effect. You may wish to start by working different stripe formations in various colors to give you a good idea of how colors work together within a design. Once you feel confident enough to work two (or more) colors simultaneously you can then try completing a sampler.

Before you start, make sure that you have all your equipment ready, have a comfortable spot in which to work, and have allowed plenty of time to work without interruption.

It is a very good idea to use a ruler or sticky "post it" note to mark off the rows you have completed. You may also want to make notes on the pattern with a pencil so that you know (for example) how many stitches of each color you will be working. Take some time to prepare your yarn bobbins, where needed, and have a pair of scissors and sewing needle at the ready to finish off your yarn ends.

To work the right side rows, follow the chart from right to left; follow the chart from left to right for wrong side rows.

Jacquard Checks

This pattern uses two colors across each row. When one block of color has been worked the redundant yarn is carried across the reverse of the work—you may choose to weave the yarn in at the reverse for a neater finish. The action of crossing the yarns over each other between use will mean that the yarn will twist and tangle, so it is a good idea to unravel them at the beginning of each row.

This pattern has a repeat of 15 stitches so the foundation chain needs to be made up of multiples of 15, plus one extra chain to allow for turning. The first stitch should be worked in the second chain from the hook.

Jacquard 2-color Repeat

When working a jacquard pattern that uses a repeated combination of just two colors you may not wish to make bobbins, but may prefer to keep the yarns in their balls instead. The action of crossing the yarns over each other between use will mean that the yarn will twist and tangle, so it is a good idea to unravel the yarns at the beginning of each row.

This pattern has a repeat of 4 stitches, plus 1 stitch, so the foundation chain needs to be made up of multiples of 4, plus 1 stitch and plus one extra chain to allow for turning. The first stitch should be worked in the second chain from the hook.

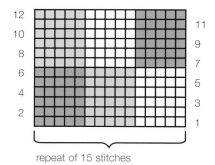

repeat of 15 stitches

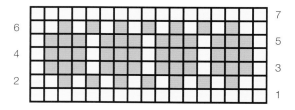

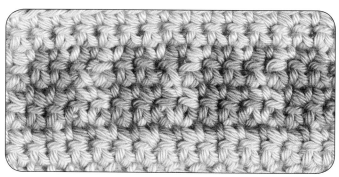

Intarsia 2-color Heart

Each square on the chart represents a color and in this sampler two colors are used to create a heart motif. It is a good idea to wind off enough yarn onto a bobbin to work the central heart motif. To do this, work out how much yarn is used to work one stitch, then multiply this length by the number of stitches used to create the complete motif. Add enough for an extra 2 stitches on each row to allow enough yarn for traveling between rows, plus an extra 8in (20cm) to allow for the tail end of yarn at the beginning and end.

To work this pattern make a foundation chain of 15 stitches, plus one extra chain to allow for turning, then work the first stitch into the second chain from the hook.

Intarsia 3-color Heart

To work this 3-color motif, calculate the yarn amounts in the same way as for the 2-color heart, making an extra bobbin for the central color. When working with more than one bobbin it is a good idea to untangle your yarns at the beginning of each row because it is inevitable that they will become twisted.

To work this pattern make a foundation chain of 15 stitches, plus one extra chain to allow for turning, then work the first stitch into the second chain from the hook.

working with color

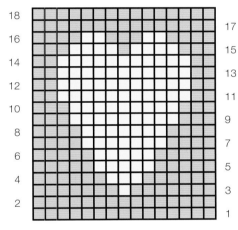

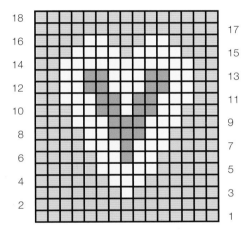

beads and sequins

Crocheting with beads is an age-old art that was particularly popular in the 18th and 19th centuries, when ladies made intricate crochet purses using very fine thread and tiny glass beads. Adding beads and sequins to your crochet can be really effective and is a relatively easy technique to achieve. Beads and sequins can be used in conjunction with one another to create some really exciting effects and can be placed randomly or to a predefined graph pattern.

working with beads and sequins

Beads come in all shapes and sizes, and in many materials—from hand made clay or papier-mâché, to machine produced plastic and glass. It is probably a good idea to avoid fragile beads or those that have sharp edges (such as cut glass), because these could affect the crocheted fabric during washing and wearing.

If you are using very fine crochet cotton for your piece, then you will be able to use quite a small bead or sequin. It thus follows that if you are going to use a more chunky yarn, the bead or sequin will need to be bigger. Either way, the hole in the center of the bead or sequin must be large enough to accommodate the yarn. Before you start a large piece of work, make a small sample using the beads or sequins and the yarn you have chosen. Establish how the beads or sequins affect the gauge (tension), whether they will snag or fray the work, and whether or not they are washable, colorfast or liable to damage.

Threading beads

You will need a strong sewing thread and a fine sewing needle. You could lay a piece of craft felt or a fine flannel over a saucer or small bowl to hold the beads, because threading from the palm of your hand or a slippery flat surface can be troublesome. The size needle you would usually use to sew a knitting yarn will be far too large to thread beads, so make your own version of a needle threader as described below to get the beads onto your knitting yarn. It is essential that the beads needed are threaded onto the yarn before you begin to crochet.

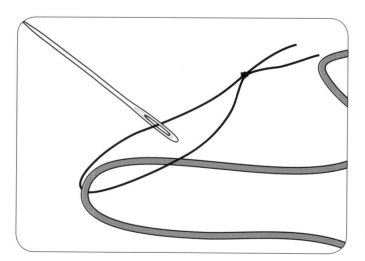

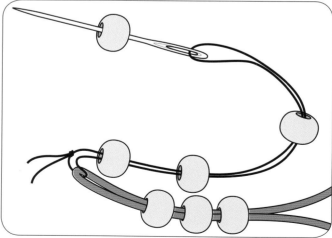

1 Thread the needle with the sewing cotton and make a small knot to join the ends and form a loop. Move the knot so that it is not in line horizontally with the sewing needle.

2 Place the end of the yarn through the loop created by the sewing thread, then pass the beads over the eye of the needle and push down onto the sewing thread and then onto the yarn. The first few beads may be a bit tricky, but so long as the beads are large enough, threading will become easier.

Threading sequins

Thread the needle and use the same technique as for beading to pass the sequins down onto the yarn, but be sure to thread the cup shaped sequins, cup side up.

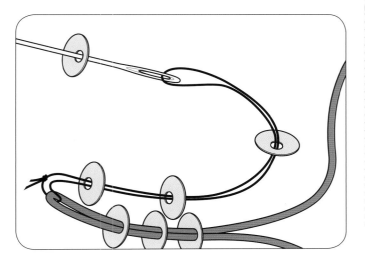

Threading many beads

Sometimes you will come across a bead with a smaller hole than the others, or a bead with a slight fault, so it is a good idea to thread the beads onto the yarn in small batches. Try threading on about five beads at a time.

If using a large number of beads it may be necessary to thread the beads onto the yarn in sections—too many pre-strung beads can make crochet difficult and can affect gauge (tension) and the appearance of the yarn.

Placing beads using single crochet (UK double crochet)

You need to place beads when you have the wrong side of the fabric facing you, because they come out on the reverse. Think ahead, because you may need to turn your work to get a bead on the right side of your work.

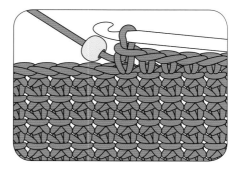

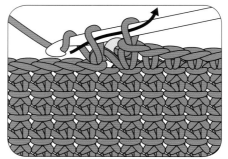

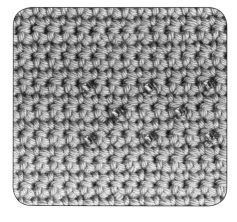

1 Work to where a bead is required. Slide the bead along the yarn so that it sits against the right side of the fabric. Put your hook through the next stitch.

2 Wrap the yarn around the hook and bring it through the stitch. Wrap the yarn around the hook and complete the stitch, holding the bead in place while you do so.

Beading in single crochet (UK double crochet).

Placing groups of beads

You can achieve some really nice effects by grouping more than one bead together. To do this work as for the method above, but bring a group of beads, (say 3 or 4) in place of a single bead.

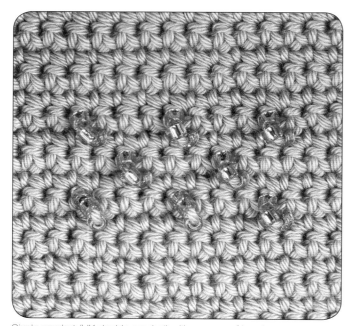

Single crochet (UK double crochet) with a group of beads.

Bead loops on a background of single crochet (UK double crochet).

Placing sequins using single crochet (UK double crochet)

You need to place sequins when you have the wrong side of the fabric facing you, because they come out on the reverse. Think ahead, because you may need to turn your work to get a sequin on the right side of your work.

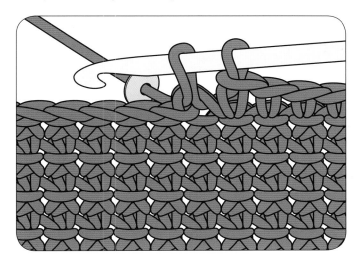

1 Work to where a sequin is required. Put your hook through the next stitch. Wrap the yarn around the hook and bring through the stitch.

2 Slide the bead along the yarn so that it sits against the right side of the fabric. Complete the stitch, holding the sequin in place while you do so.

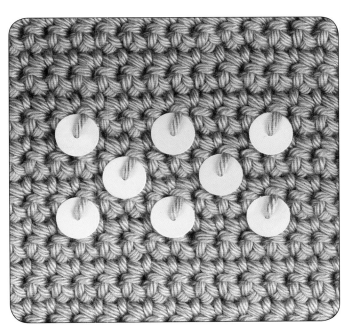

A group of sequins worked in single crochet (UK double crochet).

Beads and sequins

Sequins are available in many different shapes and sizes and a variety of different colors. Make sure the edges are not sharp or rough, or they may cut the yarn.

Be wary of plastic beads and sequins—they could melt and spoil your work if you catch them with a hot iron.

Placing beads or sequins using double crochet (UK treble crochet)

Again you need to place beads when you have the wrong side of the fabric facing you, because they come out on the reverse. Think ahead because you may need to turn your work to get a bead or sequin on the right side of your work.

When placing beads or sequins within this stitch they could push through to the wrong side of the work, so make sure you make the stitch nice and tight. This method can be used for beads and sequins alike.

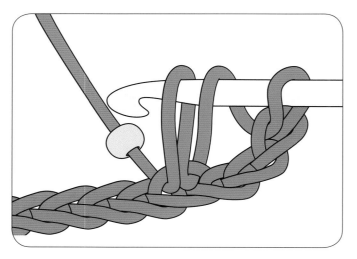

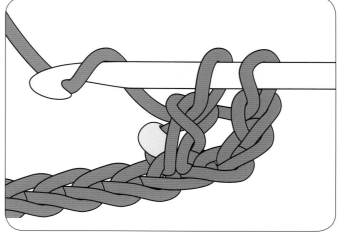

1 Work to where a bead/sequin is required. Wrap the yarn around the hook. Insert the hook into the next stitch and draw through the stitch so that 3 loops remain on the hook.

2 Slide the bead along the yarn so that it sits against the right side of the fabric. Complete the stitch, holding the bead/sequin in place while you do so.

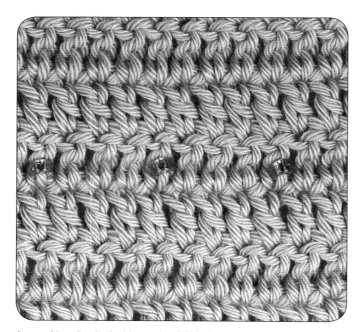

A row of beading in double crochet (UK treble crochet).

A row of sequins in double crochet (UK treble crochet).

Placing sequins or beads within a chain

This method also requires you to place the bead or sequin when you have the wrong side of the fabric facing you, because they come out on the reverse. Think ahead because you may need to turn your work to get a bead or sequin on the right side of your work. When placing beads or sequins within the chain they could push through to the wrong side of the work, so make sure you make the chain nice and tight. This method can be used for beads and sequins alike.

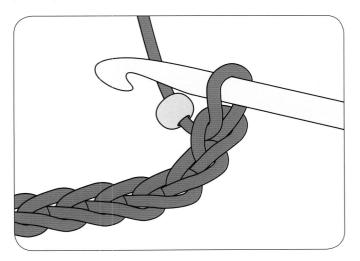

1 Work a chain until a bead/sequin is needed. Slide the bead/sequin along the yarn so it sits next to the hook.

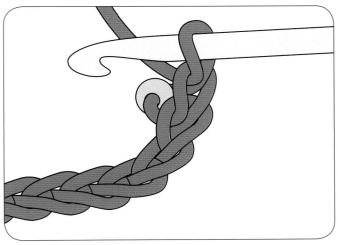

2 Complete the chain by wrapping the yarn around the hook beyond the bead/sequin and draw it through the stitch.

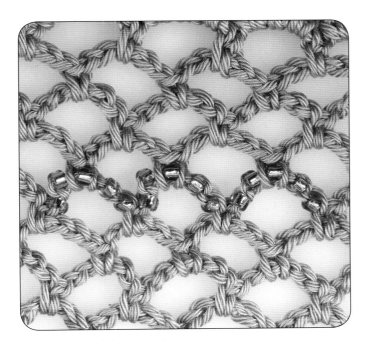

Beading on a mesh background.

Working with beads

The beads you select should not be too heavy for the yarn, or they will pull at the stitches and cause them to drop over time.

If the hole in the bead has rough edges or is slightly too small, you may be able to smooth or enlarge it with the tip of a small needle file.

Adding beads and sequins using a crochet hook

This is a great technique for when you want to add beads or sequins to your fabric without pre-threading them onto the yarn. The technique is a little fiddly, but is a fantastic method for adding beads as you go along. No pre-threading of beads is required, but you will need a really tiny metal crochet hook to thread the beads onto the crochet stitch. This method can be used for all crochet stitches, but it is more effective on those where the post of the stitch is not too long.

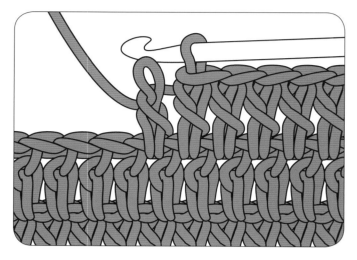

1 Work to where a bead/sequin is needed. Work the next stitch to the point where 2 loops remain on the hook. Carefully slip the yarn loop from your crochet hook, making sure not to pull on the yarn end to unravel.

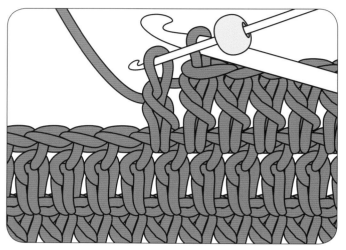

2 Push a bead onto the small crochet hook and catch the yarn loop with this hook. Push the bead from the crochet hook and onto the yarn loop.

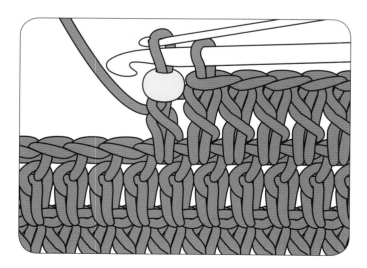

3 Slip the yarn loop back onto the crochet hook and complete the stitch.

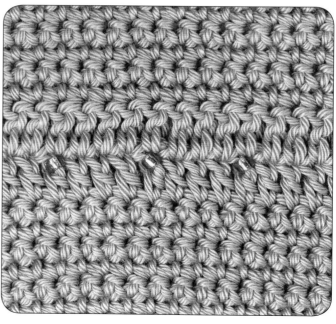

A row of beads that has been added using a crochet hook.

Following a chart

On a crochet chart, a bead or sequin is usually represented by a shaded circle over the top of the stitch symbol. Read the row where a bead or sequin is to be placed from left to right and the alternate row from right to left. This is because beads and sequins are placed on a wrong side row.

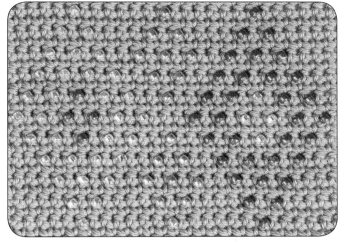

A beaded design from a chart.

Washing and care instructions for a beaded/sequin fabric

It is not a good idea to wash a beaded or sequined fabric in the washing machine. Instead, wash by hand using a mild detergent and be very careful that the beads or sequins do not cause threads to snag. When drying, avoid a rigorous spin in the machine and dry flat where possible. Beads, especially, can add a lot of weight to your fabric when used in large amounts, so do make sure you use a sturdy yarn that will withstand washing and wearing.

Be extremely careful when blocking a sequined fabric because the sequins will not tolerate a high temperature and are prone to melting. If you have chosen to recycle some beads or sequins from a vintage item be especially careful because vintage sequins are quite often made from gelatin and can simply melt away when immersed in water!

crochet edgings

Crochet fabrics have a tendency to curl, although if the piece is to be used to make a garment, curling will be restricted by the seams, button bands and collar if applicable. If the crochet piece is to be used as a flat fabric—perhaps as a table runner or panel of some kind—it may be necessary to work an edging of some sort in order to limit the capacity of the fabric to curl.

creating edgings

Edgings are not only used to stop crochet fabric from curling, they can also be used to add aesthetically pleasing effects to the crochet fabric. Crochet edgings are also sometimes used to give a decorative border to knitted fabrics—and even to woven fabric.

Creating a crochet edge on a crochet fabric

The crochet edge can be worked in a matching
or a contrasting yarn.

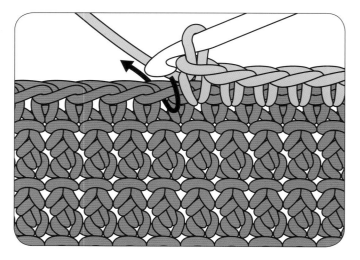

1 When working along the bottom (foundation chain) or top (final row) of a crochet piece, insert the hook into the center of each stitch from the front to back.

2 When working along a side edge of a crochet piece, insert the hook through the work one complete stitch in from the edge from front to back.

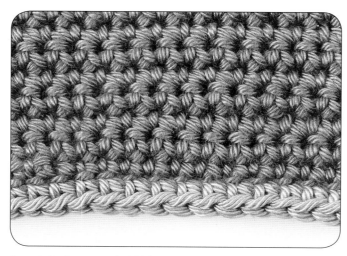

A crochet edge on crochet fabric.

Creating a crochet edge on a knitted fabric

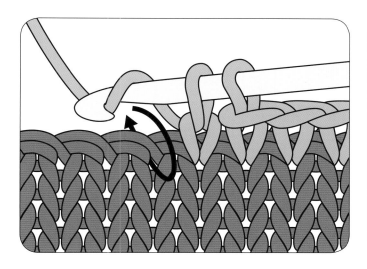

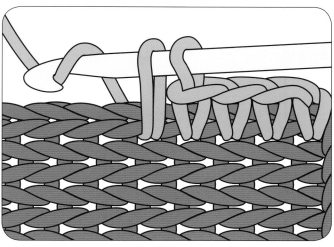

1 When working along the bottom (cast on) or top (cast off) of a knitted piece insert the hook into the center of each stitch from front to back.

2 When working along a side edge of a knitted piece, insert the hook through the work one complete stitch in from the edge from front to back.

Edging the sides

To create an even and neat pick up on the side edge of a single crochet (UK double crochet) or on a fabric that has been knitted using stockinette stitch (UK stocking stitch), pick up three stitches out of every four. Picking up every stitch will cause the fabric to stretch and thus ripple slightly, while picking up too few will cause the fabric to pucker. If you find the bottom edge of the knitted fabric is stretching, then it may be a good idea to change to a smaller hook size or work fewer stitches along the edge.

A crochet edge on knitted fabric.

crochet edgings

Creating a crochet edge on a woven fabric

A sewn stitch such as chain stitch or blanket stitch provides
a good base for a crochet edge.

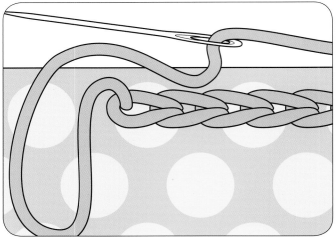

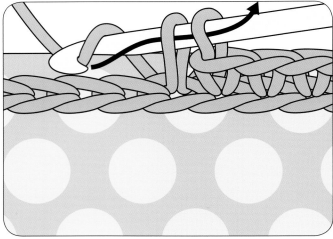

1 Make sure that the sewn stitches are regular and are
similar in size to the crochet stitches subsequently made. It
may be an idea to work a chain using the chosen yarn and hook
to get an idea of stitch size.

2 To make the crochet edge, insert the hook from front to
back through the sewn stitch.

A crochet edge on woven fabric.

Adding crochet to woven fabric

This piece of fabric has a shell edging, but you
can use any edging design that will complement
the fabric pattern.

It is also possible to make crochet edgings
independently like lengths of braid and sew
them to the fabric like the braids shown in the
photograph opposite.

basic edgings

The following are some simple edging designs, which are all quite easy to create with ordinary basic crochet stitches.

Single crochet (UK double crochet) edge

Working from right to left along the edge of the fabric, work a row of stitches into the edge of the fabric.

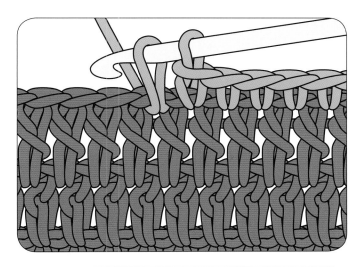

A single crochet (UK double crochet) edging.

Crochet on crochet

One of the big advantages of crocheting an edging onto your crocheted item is that you can use the same type and weight of yarn, even if you choose a contrasting color. This means that the edging will stretch and move at the same rate as the rest of the item.

Turning corners

If you need to work an edging around a corner, then you will need to make enough stitches to achieve the turn. To do this work 3 stitches into the corner stitch on the first row. You may also need to create more stitches or areas of chain on subsequent rows to achieve a neat corner.

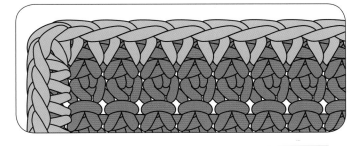

A crochet edged corner.

crochet edgings

Reverse single crochet (UK reverse double crochet) edge

This stitch is sometimes referred to as crab stitch and is worked from left to right along the edge of the fabric. It is a little tricky to begin with, because you can feel like you are working back to front. However, its attractive rope-like appearance makes it well worth the effort.

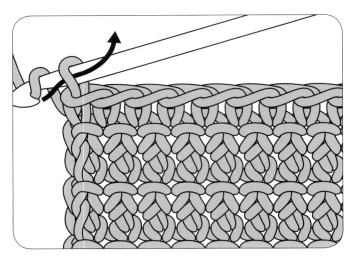

1 When working in the same yarn, make one chain at the end of the row as for a turning chain. Do not turn.

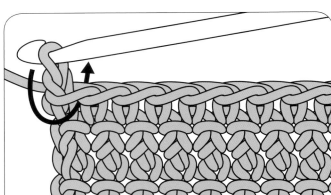

2 Keeping the yarn to the reverse of the work, insert the hook from front to back through the next stitch.

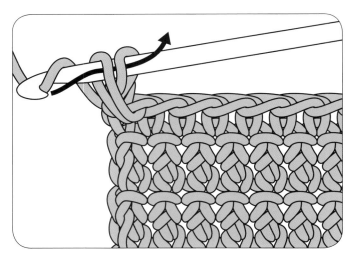

3 Wrap the yarn around the hook and draw the loop through the stitch so that 2 loops remain on the hook. Wrap the yarn around the hook and draw through the loops to complete the stitch.

Crab stitch edging, which is also known as reverse double crochet in the UK.

Shell edging

This edging is worked on top of a foundation row of single crochet (UK double crochet) that is worked along the edge first. Be careful that the right side of the shell edging ends up on the right side of the fabric, by working the initial foundation row with the wrong side of the piece facing towards you.

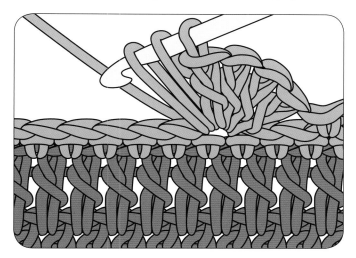

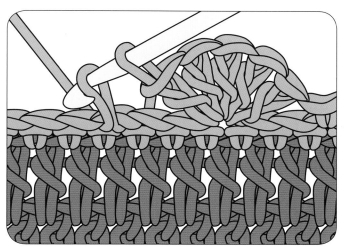

1 To work this edging, ensure that the foundation row is a multiple of 6 + 1. Work 1 chain, turn. Working from right to left along the edge, work 1 single crochet (UK double crochet) into the first stitch. *Miss one stitch then work 5 double crochet (UK treble crochet) into the next stitch, making sure that the stitches do not overlap.

2 Miss 2 stitches, work a single crochet (UK double crochet) stitch into the next stitch. Continue by repeating from * to the end of the row.

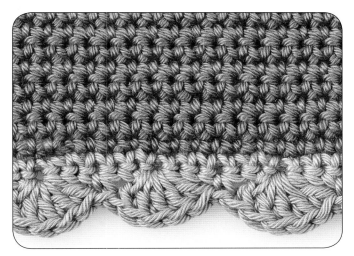

A length of shell edging

Using edgings

Edgings are a fantastic way of familiarizing yourself with various stitches and so build your crochet confidence. It is also very fashionable to embellish purchased crochet and knitwear with trims—you could use any of the designs shown in these pages or the ruffles on page 188.

crochet edgings

Picot edging

This is a simple yet very effective edging that can be worked with any number of chain between the anchor stitches. This edging is worked on top of a foundation row so, as for the shell edging on page 179, be careful to ensure that the right sides of both the crochet fabric and the shell edging match up.

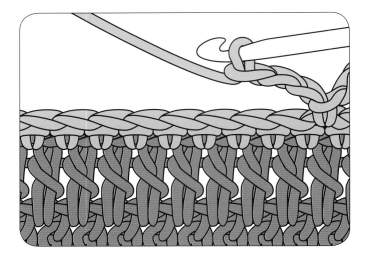

1 To work this edging, ensure that the foundation row is a multiple of 2. *Make 3 chain.

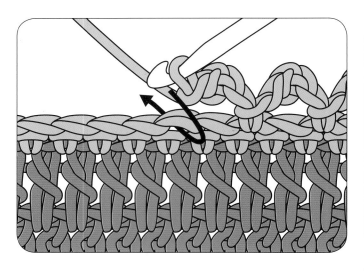

3 3ch, miss one stitch. Work a slip stitch into the following stitch and repeat from * to the end of the row.

2 Insert the hook into the back of the 3rd chain from the hook (the first of the three chain made on the previous step) and work a slip stitch into it.

A picot edging worked on every other stitch.

beaded edgings

Beads can add a lovely bit of sparkle to even the plainest piece of crochet. Remember that beads are crocheted into the fabric with the wrong side facing, so it may be an idea to do a base row along the edge of the piece first.

Placing a bead at the tip of a picot

Work out how many beads are needed for the picot edge by dividing the stitch count by 2. Thread beads onto the chosen yarn and work one row of stitching along the fabric edge. Work as for the picot edge (see opposite) catching the bead into the chain on the second of the 3 chain.

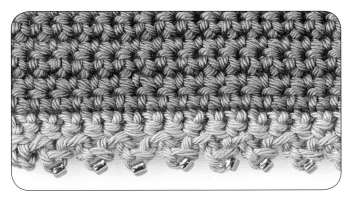

Picot edging with a single bead at the tip of each picot.

3-beaded edge

Work out how many beads are needed for the edge by multiplying the stitch count by 3. Thread beads onto the chosen yarn and work one row of stitching along the fabric edge. Using single crochet (UK double crochet), work one stitch. *Slide 3 beads up to the top of the yarn. Catch the yarn beyond the beads and complete the stitch. Repeat from *.

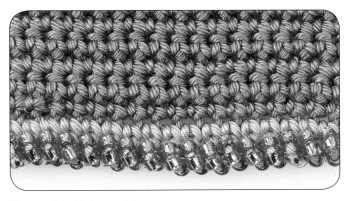

The completed 3-bead edging.

Beaded loops

Work as for 3-beaded edge, using any number of beads to create the loops. Here we have used a varying number to create uneven loop lengths.

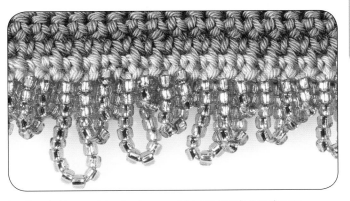

In a beaded loop edging the loops can be any length you choose.

braids

Many braids are worked in vertical strips, which are then sewn onto the base fabric. A braid edging often has shaping on both edges, or it can have one shaped and one straight edge. Braids can be used on the edge of the fabric, or as an insertion midway between two pieces.

Making a braid to the correct length

When making a vertical braid, it is a good idea to make it a few pattern repeats longer than you think it needs to be. Sew the braid in place, making sure that you do not stretch it, and unravel the braid to the right length once sewing is complete. Try to keep the braid to full or half pattern repeats if possible.

Sewing a braid to a base fabric

When sewing the braid in place, be careful not to stretch it because you could cause the piece to pucker. You could decide to use a simple over sew stitch (see page 216) or backstitch (see page 214). On straight edged pieces you may want to make a feature of the join by using an unusual sewing stitch, such as one of the two below. These are suitable for lightweight braids only.

Blanket stitch clusters

Work as for blanket stitch (see page 198) grouping the stitches together in bunches of 3 as shown here.

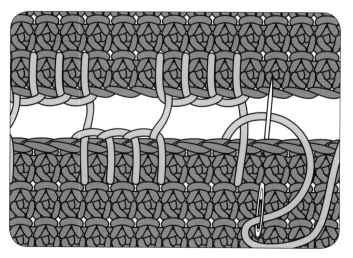

Zigzag knotted stitch

Work as in the diagram, making sure that stitches remain even and constant.

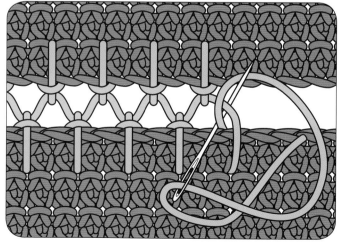

Narrow shaped edging

This edging has been made to the required length in just one color of yarn.

Section of narrow shaped edging.

Shaped edging with ribbon detail

This edging has been made to the required length in one color of yarn. Once completed an extra row of long posted stitches were added to the straight edge and a ribbon threaded through to create this lovely effect.

Shaped edging with a matching ribbon detail.

Shaped edging with beaded detail

This edging has been made to the required length in one color of yarn, but with the addition of some beads to add a little sparkle.

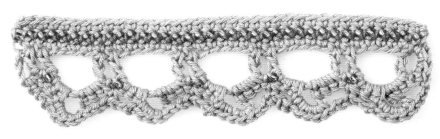

Shaped edging with a beaded top band.

Multicolored shaped edging

This edging has been made to the required length in more than one color of yarn. Once completed, extra rows of stitches were added to the straight edge to create this lovely multicolored effect.

Shaped edging made in several colors.

crochet edgings

fringes, ruffles and tassels

Adding fringes and tassels is a great yet simple way to decorate your fabric. Fringes can be made to whatever length you like in an array of exciting yarns and threads. Simple tassels are easy to make and can look great stitched to the corners of cushions or sewn onto edgings, but be aware that they do use up a lot of yarn.

Simple fringe

Cut lengths of yarn to double the length of the required fringe, plus a little more to allow for the knot.

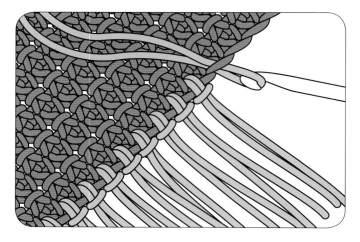

1 From the reverse of the base fabric, insert the crochet hook through the center of a stitch at the edge of the crochet piece. Catch the yarn and pull it through to the reverse, thus creating a loop.

2 Use the crochet hook to catch the yarn and bring it through the loop created on the last step. Pull gently to tighten the loop.

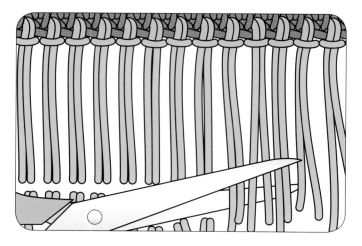

3 Lay the fringe flat and use sharp scissors to neaten the yarn ends.

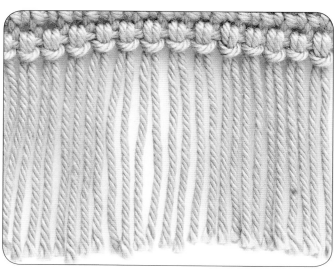

The completed fringe can be trimmed to any length.

Knotted fringe

A knotted fringe is worked using the same basic method as for the simple fringe but is subsequently knotted. Allow extra yarn for the knots. Divide every section of fringe in half and then knot each half of one together with half of the next one along.

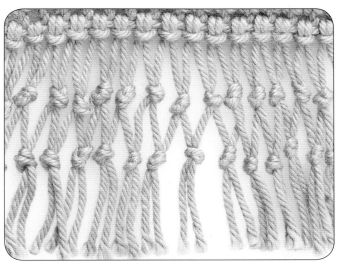

A double knotted fringe needs fairly long fringing.

Chain fringe

You can create an attractive fringe by, working between stitches, lengths of chain secured into the fabric using a slip stitch. You can choose whether to make a chain for every stitch, or whether to spread them out. Work to where the fringe is required. *Work chain to chosen fringe length. Secure to the base fabric by working a slip stitch into the next stitch. Repeat from *.

A chain fringe can be worked to any length.

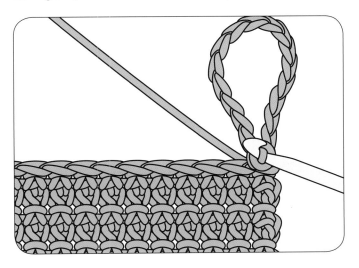

Looped chain and fringe

You could decide to make a crochet base for your fringe, as in the looped chain base shown here.

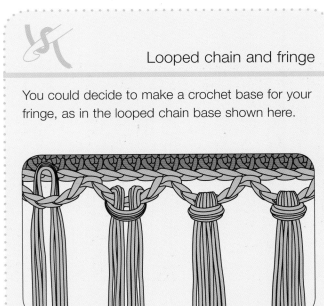

Beaded fringe

A beaded fringe can add weight to the bottom edge of a crocheted piece and creates a sophisticated, dressy effect.

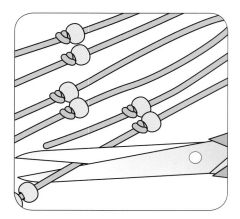 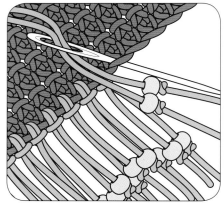 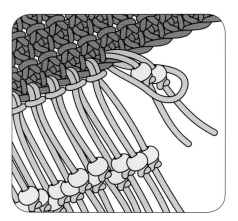

1 Thread a small needle with sewing cotton and pass the required number of beads down onto the yarn using the method as described on page 164. Cut the yarn to the lengths required for each tassel, leaving 2 beads on each length. Ensure the beads don't slip off the yarn by making a tight knot at the end of both yarn ends.

2 Fold the yarn length in half and thread through a large eyed sewing needle. Insert the needle through the edge of the fabric from front to back.

3 Remove the yarn from the needle and thread though the loop that has been created. Pull gently to tighten. Lay the fringe flat and use sharp scissors to neaten the yarn ends.

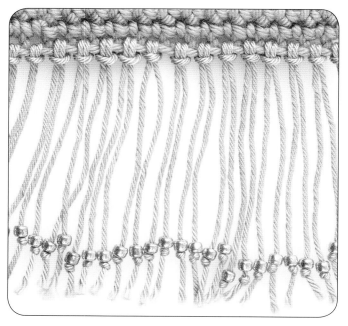

Beads add sparkle and weight to the fringe.

Corkscrew fringe

This creates a wonderful fringe, but it is time consuming and uses a great deal of yarn. *Create a chain to the required length, bearing in mind that the fringe will bounce up and thus be slightly shorter in length once complete. Work 2 stitches into every chain to end. Secure by working a slip stitch into the next stitch. Repeat from *.

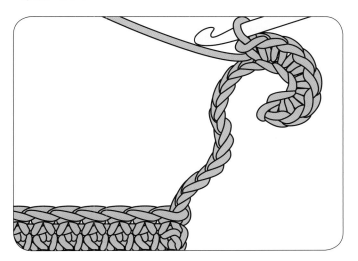

The corkscrew fringe is full of texture

Ruffles

Ruffles are really effective and are very easy to work. You can work them as an edging or as a separate piece along a foundation chain to create a scarf or throw.

Basic ruffle

A basic ruffle is made across one row by working three long posted stitches into every stitch.

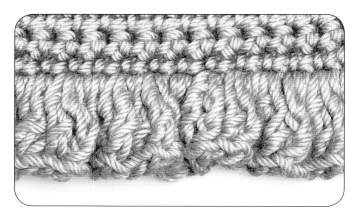

A basic ruffle.

Deep ruffle

A deep ruffle is made across 2 or more rows and is simply a repeat of the basic ruffle worked over consecutive rows.

The deep ruffle is more sculptural.

Crochet tassel

Make a foundation chain of 6 stitches—use more if you want a fatter tassel. Work 6 rows of single crochet (UK double crochet). With right side facing *make a chain to the required length of the loop. Work a slip stitch into the base of the chain to secure.

Repeat from * twice more so that 3 loops lead from one stitch. Work as set, making 3 chain loops into every stitch of the previous row. To finish, roll the piece tightly to create a tassel and sew to secure.

A tassel made of lengths of crochet chain.

Making tassels

This tassel is made in a single color of yarn, but multicolor tassels are also very effective. To make a multicolored crochet tassel, you will need to work each color separately and then assemble the tassel as described above. Making a multicolored wrapped tassel is easier; just wrap different colors of yarn in layers.

Wrapped tassel

To make this tassel, you will need to cut a piece of card to wrap
the yarn around. Any firm card will be suitable for this.

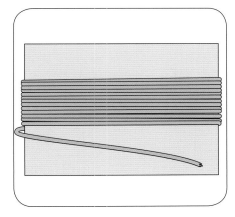

1 Wrap the yarn around a piece of card the length of the tassel required. The more yarn you decide to wrap the fuller the tassel will be.

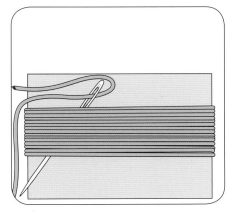

2 Thread a second piece of yarn through the top end of the tassel, between the yarn and the card, and tie to secure leaving a long end of yarn to tie around the tassel.

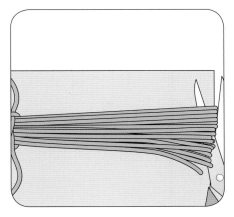

3 Using sharp scissors, cut along the yarn at the bottom edge.

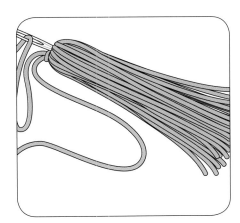

4 Remove the card. Thread the long end of yarn through a sewing needle and push it down through the center of the tassel from the top.

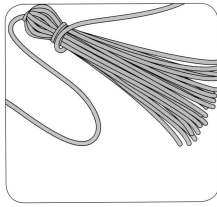

5 Wrap this end of yarn around the tassel as many times as required. Make a knot to secure. Trim the tassel ends to neaten. Use the remaining yarn end to sew the tassel to the project.

A wrapped tassel in a single color yarn.

stitch directory

Abbreviations and symbols can differ depending upon whether you are following a US or a UK pattern and can even be personal to a pattern writer or designer, so it is really important that you make sure you understand all the crochet abbreviations and symbols before you start working from this Stitch Directory.

Don't be fooled by simply reading the stitch names, because some stitch references are the same yet mean very different things. For example, US and UK patterns share stitch names (such as double crochet, or treble crochet for example), yet these names do not refer to the same stitches. Single crochet in US terminology is a dense stitch with a short post, which in the UK is called double crochet. However, double crochet in the US is a longer stitch with a post, which is perhaps twice the height of the UK stitch, and is known in the UK as treble crochet.

All patterns in this section are written using US terminology only. See page 33 for stitch abbreviations.

Cluster and Picot Loop Edging

Foundation chain: Multiples of 8 + 14
Special abbreviations: Cluster = dc3tog;
Picot = 3ch, 1sc into 3rd ch from hook

Row 1: Work a cluster into 10th ch from hook, *5ch, skip 3 ch, sc into next ch, 5ch, skip 3 ch, work a cluster into next ch; rep from * to last 4ch, 2ch, skip 3 ch, dc in next ch, turn.
Row 2: *Ch10, skip the next cluster, sc into the next sp; rep from * to end of row finishing with 10ch, sc in final sp, turn.
Row 3: Ch1, *Work 5sc into next 10ch-sp, [work a picot, 3sc into ch-sp] twice, work a picot, work 5sc into loop**, work 3sc into next 3ch-sp; rep from * to the last 10ch-sp, rep from * to **. Fasten off.

Three Petal Flower Edging

Foundation chain: The foundation base is made from multiples of 2 + 1 cluster. The clusters form the foundation base.
Special abbreviation: Cluster = tr2tog and t3tog as specified

Foundation Base: *10ch, work tr3tog into 10th chain from hook, 4ch (counts as tr) work tr2tog into 4th ch from hook; rep from * until required number of clusters are completed ending with 10ch and a tr3tog cluster, turn.
Row 1: Ss in first ch of 10ch-sp, ss into ch-sp, 4ch, work tr2tog, *5ch, tr3tog, 5ch, tr6tog by working 3tr in same ch-sp as the last cluster and working 3tr in the next ch-sp (this will mean you draw yarn through 7 loops on final stage of st); rep from * to the last ch-sp, [5ch, tr3tog] twice.
Fasten off.

Trellis and Fan Edging

Foundation chain: Multiples of 22 + 4

Row 1: 1dc in 4th ch from hook, *3ch, skip 2 ch, sc in next ch, [5ch, skip 2 ch, sc in next ch] 5 times, 3ch, skip 2 ch, 1dc in next 2 ch; rep from * to end of row, turn.

Row 2: Ch3 (counts as 1dc),1dc into in the the base of the ch, 2dc in next dc, *4ch, skip the next 3ch-sp, sc into next 5ch-sp, [5ch, sc in next 5ch-sp] 4 times, 4ch, skip the next 3ch-sp, 2dc in each of the next 2 dc; rep from * to end of row, turn.

Row 3: Ch3 (counts as 1dc), 1dc into in the the base of the ch, 1dc in each of the next next 2 dc, 2dc in next dc, *5ch, skip the next 4ch-sp, sc into next 5-ch-sp, [5ch, sc in next 5ch-sp] 3 times, 5ch, skip the next 4ch-sp, 2dc in next dc, 1dc in each of the next 2 dc, 2dc in next dc; rep from * to end of row, turn.

Row 4: Ch3 (counts as 1dc), 1dc into in the the base of the ch, 1dc in each of the next 4 dc, 2dc in next dc, *5ch, skip the next 5ch-sp, sc into next 5ch-sp, [5ch, sc into next 5ch-sp] twice, 5ch, skip the next 5ch-sp, 2dc in next dc, 1dc in each of the next 4 dc, 2dc in next dc; rep from * to end of row, turn.

Row 5: Ch4 (counts as 1dc and 1ch), 1dc into in the the base of the ch, [1ch, 1dc in next dc] 6 times, 1ch, into the next dc work 1dc, 1ch, 1dc, *6ch, skip the next 5ch-sp, sc into next 5ch-sp, 5ch, sc into next 5ch-sp, 6ch, skip the next 5ch-sp, into the next dc work 1dc, 1ch, 1dc, [1ch, 1dc in next dc] 6 times, 1ch, into the next dc work 1dc, 1ch, 1dc; rep from * to end of row, turn.

Row 6: Ch2, 1sc in next 1ch-sp, [2ch, sc in next 1ch-sp] 8 times, 2ch, sc into the next dc, *6ch, skip the next 6ch-sp,1sc in next 5ch-sp, 6ch, skip the next 6ch-sp, 1sc in into the next dc, [2ch, 1sc in next 1ch-sp] 9 times, 2ch, 1sc into the next dc; rep from * to end of row.

Fasten off.

Stepped and Pointed Fan Edging

Foundation chain: 11

Row 1: 2dc in 4th ch from hook, 2dc into each of the next 6 ch, 1dc in final ch, turn.

Row 2: Ch3 (counts as 1dc), 1dc in next 7dc, [1ch, 1dc in next dc] 8 times, turn.

Row 3: Ch3 (counts as 1dc), 1dc in first sp, *3ch, 4dc around the post bar of dc just made, 1sc in next 1ch-sp, 1dc into the next 1ch-sp; rep from * until 4 points have been made, 9ch, skip 7 dc, 1sc into top of 3-ch tch.

Row 4: Ch3 (counts as 1dc), 15dc into 9ch-loop, turn.

Rows 5–7: Repeat Rows 2–4.

Row 8: Work as for Row 2. Do not turn. Work a ss in last point of previous group, thus joining scallop. Continue to work in this eight-row repeat until work is required length.

Fasten off.

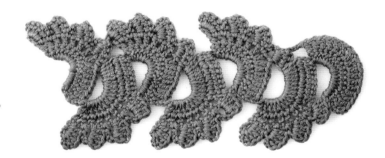

embellishments

A dense crochet fabric makes a really good base for sewing stitches and simple embroidery adds a personal touch that can transform a plain crochet piece into a unique, distinctive piece. Surface crochet is also a nifty way of adding detail to your work using the crochet hook instead of a sewing needle. This chapter also covers several different cords, and finally pompoms.

sewing stitches

Because a tight crochet stitch such as single crochet (UK double crochet) produces uniform stitches in a grid-like pattern, the fabric produced can be used in much the same way as a sewing or tapestry-type canvas. For sewn stitches, it is a good idea to use a sharp sewing needle and a relatively strong thread.

Cross stitch

Using cross stitch on a background of tight crochet can be a very effective way of adding adornment to the crochet piece. You may want to work to your own design or to a suitable traditional cross stitch pattern.

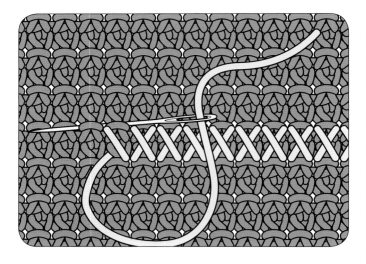

On a graph the cross stitch occupies the space of one or a multiple of squares on the grid, these are usually indicated by either a block of color or a symbol of some kind.

With the right side facing, bring the needle through from the back and make a diagonal stitch to the upper left corner of the crochet stitch. Bring the needle through the work from back to front at the base of the left side of the crochet stitch. Pass over the first part of the stitch to the upper right corner of the crochet stitch. Insert the needle from front to back through the work to complete the stitch.

Embroidered cross stitch motif in several colors on a background of single crochet (UK double crochet).

Basting stitch (UK running stitch)

This is probably the easiest of all the embroidery stitches and as such is one that most people are familiar with.

With the right side facing, bring the needle through from the back. *Insert the needle through the work from front to back a short distance along to the left—keep this distance uniform, perhaps one or two stitches. Bring the needle through the work from back to front the same distance along to the left. Repeat from *.

Backstitch

This is another common stitch and is one that many people use for putting together crochet or knitted garments. Backstitch is useful for creating outline details and lines.

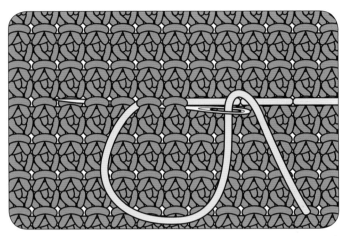

With the right side facing, bring the needle through from the back of the fabric, just to the left of where the stitching is to begin. Insert the needle through the work from front to back a short distance along to the right—keep this distance uniform, perhaps one or two stitches. *Bring the needle through the work from back to front the same distance along to the left from where it last emerged. Continue by inserting the needle through from front to back at the point where the last stitch emerged. Repeat from *.

Working embroidery

Embroidery is best worked on an even, flat crochet stitch with a short post. It can also look really good when used to embellish textured work, lace work—and even to add a little more detail to color work.

A smooth yarn is more suitable; a yarn with a slub or pile may stick or snag. Make sure that your chosen yarn will not shrink or color run and that it is comparable in weight and fiber content to your crochet yarn; it is also a good idea to use a large sharp sewing needle.

When working complicated embroidery ideas, you may want to draw your design onto a piece of light-weight non-fusible interfacing. This can be either pinned or sewn onto the crochet fabric and removed by tearing or cutting it away once the embroidery is complete.

Not all stitches are suitable for use on a crochet fabric. Very heavy embroidery can stretch the fabric and make it stiff and unwieldy.

Stem stitch

This stitch creates an overlapping line of stitching that can travel in any direction; it is useful for outlining motifs and is worked in a very similar way to backstitch. It is often used to replicate plant stems and leaf outlines.

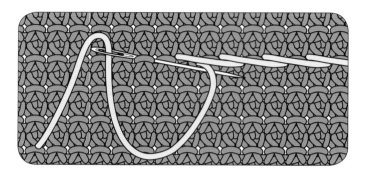

With the right side facing, bring the needle through from the back. Insert the needle through the work from front to back a short distance along to the left—keep this distance uniform, perhaps one or two stitches. *Bring the needle through the work from back to front approximately half the distance along to the left. Continue by inserting the needle through from front to back at the half way point of the last stitch. Repeat from *.

Chain stitch

A sewn chain stitch looks like a crochet chain but is bonded to the fabric. It is good for making bold outlines or for filling in embroidered shapes. It is worked by wrapping the yarn loop around the needle before the stitch is completed.

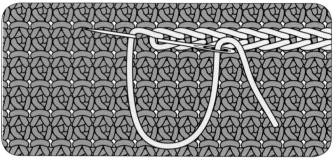

With the right side facing, bring the needle through from the back. *Insert the needle through the work from front to back at the point where the thread emerges from the fabric, leaving a small loop of thread at the front. To secure the loop, bring the needle back through to the front of the work a short distance along to the left and through the center of the loop. Tighten and repeat from *.

Daisy stitch

A variation on chain stitch, daisy stitch is worked in a circle and provides a speedy way to creating the appearance of a stylized flower.

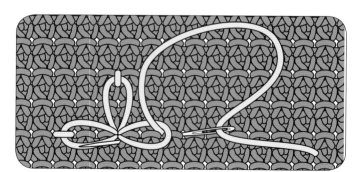

With the right side facing and working from a central point, work chain stitch but instead of making a running sequence of stitches, work each chain stitch out from the central point. To secure each chain in place, sew a small stitch over the top of the sewing thread loop. Repeat so each chain represents a petal.

Satin stitch

Satin stitch is a very firm embroidery stitch and is used to completely cover a defined area. It is a good stitch to use to fill small spaces, but be careful not to pull the stitches too tightly, because this could cause the base fabric to pucker.

With right side facing, sew small diagonal stitches as close together as possible by bringing the needle through from the back and then working from front to back. Make sure the stitches sit neatly next to each other and do not overlap.

French knot

French knots are great for adding a little bit of extra relief work to the fabric.

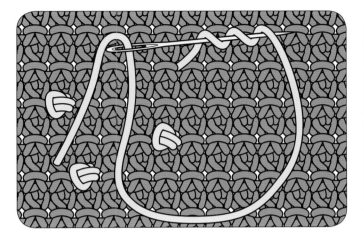

With the right side facing, bring the needle through the work from back to front. With the needle close to the work, wrap the thread around the needle two or three times. Insert the needle through the work from front to back at the point where the thread emerges from the fabric. Gently pull the needle through to the back of the work, thus creating a knot around the sewing thread.

Bullion stitch

An embroidered bullion stitch is a variation of a French knot and is the sewing equivalent of its crochet counterpart.

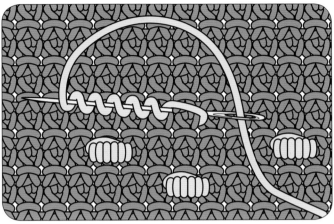

With the right side facing, bring the needle through the work from back to front. Insert the needle through the work from front to back, at the point where the thread emerges from the fabric. Bring the needle through to the right side of the work again as if to make a chain stitch. Wrap the thread around the needle 5 or 6 times. Hold the thread wraps in place and draw the needle through the loops as if making a French knot. Gently pull on the thread to tighten, then insert the needle through to the back of the work at the starting point of the first step of the stitch.

Combining stitches

Several different embroidery stitches can be combined to make a more complex design or a border. You could also try weaving a contrast yarn in and out of the stitches of the embroidery for extra interest.

Make sure the yarn or floss you use for the embroidery is of the same or similar composition as the yarn used to make the project, or it may cause problems when washing the item.

Serveral embroidery stitches on a background of single crochet (UK double crochet).

Buttonhole/blanket stitch

This stitch can reinforce the edge of a crochet fabric and reduces the likelihood of the fabric edge curling. It can also be used to act as a base for crochet stitches on woven or jersey fabrics.

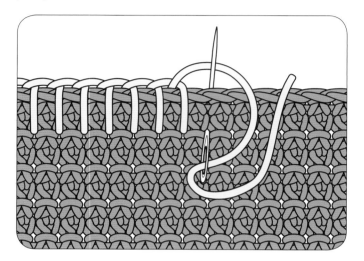

With the right side facing, bring the needle through the work from the back to front approximately one row in from the edge of the fabric. *Insert the needle from front to back of the work one stitch along to the right, point the needle upward and catch the loop of the yarn around it and pull through. Repeat from *.

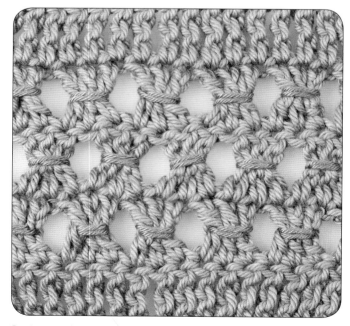

Sewing round posts in a matching yarn.

Sewing around posts

You can add color to your crochet fabric very easily by sewing around the posts of the stitches. This is best worked on stitches that have very long posts.

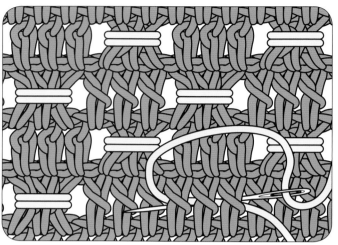

Here the posts of the stitches have had a contrast yarn wrapped around and secured with a sewn stitch. Groups of 3 posts have been sewn together to form an exciting textured pattern.

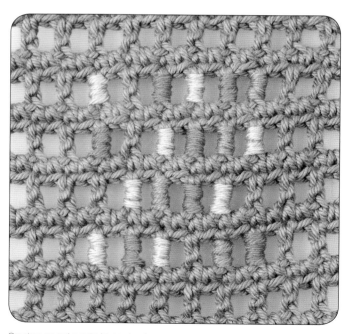

Sewing round posts in contrast yarns.

surface crochet

The stitches produced by surface crochet are the same in appearance as sewn chain stitch. To do this technique you will first need a base fabric on which to work. A sturdy stitch with a short post is probably best, or you could opt to use a background mesh fabric (see pages 104–106).

Surface crochet on a mesh fabric

Using a mesh as a base fabric means that you can easily see the yarn at the back of the work.

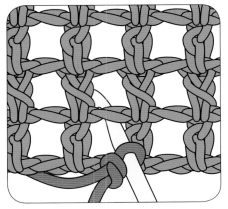 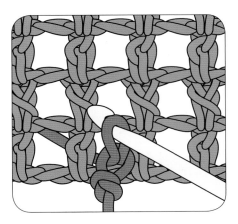 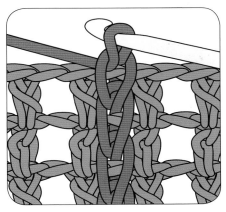

1 Work the mesh fabric. Using the contrast yarn, place a slip knot on the crochet hook. *Insert the hook through the chosen space on the mesh background fabric.

2 Hold the yarn to the reverse of the work. Wrap the yarn around the hook and draw through the slip knot on the hook and thus through to the front of the fabric.

3 Repeat from *, drawing the yarn through each stitch as required. When the design is complete, cut the yarn and pull it through the final stitch to secure.

Lines of surface crochet on a mesh background.

Surface crochet on single crochet (UK double crochet) fabric

Using a dense and sturdy stitch for the base fabric will give you a good base for surface crochet. Using this method you will be able to make your stitches travel in any direction.

Work as for using a mesh fabric, inserting the hook through the gaps between stitches instead of into the larger mesh spaces.

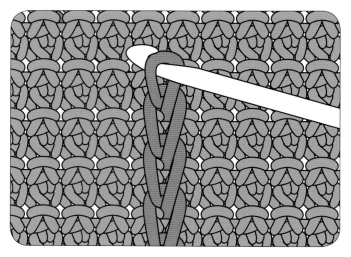

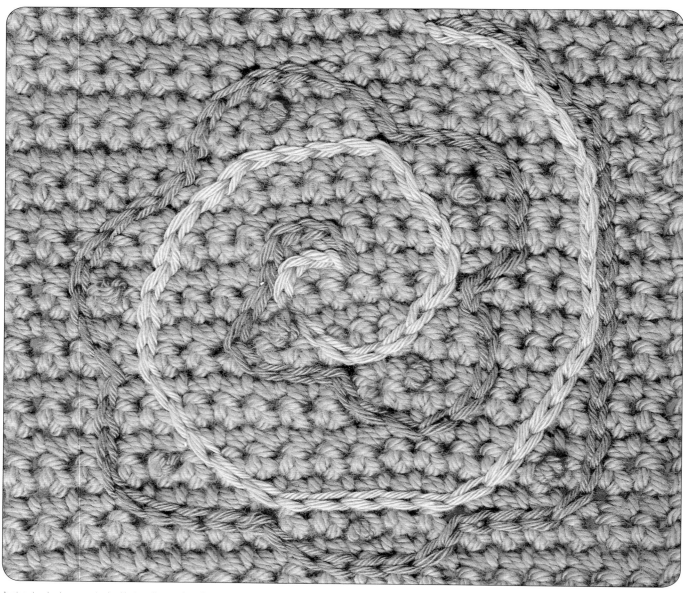

A simple design created with two lines of surface crochet combined with French knots.

decorative flowers

Because many crochet motifs are made in the round and because the craft by nature produces intricate feminine pieces, it is logical that it lends itself perfectly to the production of decorative features such as flowers, leaves and foliage. Crochet flowers can make wonderful embellishments for your projects and can be made as corsages for your favorite outfits.

Choosing the right yarn and materials

Make sure you choose a suitable yarn for your chosen crochet piece, and use the correct hook. Working an intricate lace flower in a bulky or hairy yarn will mean that stitches are less defined and that the detail of the stitching is unclear.

Making a frilled flower

Frilled flowers are very simple to make, and you can make each petal in a different color if you wish. This flower is made using double crochet (UK treble crochet).

1 Make 6 chain, join with a slip stitch to form a ring. Work 3 chain in order to reach the height of the stitch. Work 3 further stitches into the center of the ring.

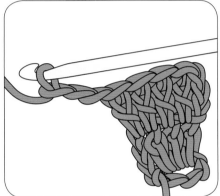

2 *Turn. Work a further 3 chain to reach the height of the next row. Work a stitch into each stitch of the previous row. Work 3 chain.

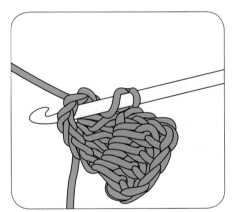

3 Turn the piece again so that the right side is facing. Bring the yarn behind the petal and hold at the reverse of the work. Work 3 stitches into the center of the chain to form the base of the next petal. Repeat from *.

Making flowers

When working a 3D flower, make sure you use a yarn strong enough to hold the shape of the crochet piece and a hook small enough to make firm stitches.

When making a corsage make sure you have thought through the method for attaching it to your garments. You can buy brooch backs and pins that can be sewn in place on the reverse of the flower.

If adding beads, be sure to plan ahead and thread them onto the yarn before you start.

Making a layered flower

To get a 3D effect you can work into the reverse side of a flower motif in order to create a framework for the subsequent row. You may be asked to work around the posts of the previous row in order to do this, or you may have to make stitches into the back of petals made on the previous round.

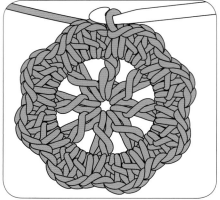

1 The example here shows a flower worked with a central wheel made of long post stitches. This will form the base for the framework.

2 Once the flower is complete, fasten off the yarn and sew in any ends on the reverse side of the work.

3 With the back facing, work a frame work for the next row by securing the yarn to a post with a slip stitch. *Work a chain long enough to travel around the outside of the flower in line with the next spoke of the wheel. Work a slip stitch around the corresponding spoke. Repeat from * until the framework is complete.

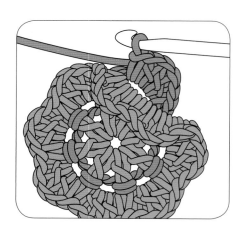

4 With the right side facing, work the next set of stitches for petals into the spaces created by the chain on the previous round.

A layered flower in three colors.

making cords

Cords can be used in many different ways: to add embellishment to a crochet fabric by sewing them into patterns, to make shoulder straps and handles for bags, or to tie a garment or other item closed. You can make a variety of pretty cords very easily—and can even use them to mimic features such as cables.

Slip stitch cord

When worked in succession through a foundation chain slip stitches can become a little loose, so it may be a good idea to use a slightly smaller hook on the return row.

Make a foundation chain to the required length. Change hook to a smaller one, if desired. Make one chain. Work a slip stitch into every chain to the end.

Double slip stitch cord

Work as for the slip stitch cord to begin with, then continue as follows.

At the end of the first row of slip stitching, work an extra slip stitch into the last stitch then work along the second side of the foundation chain, working a slip stitch into every chain to the end.

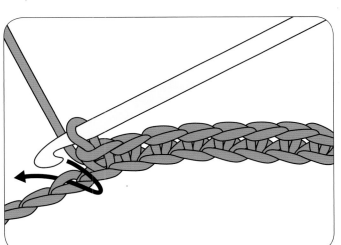

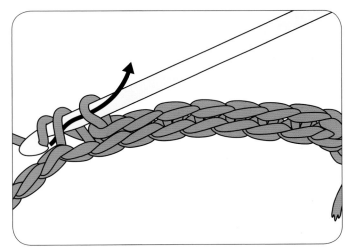

A slip stitch cord.

Double slip stitch cord.

Wide cord

You can make a wider cord by working in the same way as for the double slip stitch cord, only using a slightly higher stitch—such as single crochet (UK double crochet).

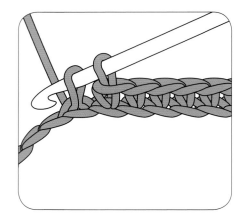

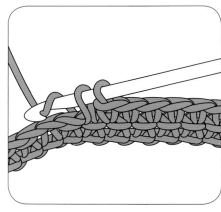

1 Make a foundation chain to the required length. Make one chain. Work a stitch into every chain to the end.

2 At the end of the first row, work 3 stitches into the first foundation chain, then work along the second side of the foundation chain, working a stitch into every chain to the end. Work 3 stitches into the final foundation chain. Join with a slip stitch into the first stitch.

A cord made with single crochet (UK double crochet).

Wide cord with surface crochet

You can add detail to the wide cord by adding a row of surface crochet along the center in a contrasting color.

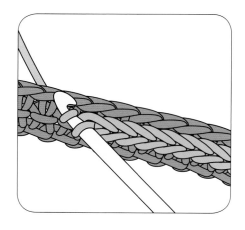

Work the cord as for the wide cord. Using a contrast yarn and a slightly larger hook, work a row of surface crochet along the center of the cord.

A cord in single crochet (UK double crochet), with a row of surface crochet down the center.

Tubular cord

You can make a chunky cord by working around a central
ring in a spiral using a stitch such as single crochet
(UK double crochet)

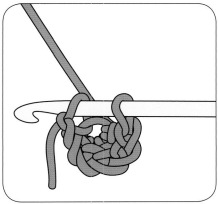

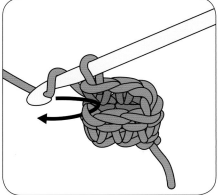

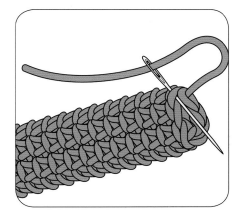

1 Make 2 chain. Work 5 stitches into the first chain. Join with a slip stitch to form a ring.

2 Work one stitch into the top loop of each of the foundation chains. Then, working in a spiral, work a stitch into just the top loop of every stitch of every round until the cord is the required length.

3 To finish, cut the yarn and fasten off. Thread the yarn end through the eye of a large needle. Sew a running stitch around the final row of stitches and pull to tighten.

A length of tubular cord.

Using cords

Cords are quite versatile because they can be used alone as tie
fastenings or as a narrow belt, for decoration, or to attach hanging
tassels (see page 188), pompoms or toggles (see page 233).

It is best to try and work cords with a fairly medium gauge (tension)
so they are not too open and floppy, or too tight and stiff.

stitch directory

Abbreviations and symbols can differ depending upon whether you are following a US or a UK pattern and can even be personal to a pattern writer or designer, so it is really important that you make sure you understand all the crochet abbreviations and symbols before you start working from this Stitch Directory.

Don't be fooled by simply reading the stitch names, because some stitch references are the same yet mean very different things. For example, US and UK patterns share stitch names (such as double crochet, or treble crochet for example), yet these names do not refer to the same stitches. Single crochet in US terminology is a dense stitch with a short post, which in the UK is called double crochet. However, double crochet in the US is a longer stitch with a post, which is perhaps twice the height of the UK stitch, and is known in the UK as treble crochet.

All patterns in this section are written using US terminology only. See page 33 for stitch abbreviations.

Daisy Bloom

Base ring: 8ch, join with ss.
Round 1: Ch3 (counts as 1dc), 1dc into ring, [6ch, 3dc into ring] 5 times, 6ch, 1dc into ring, ss to top of 3-ch.
Round 2: *Ch1, [1sc, 1hdc, 7dc, 1hdc, 1sc] into next 6ch-sp, 1ch, skip 1dc, ss into next dc; rep from * 5 more times placing last ss into top of 3-ch at beg of previous round.
Fasten off.

Fern Leaf

Row 1: 18ch, ss to into 2nd ch from hook, 1sc into next ch, 1hdc into next ch, 1dc into each of next 4 chs, 1tr into each of next 5 chs, 1dc into each of next 2 chs, 1 hdc into next ch, 1sc in next ch, ss into next ch.
Fasten off. Do not turn.
Row 2: Join yarn in first sc of row 1, 1sc into next st, 1hdc into next st, 1dc into each of next 5 sts, 1hdc into each of next 3 sts, 1sc into each of next 2 sts, ss into each of next 3 sts.
Fasten off.

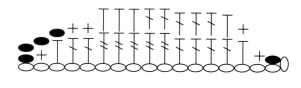

Anemone

Special abbreviation: Picot = 3ch, ss into first of these ch

Base ring: 8ch, join with ss.

Round 1: 3ch (counts as 1dc), 15dc into ring, ss into top of 3-ch.

Round 2: Ch5 (counts as 1dc, 2ch), [1dc into next dc, 2ch] 15 times, ss to 3rd of 5-ch.

Round 3: Ch1, 3sc into each of next 16 2ch-sps, ss to first sc.

Round 4: Ch1, 1sc into same sc as last ss, *6ch, skip 5 sc, 1sc into next sc; rep from * 6 more times, 6ch, ss to first sc.

Round 5: Ss into first 6ch-sp, 1ch, [1sc, 1hdc, 6dc, 1hdc, 1sc] into each of the 8 6ch-sps, ss to first sc. (8 petals worked)

Round 6: Ch1, working behind each petal of previous round, 1sc into first sc on 4th round, *7ch, 1sc into next sc on 4th round; rep from * 6 more times, 7ch, ss to first sc.

Round 7: Ss into first 7ch-sp, 1ch, [1sc, 1hdc, 7dc, 1hdc, 1sc] into each of next 8 7ch-sps, ss to first sc.

Round 8: Ch1, working behind each petal of previous round, 1sc into first sc on 6th round, *8ch, 1sc into next sc on 6th round; rep from * 6 more times, 8ch, ss to first sc.

Round 9: Ss into first 8ch-sp, 1ch, [1sc, 1hdc, 3dc, 1 picot, 3dc, 1 picot, 3dc, 1hdc, 1sc] into each of the 8 8ch-sps, ss to first sc.

Fasten off.

Springtime Blossom

Base ring: 6ch, join with ss.

Round 1: Ch3 (counts as 1dc), 15dc into ring, ss to top of 3-ch.

Round 2: Ch5 (counts as 1dc and 2ch), 1dc into same st as last ss, *1ch, skip 1dc [1dc, 2ch, 1dc] into next dc; rep from * 6 more times, 1ch, ss to 3rd of 5-ch.

Round 3: Ss into first 2ch-sp, 3ch (counts as 1dc), [1dc, 2ch, 2dc] into same sp, *1ch, [2dc, 2ch, 2dc] into next 2ch-sp; rep from * 6 more times, 1ch, ss to top of 3-ch.

Round 4: Ss into next dc and first 2ch-sp, 3ch, 6dc into same sp as last ss, 1sc into next ch-sp, [7dc into next 2ch-sp, 1sc into next ch-sp] 7 times, ss into top of 3-ch.
Fasten off.

Bird of Paradise

Flower petals: *Ch20, skip 2 ch, 1sc into each of next 2 ch, 1hdc into next ch, 1dc into each of next 2 ch, 1tr into each of next 2 ch, holding back last loop of each tr, 1tr into each of next 2 ch, yo and draw through all 3 loops on hook, 1dc into each of next 3 ch, 1hdc into next ch, ss into each of last 5 ch; rep from * 5 more times. (6 petals made).

Flower base: Ch1, 1sc in base of each of 6 petals, 5ch, turn. Holding back last loop of each tr, 1tr into each of first 5 sc, 2tr into last sc, yo and through all 8 loops on hook.

Stem: Ch30, skip 2 ch, 1hdc into each ch to base of flower, ss to base of flower. Fasten off.

professional finishing techniques

Once you have mastered the craft of crochet you will probably find that you are addicted to making exciting and innovative fabrics. However, once these pieces are complete it is important that you learn to finish them off in a professional and neat way. Bad finishing can completely spoil the outcome of an otherwise perfectly made piece of crochet.

sewn seams

Allow plenty of time to do your finishing, because rushing may lead to untidy seams or mistakes. Sew all yarn ends in neatly first and ensure that pieces have been blocked before you start assembling them together. You can use a variety of sewn stitches to join your crochet pieces. Some of these can be a little time consuming, but when done neatly they are a very effective way of finishing off.

Backstitch seam

Backstitch uses quite a lot of yarn, but rather than using one long length it is a good idea to work with relatively short lengths and rejoin when needed.

Hold the crochet pieces together with the right sides of the work facing inwards. Work a row of backstitch from right to left, making sure the stitches run in a straight line. The sewn seam can be either one or two stitches in from the edge of the work, depending upon which looks neater.

Chain stitch seam

Chain stitch creates a sturdy sewn seam, although again it uses a fair amount of yarn. Chain stitch can be a little bulky and you need to be careful not to over tighten your stitches.

Hold the crochet pieces together with the right sides of the work facing inwards. Work a row of chain stitch from right to left (see page 196), making sure the stitches run in a straight line. The sewn seam can be either one or two stitches in from the edge of the work, depending upon which looks neater.

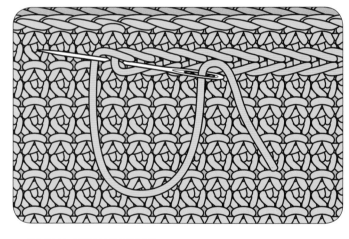

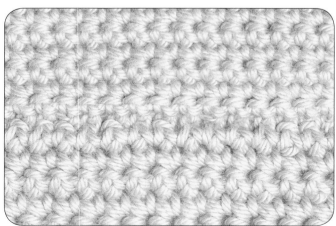

A backstitch seam from the right side.

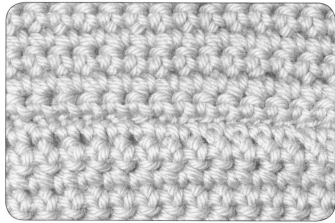

A chain stitch seam from the right side.

Mattress stitch seam

This is an almost invisible sewn seam, which is suitable for crochet and knitted fabrics alike. It uses less yarn than backstitch and chain stitch and is done with the fabrics lying flat and face up. It is a good idea not to start this seam at the very beginning of the seam; instead start a few rows or stitches in from the end of the work. Leave a long tail end of yarn (without a knot) at the beginning and use it to finish off the first section of the seam once the majority of its length is complete.

Lay the crochet pieces flat on a table or work surface with right sides facing. Working one stitch in from the edge of the left hand piece, insert the needle through the work from front to back approximately four rows or stitches up from the lower end of the seam. Bring the needle through to the front of the work one stitch up. *Insert the needle into the corresponding stitch on the right hand piece from front to back, then out to the front of the work one stitch higher. From the front, insert the needle into the stitch on the left hand piece where the yarn from the previous stitch emerges. Bring the needle back through to the front of the work one stitch higher. Repeat from * tightening the sewing every few stitches.

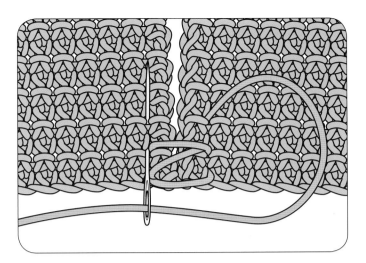

A mattress stitch seam from the right side.

Making neat stitching

It is important that you choose the correct needle and yarn for a sewn seam. If you have used a slub or hairy yarn for the crochet work—or a yarn that is liable to break easily—then use a stronger, smoother yarn in the same shade to do your sewing up. Choose a blunt knitter's sewing needle with a large eye to stitch with.

When working with the wrong side facing, always check your stitching on the right side of the work every few stitches to ensure that you have not made a mistake that will show.

You may want to use pins or markers to ensure that you match the seam correctly.

Ladder stitch seam

This is worked in a similar way to mattress stitch. It is a less bulky seam, although stitches do show on the right side of the work.

Lay the crochet pieces flat on a table or work surface with the right sides facing. Working one stitch in from the edge of the left hand piece, insert the needle through the work from front to back approximately four rows or stitches up from the lower end of the seam. Bring the needle through to the front of the work one stitch up. *Insert the needle into the corresponding stitch on the right hand piece from front to back, then out to the front of the work one stitch higher. From the front, insert the needle into the left hand piece one stitch higher than where the yarn of the previous stitch emerges. Bring the needle back through to the front of the work one stitch higher. Repeat from * tightening the sewing every few stitches.

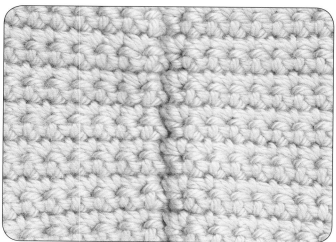

A ladder stitch seam from the right side.

Over sewn seam

This is quite a quick way of sewing crochet pieces together. It is important that you try and keep the stitch size as even and regular as possible, otherwise stitching can look messy on the right side of the work.

Hold the two crochet pieces together with right sides facing inwards. Place your left index finger between the two pieces to open the seam and make small sewn stitches around both edges to join. Where possible join stitch for stitch.

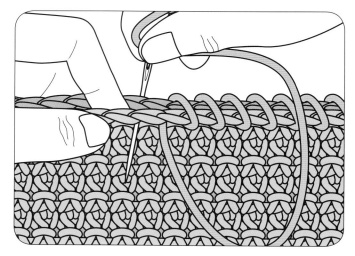

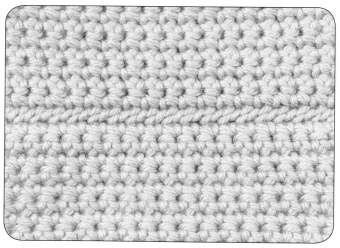

An over sewn stitch seam from the right side.

crochet seams

Some crochet stitches can be used to join crochet pieces once complete, or you can join pieces using crochet stitches as you work the piece, which is especially effective when joining blocks.

Slip stitch seam

This is the crochet equivalent of chain stitch and can be worked in a matching or a contrasting yarn.

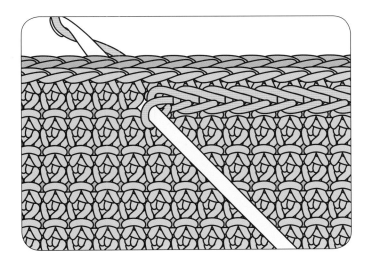

Hold the crochet pieces together with the right sides of the work facing inwards. Work a row of stitches from right to left by inserting the crochet hook through each stitch and catching the yarn held at the back of the work. Draw the yarn through the fabric and create a slip stitch. Make sure the stitches run in a straight line.

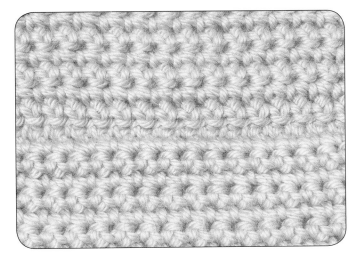

A slip stitch seam from the right side.

Alternating slip stitch seam

This stitch can create a feature on the right side of the work when worked with the right sides of the fabric facing. It can look especially effective if worked in a contrast color.

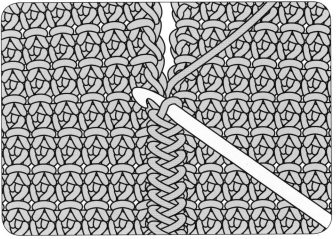

Lay the crochet pieces flat on a table or work surface with the wrong sides facing. Work a slip stitch into the first stitch on the left hand piece, *work a slip stitch into the corresponding stitch on the right hand piece. Work another slip stitch into the next stitch along on the left hand piece. Repeat from *.

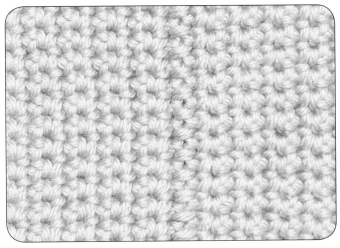

An alternating slip stitch seam from the right side.

Single crochet (UK double crochet) on a side seam

Using crochet stitches to join pieces is a very quick way of assembling them together. Be careful not to make the stitches too loose or tight because this can affect the final neatness of the join.

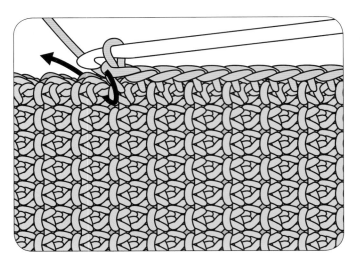

Hold the two crochet pieces together with right sides facing inwards. Place your left index finger between the two pieces to open the seam. Insert the hook through a stitch on the front piece then through its corresponding stitch on the back piece. Draw the yarn through from the reverse of the work and complete a stitch. Where possible join stitch for stitch.

A single crochet (UK double crochet) side seam from the right side.

Single crochet (UK double crochet) on a top seam

Crocheting along a top seam is quick and easy; where possible, join stitch for stitch. If the stitch count differs between the pieces, then decrease by working stitches together where needed.

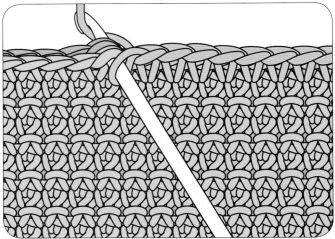

Hold the two crochet pieces together with right sides facing inwards and the top seams running parallel to each other. Place your left index finger between the two pieces to open the seam. Insert the hook through a stitch on the front piece then through its corresponding stitch on the back piece. Draw the yarn through from the reverse of the work and complete a stitch.

A single crochet (UK double crochet) top seam from the right side.

Single crochet (UK double crochet) and chain seam

This is quite an open seam that creates small holes between stitches. It is good for joining lace and openwork motifs.

Work as for the single crochet (UK double crochet) seam opposite, working one chain between each stitch and inserting the hook through the work every alternate stitch.

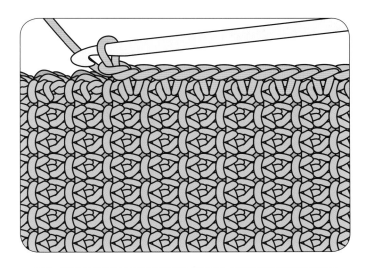

A single crochet (UK double crochet) and chain seam from the right side.

Making neat seams

Ideally seams in crochet should be as invisible as possible. The pattern you are following may suggest a certain type of seam that will work best for the design, but otherwise choose the method that you feel will give the best results.

Very large and heavy pieces of crochet may drop over time, and for such items a crocheted seam is more likely to drop at the same rate than a sewn one. It is a good idea to hang large pieces on a padded hanger between crochet sessions, so the work can drop if it is going to before you come to make the seams.

joining circles together

When joining circular motifs or shapes with lots of curved edges, there are a few specific techniques you can use that will give a better result.

Joining circular motifs

Because circular motifs—or motifs with very curved edges—do not have straight sides, they are not as easy to join together as angular shapes such as squares and triangles.

The best way to join circular shapes is to work a few sewn stitches in a matching yarn just where the circles touch.

Circular motifs only need to be joined where they touch.

Fastening off on rounds

To get a neat finish when working circular rounds, fasten off the last stitch of the round using a sewn stitch instead of a slip stitch.

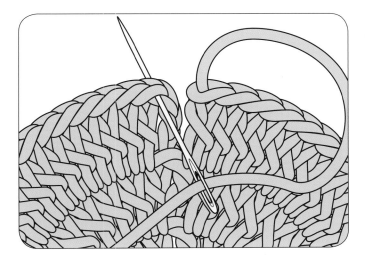

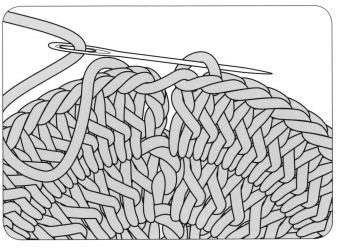

1 Draw the yarn through the final stitch of the round and cut the yarn leaving a long end. Thread the end through a sewing needle. Insert the needle under the chain created by the next stitch.

2 Insert the needle through the center of the chain created by the fastened off stitch, in order to mimic a chain.

Neat rounds

Before starting to join motifs together, block and press them into the correct shape as described on page 245. If many motifs have been made over a period of time they may be slightly different sizes due to varying gauge (tension) at different times of working, but blocking and pressing can correct such minor variations.

When working with lots of motifs that are all supposed to be identical, draw a template in waterproof pen on a piece of fabric and pin the motifs out using the template as a guide.

professional finishing techniques

joining blocks together

You can join blocks using either a sewn or a crochet stitch. When you join more than two blocks together you will need to deal with the areas where all the blocks meet.

Joining four square motifs with sewn stitches

For a neat join, work your sewn stitches through just one side of the chain created by the stitch. For a stronger seam, work your stitches through the complete chain.

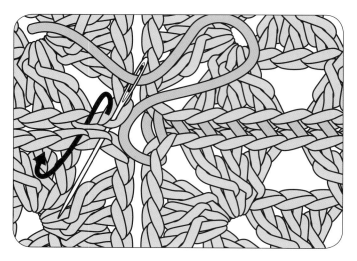

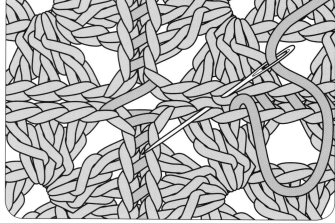

1 Join the first two blocks using the preferred sewing stitch. At the end of the straight edge, position two more blocks in place. Thread the sewing needle through the first stitch on both of the blocks in order to join all four together. Continue to sew blocks together in this way to end.

2 Turn the work so that the open seam is horizontal. Use the chosen sewing stitch to work along this seam to end.

These four motifs have been sewn together.

Joining four square motifs with slip stitch

You can make a nice feature of the slip stitch by working
it in a contrast color.

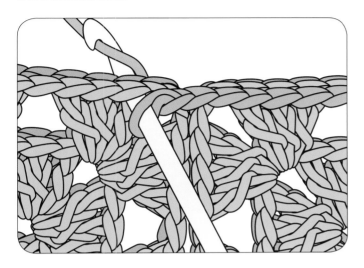

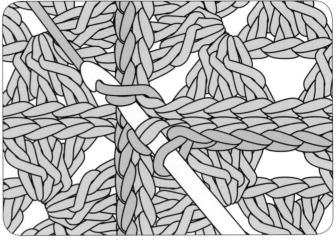

1 Join the first two blocks using slip stitch. At the end of the
straight edge, position two more blocks in place. Insert the
hook through the first stitch on both of the blocks in order to join
all four together. Continue to crochet blocks together in this way
to end.

2 Turn the work so that the open seam is horizontal. Use
the chosen crochet stitch to work along this seam to end.
Where the blocks meet, carry the yarn across the ridge created
by the seam and pull gently in order to work a tight, strong stitch.

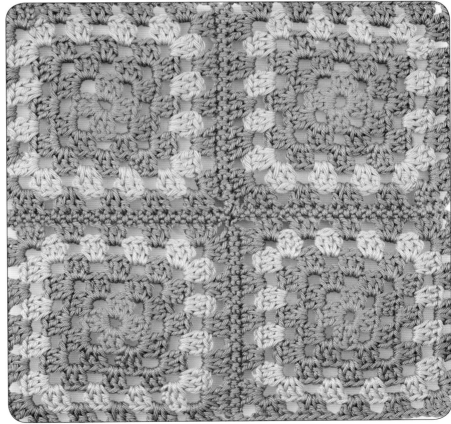

These four motifs are crocheted together
using slip stitch. In this case, the slip stitch
chain is on the reverse.

Joining motifs as you work

Depending upon the chosen motif, it may be possible to join the crochet pieces to one another as you complete the final round of each one. It is a good idea to piece the motifs together in long strips first, which can then be joined to each other using a further row of stitching.

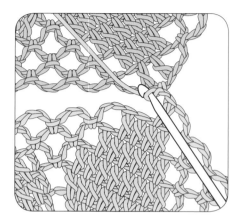 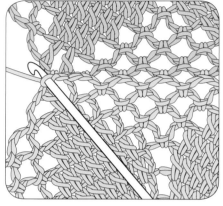 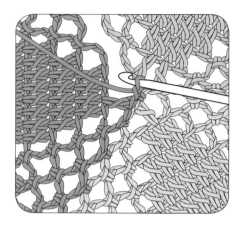

1 Complete one motif. Work the second motif until you reach the final round. Work according to the pattern down one side of the motif. At the corner, line up the first motif with the second one and work a stitch into the corner space of both motifs simultaneously.

2 Work according to the pattern around the second motif, working joining stitches with areas of chain in between, where possible, in order to attach the first motif.

3 Finish the final round of the second motif. Join further motifs in the same way.

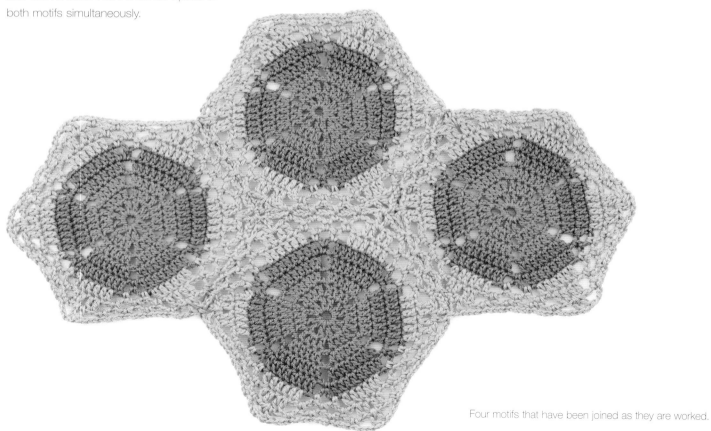

Four motifs that have been joined as they are worked.

making shapes fit together

Many different shapes can be fitted together to make a fabric. Some shapes (such as circles) will have open areas between them; others will interlock to create a fabric with no holes—such as squares and triangles. Many geometric shapes that do not join perfectly with each other can be combined with others to create solid fabrics. Octagonal shapes, for example, can be pieced together with squares and triangles to create a fabric with no gaps.

Circular blocks

Circular blocks can be sewn together in random patterns or in strips. When joined together in strips they create small areas where there is no fabric. These spaces can be filled in more with smaller circles.

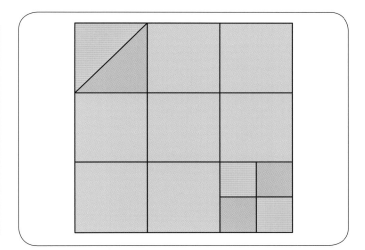

Square blocks

Squares will piece together easily to make a fabric with no open areas. You can also use triangles or smaller squares joined to make a bigger square block.

Joining shapes

Mosaic and tiling designs can often give you some new ideas on how to fit different geometric shapes together successfully. If you want to create quite a complex design, try working out how the shapes will fit together on graph paper first.

professional
finishing
techniques

Triangular blocks

Many triangle shapes will piece together to make a complete fabric. You can also try making four smaller triangles pieced together to form one larger one.

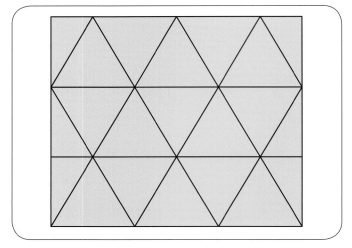

Hexagonal blocks

Hexagons will also create a solid fabric with no gaps when pieced together. In order to create straight outer edges, you will need to create half hexagons to fill in the spaces.

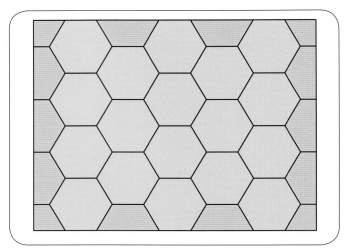

Octagonal blocks

Octagonal shapes are best joined together one by one, rather than in strips. You can use small squares and triangles to fill in gaps and edge spaces, if you want to create a complete fabric.

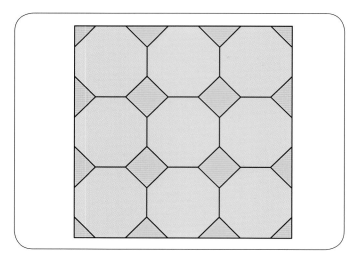

Creating fabric

Crochet can be quite a dense fabric, but it can also be light and airy—particularly the more lacy designs. It's not essential to create a solid fabric when joining motifs, so don't be afraid to leave gaps between shapes if you think it will add an extra dimension to the design.

buttons and buttonholes

Buttons tend to be the most popular way of fastening crochet garments. Most are lightweight, easy to attach and do not stretch the crochet fabric.

Take plenty of time to choose the correct button; make sure it is colorfast, smooth and of a good quality, and that it fits through the matching buttonhole. Remember to match the button to the style of your project—for example, a crochet garment made with chunky yarn will require a large button, preferably with a shank, and therefore will need a large buttonhole; a crochet garment in lightweight fine yarn will require a smaller button and therefore a smaller hole.

Buttonholes

You can make several different styles of buttonhole using crochet stitches, although it is an advantage to make the button band in a sturdy dense stitch and not use one that creates long posts. The hole needs to be just big enough for the button to slip through, bearing in mind that a crochet fabric will stretch slightly.

Making a buttonhole within a piece

If you are making a garment that requires buttons, you will need to make the band for the buttons to be sewn onto before you make the buttonhole band. Mark on the button band where the buttons are to be sewn, because this will determine where you make holes on the subsequent buttonhole band. Be sure to space the holes evenly and to work throughout in a consistent stitch such as single crochet (UK double crochet).

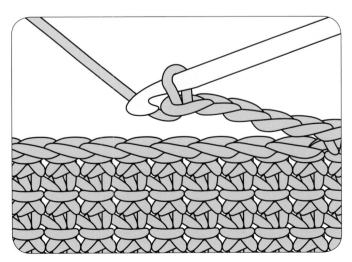

1 Work to the position of the required buttonhole. Decide how many stitches to skip and make a chain to the same length.

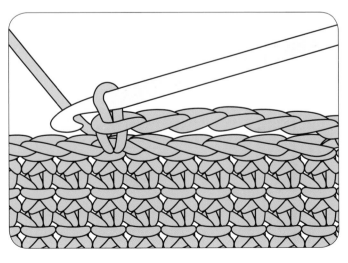

2 Secure the chain in place by working a stitch into the next stitch. Continue along the row, making chains to create subsequent holes where required.

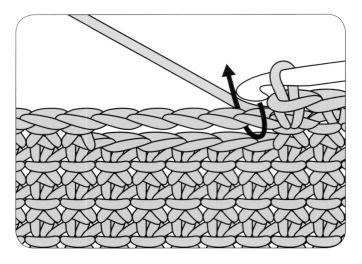

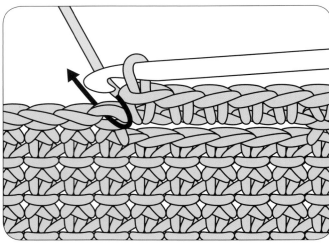

3 On the return row, work stitches around the chain that was made on the previous row. Make the same number of stitches around the chain as were used to make the chain.

4 At the end of the chain, work a stitch into the next stitch of the row. Continue along the row, working into the spaces made by each chain on the previous row.

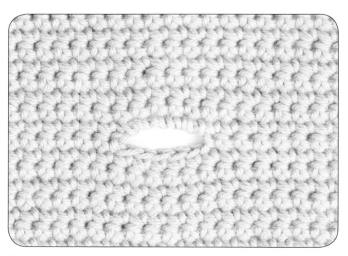

The finished buttonhole is neat and even.

Sizing buttonholes

Choose your buttons before you begin making your buttonholes, so the hole can be made to fit the button rather than the other way round.

After making the first buttonhole, check it fits the button correctly before making more; if not you can adjust the size for the remaining holes. It may not be necessary to remake an incorrect first buttonhole—if it is too tight it may stretch a little, if too loose sew a stitch across the end.

Making button loops

Button loops are made on the last row of the button band and are usually a little more ornate so are a nice way of adding some extra detail. Bands for button loops are normally narrower than for buttonholes within a fabric. With wrong side facing, first work to the position of the required button loop.

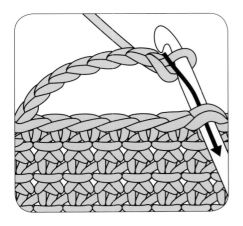

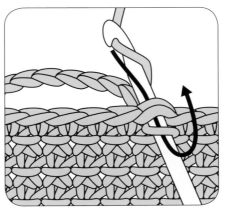

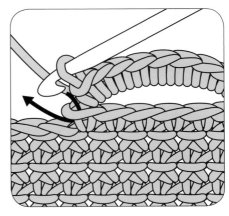

1 Place a stitch marker in the last stitch, then work a few more stitches (here a further 6 stitches are shown). Make a chain long enough to go over the button, remembering the loop will stretch slightly. Slip the yarn loop from the hook and thread the hook through the marked stitch from front to back. Place the loop back on the hook and draw through the stitch.

2 Insert the hook back through the same stitch. Wrap the yarn around the hook and draw through to the front.

3 Work enough stitches around the chain to fill the loop. Work the final stitch of the loop into the stitch at the base of the chain, as shown by the arrow in the illustration.

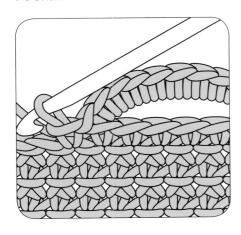

4 Insert the hook into the next stitch beyond the button loop and continue along the row, making subsequent loops where required.

A completed button loop adds extra detail to an edge.

making your own buttons

In some cases it may not be possible to purchase a button that is suitable for your project. A wonderful alternative is to make your own buttons, thus creating a truly original and personal project.

Ball button

You can quite easily make a crochet covering for a large bead or an existing rounded button to make your own ball button. This method can also be used to cover beads for necklaces, or even to cover Christmas tree baubles. The ball covering is made using single crochet (UK double crochet).

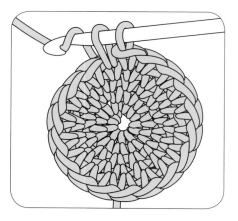  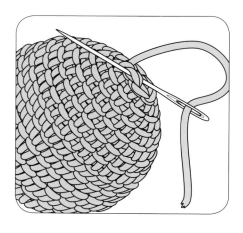

1 Make 2 chain. Work 6 stitches into the first chain to create a small ring. Do not work a slip stitch to join the ring, instead continue to work in a spiral. Work 2 stitches into every alternate stitch until the crochet piece is large enough to accommodate the bead.

2 Hold the bead inside the crochet piece and continue to crochet around in spirals until approximately one third of the bead is visible. Decrease the stitch count by working 2 stitches together every alternate stitch. When the bead is very nearly covered work 2 stitches together into every stitch until the bead is no longer visible.

3 Cut the yarn to approx 6in. (30cm) and use the end to secure the ball button, using a sewing needle and a few tight stitches. Use the yarn end to sew the ball button in place.

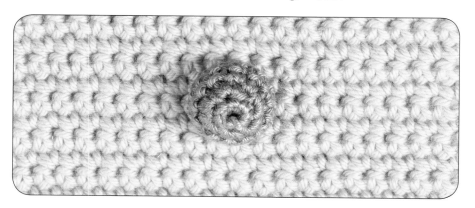

Crocheted ball buttons can be made in any color.

Dorset button

Dorset buttons were traditionally made using small pieces of goat's horn cut in slices to create rings. Contemporary Dorset buttons can be made using plastic curtain rings or window blind rings. They can be created in an almost endless permutation of color and types of yarn and are extremely quick to make.

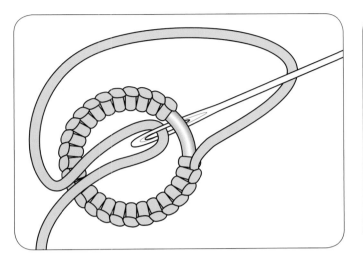

1 Using a long end of yarn, sew around the edge of the curtain ring using buttonhole stitch (see page 198). Holding the tail end of the yarn close to the ring, sew over both the ring and the tail until it is hidden. Secure once the ring is full and turn the hem edge of the blanket stitch to the inside of the ring.

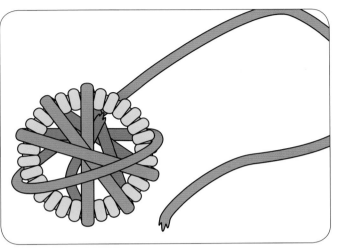

2 Using a contrast yarn, sew across the ring to create the spokes of a web. Using two or three stitches, over sew the center of the spokes and secure the yarn.

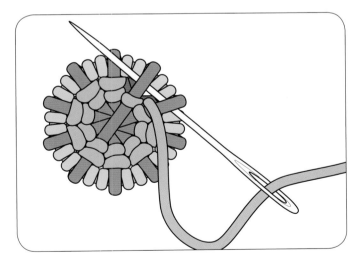

3 Using a third yarn color, thread the needle through from the back to the front of the button, close to the center of the spokes created by the previous yarn. Fill in the center of the ring by working backstitch around the spokes of the web. Fasten off the yarn.

A selection of different Dorset buttons.

sewing a button into place

If a button is not attached to the crochet piece correctly it can pull and stretch the fabric. Use a strong lightweight yarn in the same color to stitch the button on, or use a specific button thread that can be found in most haberdashery shops. It is a good idea to buy an extra button and sew it to the inside of a side seam, in case it is needed later to replace a lost button.

Attaching a shank button

A shank button has a solid front and a small ring on the back that you stitch through to secure the button to the fabric.

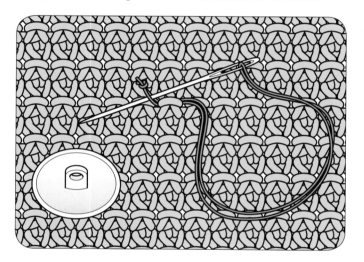

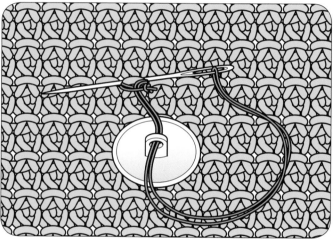

1 Thread a sewing needle with desired sewing thread, double up the sewing thread and make a knot in the end. From the front insert the needle through the crochet fabric in the position where the button is required. Bring the needle back through to the front of the fabric just slightly to the right side of the knot. Insert the needle between the two sewing threads just under the knot and pull gently to tighten.

2 Working small stitches close to the knot, being careful not to pull on the crochet fabric, to secure the button in place. Fasten off the sewing thread at the reverse of the work by making small over sewn stitches.

Attaching a button with holes

Many buttons have either two or four holes—or very occasionally an odd number such as three—that you sew through to secure the button to the fabric. You will need to create a short thread shank behind this type of button to hold the back of it slightly above the surface of the fabric, so there is room behind the button for the layer of fabric containing the buttonhole.

 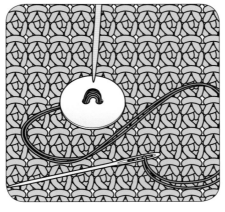 

1 Secure the sewing thread to the crochet fabric in the same way as for a shank button. Hold a small knitting needle, a matchstick or other such object on top of the button and sew over this and through the button holes to secure.

2 Remove the needle or matchstick, which will have created extra thread in the stitches holding the button in place.

3 Gently pull up on the button so that the extra thread is taken to the underside. Take the needle and thread through one of the holes to the back of the button and wrap the thread around the base of the stitches several times to strengthen the shank you have created. Fasten off the sewing thread at the reverse of the work by making small over sewn stitches.

Toggles

If you can find toggles with large enough holes, you can use small lengths of crochet chain, or even a crochet cord (see page 205), to secure them into place on the fabric.

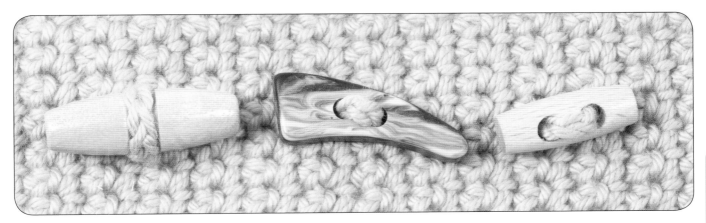

Toggles come in a variety of different designs.

zippers

If you would rather not use buttons to fasten your project, you could opt instead to use a zipper. Inserting a zipper can be a little tricky, because crochet fabric is by nature elastic and slightly stretchy, while a zipper is not.

Inserting a zipper

If the zipper is not inserted carefully the crochet fabric can either become stretched or puckered.

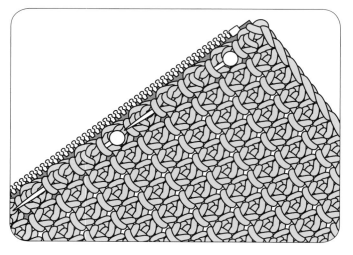

1 Open the zipper and pin into place, making sure that the edge of the crochet fabric lines up with the zipper teeth.

2 Using a fine sewing thread, work backstitch to join the zipper to the crochet fabric one stitch in from the edge of the work.

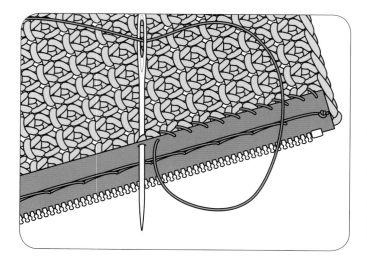

3 Using the crochet yarn (if possible), over sew neatly around the zipper edge on the reverse side of the work, making sure that no stitching is visible on the right side of the work.

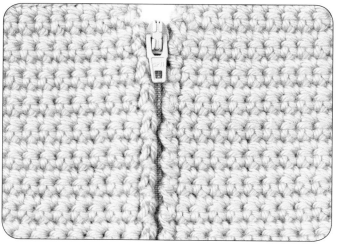

The zipper from the front side.

shaping

When making a garment, or following a crochet pattern—such as when working chevron designs, for example—you may need to either increase or decrease the number of stitches in the row. Increasing and decreasing can be done either partway through a row, or at either end.

Increasing stitches within a row

If the increasing is to be done partway through a row, the pattern will usually tell you exactly where to create more stitches.

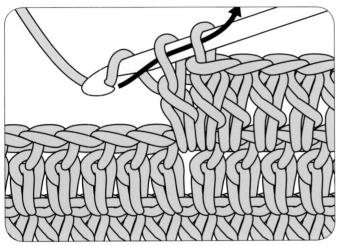

1 To make one extra stitch, work to where the increase is required. Work 2 stitches into the next stitch.

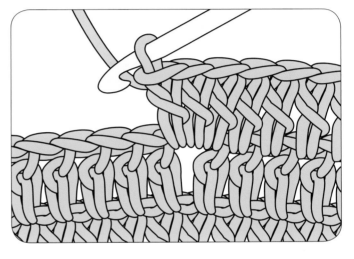

2 To make more than one extra stitch, work to where the increase is required. Work 3 (or more stitches) into the next stitch.

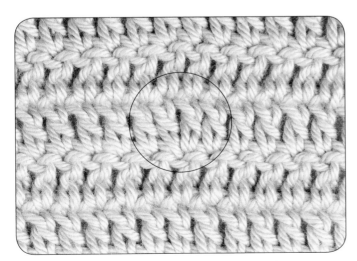

Detail of a one-stitch increase, in which two stitches have been made from one.

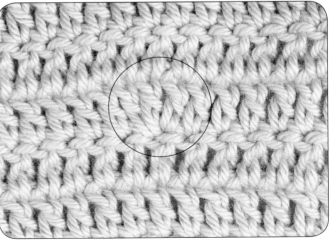

Detail of a two-stitch increase, in which three stitches have been made from one.

Decreasing stitches within a row

To decrease by one stitch within a row, work to where the decrease is required as noted in the knitting pattern. Decreases can be made using any stitches. In the

illustrations shown step 1 shows a decrease made within single crochet (double crochet UK) and step 2 shows a decrease within double crochet (treble crochet UK).

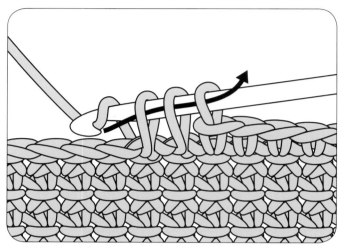

1 Work an incomplete stitch, by stopping before the last step of each stitch, into the next 2 stitches to leave 3 loops on the hook.

2 Wrap the yarn around the hook and draw through all the loops.

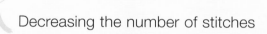

Decreasing the number of stitches

Decreases can be made using any stitches. In the illustrations shown step 1 shows a decrease made within single crochet (double crochet UK) and step 2 shows a decrease within double crochet (treble crochet UK).

Detail of a one-stitch decrease, in which two stitches have been reduced to one.

Increasing stitches on the right hand side of the fabric

To increase on the right hand side of the fabric you will need to add an area of chain in which to work the subsequent row. This chain is added at the end of a reverse side row.

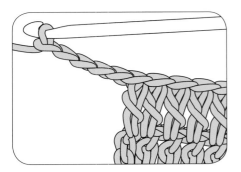

1 Work to the end of the reverse side row. Make the required number of chain, remembering to add enough to allow for any turning chains needed.

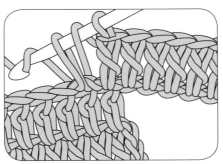

2 Turn and work the next row of stitches into the chain and then into the subsequent stitches of the previous row.

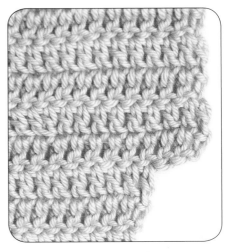

Increasing on the right hand side.

Increasing stitches on the left hand side of the fabric

When using a stitch with a long post you may need to create the shaping at the beginning and the end of the same row, to avoid shaping on the left side being a row higher.

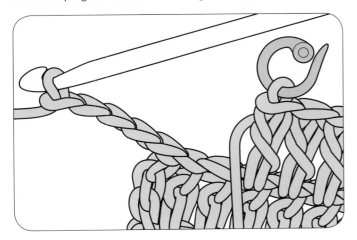

Work to the last few stitches of the row. Remove the working stitch from the crochet hook place on a stitch holder. Join a length of yarn to the final stitch of the row and work the required number of chain. Fasten off the chain. Insert the hook back into the held stitch and work to the end of the row, working the final few stitches into the previous row, then subsequent stitches into the added chain.

Increasing on the left hand side.

professional finishing techniques

Reverse shaping

Crochet patterns have set ways in which they communicate instructions. To save space, many patterns will ask you to "work as set" for example, so that each row of the pattern does not need to be written. One instruction that often confuses crocheters is that to "reverse shaping." This instruction is usually given when working a neckline, but can also be used when shaping sleeves or other design features.

To reverse the shaping you will first have worked a piece from the pattern, but you now need to work a second piece as a mirror image of the first. This will mean working the shaping as instructed for the first piece, but at the opposite end of the row. A way to keep track of where you are is to draw out the shape required on a piece of paper.

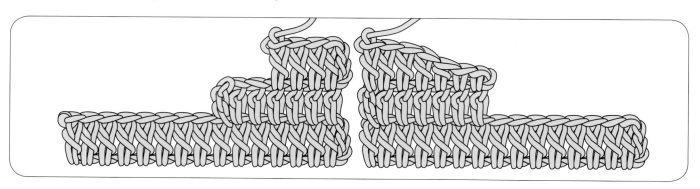

Gradual shaping

When using a stitch with a long post, shaping can look a little clumsy with the edges of the crochet fabric stepped. You may prefer to work gradual shaping in order to achieve a slope instead.

Work a sequence of stitches with smaller posts into the first few stitches, as shown in this illustration.

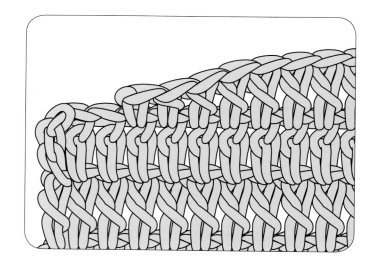

picking up stitches

Many crochet pieces will require an edging, border or fancy trim of some kind, which is created directly on the edge. To do this you will probably need to pick up some stitches.

Marking the edge

If you have a set number of stitches to pick up across the edge, it is a good idea to place markers at regular intervals to ensure that you achieve an even pick up.

Measure the crochet edge. Decide how frequently a marker needs to be placed—for example, every 2in. (5cm)—and mark the edge with stitch markers, tied yarn or sewn stitches. Count how many spaces there are between the markers, then divide this number into the stitch count. For example, if there are 10 spaces and the pick up requires 50 sts, then the calculation will be 50 divided by 10 = 5 stitches to be picked up between each marker.

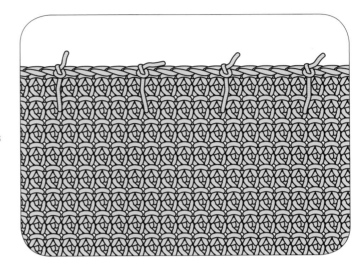

An edge marked for picking up stitches.

Where to put the hook

If you are picking up stitches along an edge, start by placing the hook as shown.

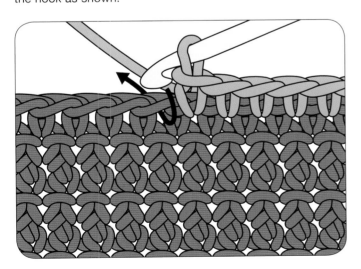

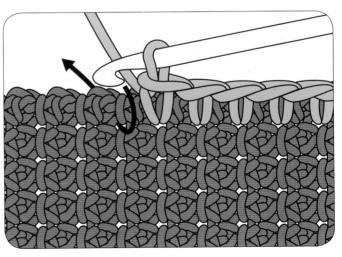

1 When working along the bottom (foundation chain) or top (final row) of a crochet piece, insert the hook into the center of each stitch from the front to back.

2 When working along a side edge of a crochet piece, insert the hook through the work one complete stitch in from the edge, from front to back.

professional finishing techniques

Picking up stitches using single crochet (UK double crochet)

The quickest way to pick up stitches is to do so by working single crochet (UK double crochet) around the outside of the crochet fabric one stitch in from the edge. This stitch will bind the edge of the crochet piece, so it is important that you keep edge stitches neat and even. Once the row of single crochet (UK double crochet) is complete, it can be used as the base for the required edging or border.

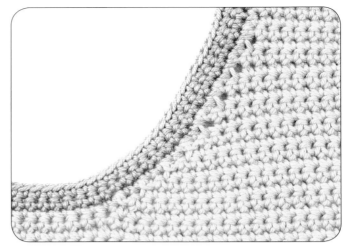

An edge that has been finished by picking up stitches with single crochet (UK double crochet).

Picking up stitches using slip stitch

Working a row of slip stitch through the crochet fabric one stitch in from the edge (as for surface crochet on pages 199–200) is a neat way of creating a base for the required edging or border. The fabric edge is not bound by the stitches and will create a seam on the reverse side of the fabric.

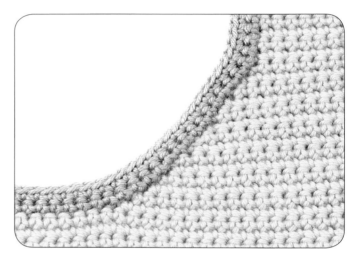

An edge that has been finished by working slip stitch one stitch in.

Picking up stitches using Tunisian crochet

Work along the edge of the crochet piece, picking up the required number of stitches on a Tunisian hook as for the pick up row on page 138. When you reach the end of the row, fasten off the stitches as for the return row on page 137.

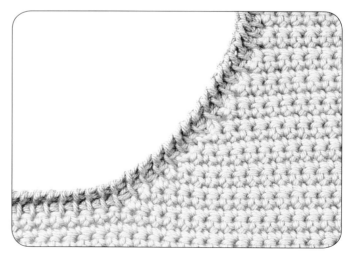

An edge finished by picking up stitches using a Tunisian hook.

pockets

Crochet pockets can be used as a great addition to garments of any description; they could be added as a detail on a knitted or crochet project, or could be used to decorate a woven item of clothing, such as a pair of denim jeans or a jacket. Using the shaping techniques described on pages 235–239 you can make a variety of differently shaped pockets, depending upon the style you wish to achieve. It is probably best to use single crochet (UK double crochet) for a pocket, because this creates a dense fabric that will not allow items to slip through. When completed, sew the pocket into place using a strong color-matched thread.

Working out how many stitches to use

It is important that you take some time to think about what the pocket is going to be used for before you begin, so that you make it to the correct size. If it is purely decorative then a small pocket will suffice; however, if it needs to hold items such as keys, wallets, or even a remote control of some kind, then you will wish to avoid the mistake of making it either too small or too flimsy. In order that your pocket comes out to the correct size it is wise to do a little preparation and make a gauge (tension) square using the desired yarn and its compatible hook. Work out how many stitches and rows to 1in. (2.5cm) by measuring your gauge (tension) with a ruler, as described in more detail on page 46. This calculation can then be multiplied out to achieve the correct number of stitches and rows needed for your pocket design.

Rectangular pocket

This is probably the easiest pocket to make. Make the foundation chain to the required length and work repeated rows until the pocket reaches the required length. For extra interest you may want to add in a buttonhole as a feature (see pages 227–229), or stitch the pocket in place so that the rows sit vertically instead of horizontally.

A pocket made so that the rows run vertically, with added woven ribbon decoration and a button.

Shaped pocket

Start with fewer stitches than are required by the widest part of the pocket, and increase by working 2 stitches into the first and last stitch of each of the first few rows and then every alternate row until the required width is achieved. In this example a beaded border has been added for decoration.

A few lines of beading can add both texture and color.

Triangular pocket

Start with only 3 stitches and increase by working 2 stitches into the first and last stitch of every row until the optimum width is required. Continue to work straight until the pocket length is achieved. Here we have also added a triangular flap with button detail to create a handy and safe pocket design.

Shaped pockets are easy to make.

Placing pockets

Before you start sewing the pockets into place, it is a good idea to pin or even tack them in place and check whether or not you have chosen the correct positioning. Why not try adding pockets to unusual places—such as on the sleeve of a sweater, the inside of a garment, or even onto a cozy blanket or throw.

Perfect pockets

When making pockets it is a good idea to work to a tighter gauge (tension) than normal, because this will give the pocket extra durability.

care essentials

Having spent large amounts of time creating a beautiful piece of crochet, you will want to be sure that it is not spoilt by poor care. When made using a quality yarn, a crochet piece can last for many years if cared for correctly. Before making any decisions about how to wash, block or steam an item, always check the ball band for as much information as possible.

Washing

The most common outcome of poor care when washing is felting, which is caused by a combination of friction, agitation and heat. Different types of yarn require different kinds of care, but for most the same principles apply when washing.

Hand washing

Before emerging an item in water, remove any trims that are not washable such as special buttons, beads that may dissolve or trims that may not be colorfast. Do not use biological detergent or the type with added "brighteners" because these can prove too harsh for many yarns, especially luxury yarns such as cashmere and silk. Soap flakes, mild detergent such as baby shampoo, and specially formulated liquids for yarn are usually best. If in doubt when using a detergent, test it out on the gauge (tension) swatch first.

Make sure the water is cool and that detergent is completely dissolved. Wash one large crochet piece at a time, and change the water after every piece. Do not wring, twist, or rub the fabric and never use a brush to remove spots or stains. Wash the garment as quickly as possible, although some pieces can be left to soak for short lengths of time. Make sure the water runs clear after the final rinse.

Machine washing

If washing the item in a machine, use a delicate or wool cycle at a low temperature. The cycle should have as little fast spin action as possible. Putting the garment in a net bag for washing, which can be purchased from good general stores, will reduce friction. A white cotton pillowcase, tied at the end, will work equally well.

Folding and storing

Crocheted garments need to be stored flat and as loosely as possible. Moths are especially attracted to dirt, oils and animal proteins so take special care of yarns with lanolin and natural oils. When storing garments for long periods of time—for example, over the winter—wrap in tissue or brown paper then cover with a clear polythene bag. To discourage moths, place pieces of cedar or mothballs in the bag. Hang dry cleaned garments out to air for a while before storing to remove chemical odors.

Yarn care

If you don't have the yarn care information from the ball band, it is best to try hand washing first rather than putting the finished item into the washing machine.

Never dry items in bright sunlight as it may cause fading or yellowing of the colors.

If you know an item will need to be washed regularly, choose suitable washable yarns and trims to begin with.

Drying and blocking

Remove as much water from the crochet fabric as possible before laying it out to dry. A good way to do this is to wrap the item in absorbent toweling and quickly spin it in the washing machine. Repeat this process again with a piece of dry toweling, if necessary.

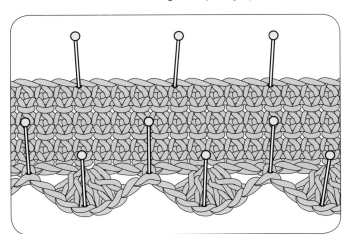

1 Blocking is the term used to describe the laying out of the crochet piece prior to sewing it together, or in order to reshape it once it has been washed. It is an idea to keep in mind the original measurements of the piece before blocking. It may be necessary to pin the item down if it is prone to curling or if it needs to be slightly stretched back into size or shape. Pieces to be joined together should be blocked with right side facing down and secured using large headed pins. If necessary, ease the fabric to achieve the correct measurements. Leave to dry away from direct sunlight or a heat source and turn occasionally.

2 Careful blocking whilst damp should eliminate the need to steam or press once dry, but if you do not have the time to wash your crochet pieces spray them gently with clean water and leave to dry. When using an iron be extremely careful that the hot baseplate does not touch your crochet fabric; hold the iron at least 1in. (2.5cm) away from the piece and use the steam setting, allowing the crochet fabric to absorb the hot steam. Leave to dry before unpinning.

An unblocked crochet square.

A blocked and pressed crochet square.

troubleshooting

Even the most seasoned crocheter will find that they make mistakes or stumble across things they don't understand. There are a few common mistakes that befall beginners, which may even have experts stumped. Mistakes are often made when the pattern instructions are not read or followed correctly, so be sure to use your stitch markers and row counters to good effect and do not try to crochet when you are distracted or very tired.

Stitches do not match the illustrations

The most common reason for this is that you are working to the wrong abbreviations and symbols. These can differ depending upon whether you are following a US or UK pattern and can even be personal to a pattern writer or designer, so be really careful to make sure that you have understood the instruction.

US and UK patterns share stitch names (such as double crochet and treble crochet, for example), but beware as these names do not refer to the same stitches. A double crochet in UK terminology is a dense stitch with a short post (the same as single crochet in the US), but in US terminology double crochet is a longer stitch with a post that is perhaps twice the height of the UK stitch (the same as treble crochet in the UK).

Stitches are too tight or too loose

Achieving an incorrect gauge (tension) will not only affect the size and shape of your crochet fabric, it will also affect your ability to work the fabric easily. It might also mean you will use a different amount of yarn than the pattern suggests. Stitches that are too tight can be difficult to insert your hook into, whereas stitches that are too loose might become baggy and over stretched.

If you do not achieve the correct gauge (tension) with the given hook size, change your hook size either to a larger size (if too tight) or a smaller size (if too loose)—see gauge (tension) on pages 46–47. If you find you are consistently working too tight, even on a larger hook, then you may not be taking the stitch high enough up onto the shaft of the crochet hook at the end of each stitch before you start the next one. Try making a concerted effort to move the stitch up onto the main part of the hook between working each stitch to see if this relieves the problem.

US or UK?

Since some stitch names are the same in both US and UK terminology, it can be hard to know which terms a pattern from an unknown source is written in. One good pointer is to look for mentions of either "single crochet" or "half double crochet", since both these only exist in US terminology.

If the pattern includes charts, the problem is resolved since the chart symbols are universal—see page 22–23 for details of what the most commonly-used chart symbols stand for.

Keeping a motif flat when working in the round

When working in the round it is quite common for the piece to become a little bit frilly. This could be either because you have increased too many times, or are achieving an incorrect gauge (tension) in your work. If you are following a pattern and find that your motifs are consistently wavy, try using a smaller hook. If you are working on a motif of your own design work a full row of a dense stitch with a short post, such as single crochet (UK double crochet), without increasing. This row may bring the motif back under control.

A circular motif that has beome frilly.

A perfectly flat circular motif.

Neatening a slip stitch at the end of a round

Many crocheters worry that the slip stitch made at the end of a round is loose or a little sloppy. If this is consistently the case, then the slip stitch can be quite obvious and can form a repeated inconsistent stitch on the right side of the piece.

Remove the hook from the last stitch worked and place on a stitch marker. From the reverse of the piece, insert the hook through the stitch that you intend to make the slip stitch into. Place the held stitch back on the hook and draw through the stitch to the reverse side.

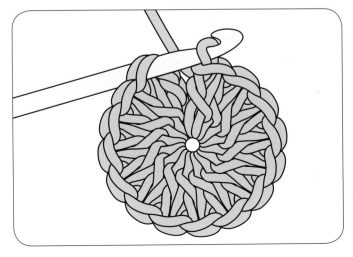

professional finishing techniques

Working a multicolor motif

When working a motif where the color is changed on every row you can achieve a much neater appearance by fastening off one color then rejoining another in a different position.

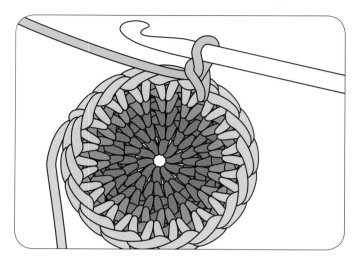

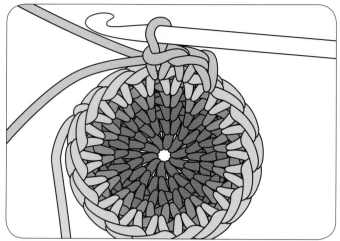

1 At the end of the first round work a slip stitch into the first stitch of the row. Cut the yarn and fasten off. Join the next color using a slip stitch at another point of the motif.

2 Work the required number of chain for the height of the stitch. Hold the tail end of yarn in line with the top of the last row and work the next few stitches over the top of it in order to weave it in.

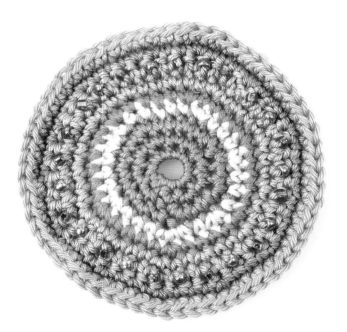

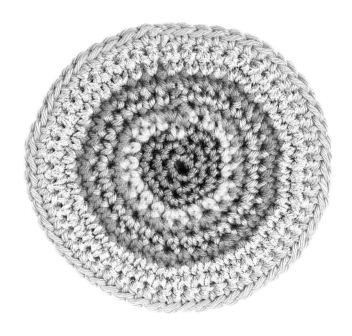

A circular motif in which the colors have been fastened off and rejoined at a different point.

Here the colors have been joined in at the end of the round—note that the first stitch of the new color intrudes into the previous one.

Keeping the correct stitch count

When working stitches with a long post such as double crochet (UK treble crochet) it is very common to get a decreasing stitch count and end up with a piece of work rather more triangular in shape than rectangular. The usual reason for this is that the final stitch of the row has not been worked into the top of the turning chain made at the beginning of the previous row. To keep the stitch count correct, always count your stitches at the end of every row and be sure to work the final stitch into the top of the turning chain.

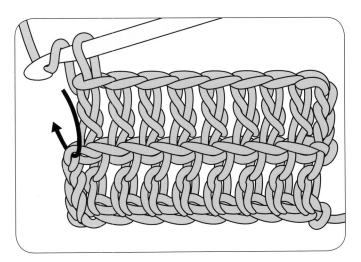

Correcting skewed motifs and blocks

There are a several reasons why blocks may not turn out the right shape and why they may be irregular or skewed to one side.

Turning chains

Make sure that the turning chains are the correct height for the stitch. Even if you are achieving the correct gauge (tension) for the stitches you may find that your turning chain is too loose, thus creating a large loopy space that makes the piece baggy, or is too tight and is causing stitches to stretch to accommodate it.

Yarn that biases the fabric

A poorly spun yarn that has a loose twist or one that has become unraveled may cause your fabric to bias. Working the yarn from the other end of the ball could help alleviate this problem because it can tighten the twist on the yarn.

Avoiding mistakes

Always buy good quality yarn—cheap yarn is a false economy. If you are going to spend hours making something by hand, you will want it to look fabulous for many years to come. Cheap yarn will often not make up well, and may not be very pleasurable to work with.

Read through the whole pattern before you begin—knowing what comes next will often help you avoid making a mistake when following the instructions.

glossary

abbreviations Shortened words to describe an instruction, used in a pattern to save space.

Amigurumi Japanese craft of making small "cute" crochet toys.

ball band Wrapper used to keep lengths of yarn intact and relay essential information such as yarn origin, weight, and content.

bead crochet Technique of adding beads as the fabric is made.

block/blocking Process of flattening and neatening the crochet fabric once completed, by pinning out and steaming/dampening then leaving to cool/dry.

bobbins Small lengths of yarn wound into manageable bundles or around plastic holders for use in color work.

bobble A decorative textural stitch that creates a rounded bump in the crochet fabric, made by increasing and decreasing stitches.

border A finishing of some description added to the edge of a crochet fabric, such as a "lace border" for example.

braid A decorative edging that can be sewn to the edge of a crochet fabric—or to the edge of a woven fabric.

cable A stitch formation in which stitches are purposely crossed over each other to create a twisted design.

chain The loops created by passing one loop of yarn through another using a crochet hook.

chain space The space created by working an area of chain between stitches.

chart A drawn design plotted onto squared paper.

chevron A zigzag design crochet fabric made by working increases and decreases at regularly repeated points in a row.

cluster A group of stitches worked in close proximity to create a decorative bump in the crochet fabric.

contrast (color) A secondary color used in conjunction with a main color of yarn.

cord A long thin length of crocheted, knitted or woven yarn, used to make tie fastenings, a belt or as a decoration.

decrease Reducing to fewer stitches by either fastening off or working several stitches together.

Dorset button A decorative fastening made by wrapping yarn around a circular frame.

dye lot The number/reference that indicates which batch of dye was used for the yarn. The same color yarn will vary across different dye batches, so buy all the yarn for a project at one time and check all balls are from the same batch.

embellishment Techniques and items used to decorate the crochet fabric.

extended stitches Stitches worked with an extra step to make them longer than the standard versions.

fan Groups of stitches worked from one stitch to create the formation of a fan shape.

fasten off Finishing off the last stitch in a way that prevents stitches from unraveling.

Fair Isle A knitting method in which more than one color is used to create a repeated pattern across the rows.

fiber Filament thread made by spinning and processing.

filet crochet A crochet technique that creates areas of open and dense fabric to create patterns, which are often pictorial.

finishing techniques Methods used to complete garments and projects once crocheted.

foundation chain The first chain made to form the base of the crochet fabric.

foundation row The first row made into the foundation chain.

freeform crochet A way of working without regard to the constraints of a written pattern to create unique crochet fabrics.

gauge The US term for a number of stitches and rows achieved over a determined measurement. The UK term is tension.

increase Achieving a greater number of stitches by either working into new chain, or working more than one stitch into the same place.

intarsia Creating an area of contrasting colored fabric inside the main color to create motifs and patterns.

Irish crochet Lace-type crochet originating in Ireland, often using very fine yarns worked around cords to create relief designs.

jacquard A method of color work used to describe a repeating pattern using few colors across a small number of stitches.

knitting The craft of making a fabric using yarn and a pair of long pointed sticks.

lace A delicate fabric, often with open areas to create decorative holes between denser areas of stitches.

measure The size or extent of something; to find the size or quantity of something by using an instrument such as a ruler.

mesh A crochet fabric produced by working stitches with gaps between to achieve a "net" type of appearance.

motif A decorative design either incorporated into the crochet fabric as it is worked or attached to it (perhaps by means of sewing) once it is completed.

pattern A decorative design; a written set of instructions.

picot A decorative loop that forms a peak design, which is often used on the edge of a fabric to create a decorative edging.

ply A twisted single strand of yarn.

puff A decorative textural stitch made by increasing stitches to create a small "bump" in the fabric.

right side The side of the fabric that will be on show once completed.

round Circular in shape; a row of crochet worked in a seamless piece to create a tube or cylinder.

row A line of stitches worked along the previous one.

seam The join between two (or more) fabrics.

sequins Small plastic (metallic/shiny) discs with a central hole. Used as an embellishment and either sewn or crocheted into place.

shank The stem at the back of a decorative button that holds the button away from the face of the fabric to allow for the layer of fabric for the buttonhole.

slip knot The knot used to create a loop on the crochet hook that acts as the first stitch/chain.

spike A loop of yarn worked into a previous row to create a decorative design.

stitch A small amount of yarn that has been worked to create a loop using a crochet hook or knitting needle.

surface crochet A technique of adding

yarn stitches to the surface of the crochet fabric using a crochet hook and yarn.

symbol A drawn design used to represent an instruction, either in a crochet pattern or on a chart.

tension The term used in the UK for the number of stitches and rows achieved over a determined measurement. The US term is gauge.

texture The structure, feel, and appearance of the surface of the fabric. A textural fabric is the opposite of a smooth flat fabric.

toggle A small (often wooden peg) used in place of a button as a fastening.

tubular A crochet fabric made by continuously working in one direction to create a cylindrical piece.

Tunisian crochet A dense crochet fabric made using a long hook. Stitches are picked up on one row and fastened off on the following row.

turn Move the fabric round so that the opposite side of the work is facing.

turning chain A number of chains made at the beginning or end of a row in order to achieve the stitch height needed by the first stitch of the subsequent row.

weight The bulk of a yarn or fabric.

wrong side The side of the fabric that will not be seen once the piece is complete; the inside of a garment.

yarn A continuous strand of wool, cotton, or synthetic fiber used to create a fabric.

zipper A fastener with two rows of plastic or metal teeth, with a sliding tab that forces them to interlock as it is slid up.

resources

CROCHET GUILDS

Knitting & Crochet Guild of Great Britain
Unit 4, Lee Mills Industrial Estate
St. George's Road
Scholes
Holmfirth
HD9 1RJ
England, United Kingdom
www.kcguild.org.uk

Crochet Guild Of America
1100-H Brandywine Blvd
Zanesville
OH 43701
USA
www.crochet.org

YARNS

Coats Crafts (UK)
Green Lane Mill
Holmfirth
HD9 2DX
England, United Kingdom
www.makeitcoats.com/en-gb

Coats & Clark (US)
Consumer Services
P.O. Box 12229
Greenville
SC 29612
USA
www.makeitcoats.com/en-us

Coats GmbH (Germany)
Kaiserstr. 1
D-79341 Kenzingen
Germany
www.makeitcoats.com/de-de

Rowan Yarns (Worldwide)
Green Lane Mill
Holmfirth
HD9 2DX
England, United Kingdom
www.knitrowan.com

British Wool Marketing Board (UK)
Wool House
Sidings Close
Canal Road
Bradford
BD2 1AZ
England, United Kingdom .
www.britishwool.org.uk

Cotton Board (US)
5050 Poplar Avenue
Ste. 1900
Memphis
TN 38120
USA
www.cottonboard.org

BEADS

Debbie Abrahams Beads (UK)
26 Church Drive
Nottingham
NG5 2BA
England, United Kingdom
www.debbieabrahamsbeads.co.uk

Beadwrangler (US)
228 N Sun Ct
Tampa
FL 33613
www.7beads.com

BUTTONS AND TRIMS

Bedecked (UK)
The Coach House
Barningham
Richmond
DL11 7DW
England, United Kingdom
www.bedecked.co.uk

WEB RESOURCES

Donna Griffin (Amigurumi)
www.cutedesigns.co.uk

Jane Crowfoot (Janie Crow)
www.janeknits.blogspot.com

index

acknowledgments

I would like to thank the team at Pavilion Books for giving me the opportunity to work on this lovely project.

I would like to thank Marie Clayton for being such a great editor and having a calming influence on me at all times. Louise Leffler for designing the book so magnificently and Kuo Kang Chen for his meticulous illustrations.

I would also like to acknowledge the team at Coats Crafts UK for helping me source beautiful objects for the photography shoots and providing me with some superb yarns from Rowan to make samples. I would especially like to thank Sharon Brant for all her help and advice.

Thanks also to Annette Traves, Carole Downie, Erica Pask, Freddie Patmore, Helen Bridgwood and Sharon Tyler who helped me produce more than 200 crochet samples to illustrate the techniques within this book.

Of course this acknowledgment would not be complete without a mention of my family. Thanks to Charlie and Summer for their support and Andy for taking such a massive interest in the project despite never having held a crochet hook in his life! I would especially like to thank Scramble for her constant company whilst I slaved away at the PC or with my yarn and crochet hook and for her gentle yet persuasive insistence that my artistic flow be interrupted frequently by walkies, biscuit treats and cuddles.

Credits:

Rowan Yarns – Crochet hangers, Lace edge cardigan and Pic-nic blanket
Donna Griffin – Amigurumi bears
Helen Bridgwood – Crochet necklace
Erica Pask – Cream beaded cushion and Bolster
Heike Gittins – Crochet hooks
Jenny Stillwell – Crochet hooks
Sarah Hazell – Flower corsages, Beaded bangle and Edgings bag

Jane Crowfoot taught herself to knit and crochet after being inspired by her great-grandmother's hand-made blankets. She studied textile design at Winchester School of Art. In 1996, she became a Design Consultant for Rowan Yarns and went on to work with Debbie Bliss. Jane is a leader of the recent crochet revival, which has seen knitters all over the world put down their needles and pick up a crochet hook.

Ultimate Crochet Bible is a definitive reference for all aspects of crochet – from the first chain to the care and maintenance of your projects. The book boasts more than 400 step-by-step illustrations and stitch directory photographs to guide you through the process.

The first two chapters, "Getting Started" and "Crochet Basics", are packed with useful information, such as choosing and using a hook, how to read a pattern, holding the yarn and basic stitches. Once you are armed with the basics, you can go on to learn about a wide range of texture and lace techniques.

Traditional, lace-weight crochet is covered in "Thread Crochet". The yarn used tends to be fine and the hooks are small, but this allows you to put more detail into a piece of work. Filet and Irish crochet are covered here. "Tunisian and Entrelac Crochet" shows how elements of crochet and knitting can be combined. Entrelac is a method of creating square shapes in order to make a textured fabric that resembles basket weave.

In "Working with Color", the two main techniques of adding color to a piece of crochet – Intarsia and Jacquard – are explained. And to create some really exciting effects, you can add beads and sequins to your crochet. It's a relatively easy technique.

Other types of crochet included are Freeform (without a pattern) and Amigurumi (Japanese). In addition, there are techniques for edgings, braids, fringes and tassels. The chapter on embellishments reveals how simple embroidery can add detail to your work.

"Professional Finishing Techniques" provides all the know-how you need to take your crochet to a whole new level. But whatever your level of experience, this book will be an invaluable treasure trove of crochet techniques that you will turn to time and time again.

PAVILION

Whatever the craft, we have the book for you – just head straight to Pavilion's crafty headquarters.

Pavilioncraft.co.uk is the one-stop destination for all our fabulous craft books. Sign up for our regular newsletters and follow us on social media to receive updates on new books, competitions and interviews with our bestselling authors.

We look forward to meeting you!

www.pavilioncraft.co.uk

Also in this series:

978-1-84340-411-8

978-1-84340-502-3

978-1-84340-450-7

978-1-908449-01-6

978-1-84340-574-0

978-1-909397-18-7

978-1-84340-672-3

978-1-909397-97-2

978-1-909397-98-9

Published in the United Kingdom in 2016 by
Collins & Brown
1 Gower Street
London
WC1E 6HD

An imprint of Pavilion Books Company Ltd

Copyright © Collins & Brown 2008, 2016
Text copyright © Jane Crowfoot

Distributed in the United States and Canada by Sterling Publishing Co., Inc.
1166 Avenue of the Americas, New York, NY 10036

The moral right of the author has been asserted.

ISBN 9781910231791

A CIP catalogue for this book is available from the British Library.

10 9 8 7 6 5 4 3 2 1

Reproduction by ColourDepth UK
Printed and bound in Singapore

This book can be ordered direct from the publisher at www.pavilionbooks.com